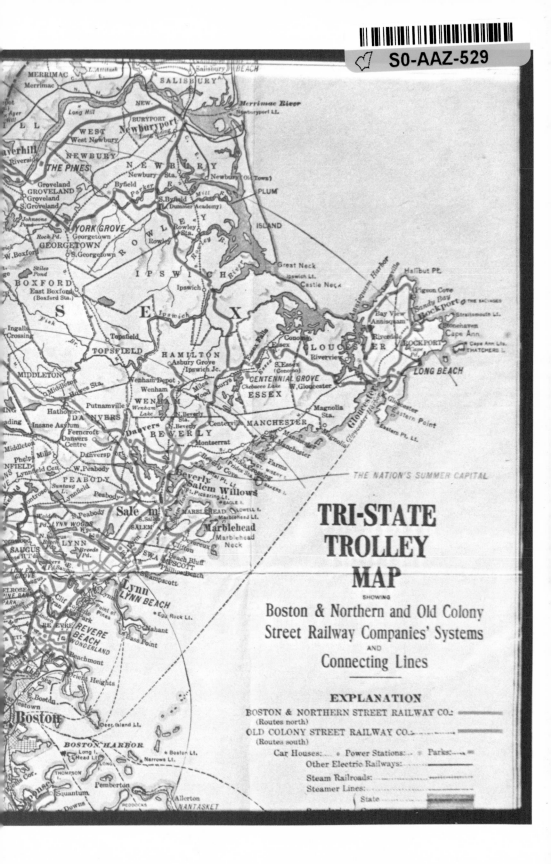

THE NATION'S SUMMER CAPITAL

TRI-STATE
TROLLEY
MAP

SHOWING

Boston & Northern and Old Colony
Street Railway Companies' Systems
AND
Connecting Lines

EXPLANATION

BOSTON & NORTHERN STREET RAILWAY CO.
(Routes north)
OLD COLONY STREET RAILWAY CO.
(Routes south)

Car Houses: • Power Stations: Parks:
Other Electric Railways:

Steam Railroads:
Steamer Lines:
State

BOSTON'S GOLD COAST

Books by Joseph E. Garland

AN EXPERIMENT IN MEDICINE: The First Twenty Years of the Pratt Clinic and the New England Center Hospital of Boston

EVERY MAN OUR NEIGHBOR: A Brief History of the Massachusetts General Hospital 1811–1961

TO MEET THESE WANTS: The Story of the Rhode Island Hospital, 1863–1963

LONE VOYAGER
(The biography of Howard Blackburn)

THAT GREAT PATTILLO
(The biography of James William Pattillo)

EASTERN POINT: A Nautical, Rustical, and Social Chronicle of Gloucester's Outer Shield and Inner Sanctum, 1606–1950

THE GLOUCESTER GUIDE: A Retrospective Ramble

THE CENTENNIAL HISTORY OF THE BOSTON MEDICAL LIBRARY, 1875–1975

GUNS OFF GLOUCESTER
(Cape Ann in the American Revolution)

BOSTON'S NORTH SHORE: Being an Account of Life among the Noteworthy, Fashionable, Wealthy, Eccentric and Ordinary 1823–1890

BOSTON'S GOLD COAST: The North Shore 1890–1929

Editor

HISTORY OF THE TOWN OF GLOUCESTER, by John J. Babson: 350th Anniversary Edition

GLOUCESTER RECOLLECTED: A Familiar History, by Alfred Mansfield Brooks

BOSTON'S GOLD COAST

The North Shore, 1890-1929

Joseph E. Garland

Little, Brown and Company   Boston   Toronto

FIRST EDITION

The photograph of President Wilson and Colonel House on page 237 is from *The Intimate Papers of Colonel House,* Charles Seymour, editor, copyright 1928, 1956 by Charles Seymour, reprinted by permission of Houghton Mifflin Company.

The photographs of President Taft on page 155 and of Eleonora Sears on page 200 are from *Myopia 1875–1975* by Edward A. Weeks and are reprinted by permission of the Myopia Hunt Club.

LIBRARY OF CONGRESS CATALOGING IN PUBLICATION DATA

Garland, Joseph E.
Boston's Gold Coast.

Sequel to: Boston's North Shore.
Includes index.
1. Boston region (Mass.)—Social life and customs. I. Title.
F73.5.G34   974.4′61   81–13730
ISBN 0-316-30430-1   AACR2

MV

Designed by Susan Windheim
Published simultaneously in Canada
by Little, Brown & Company (Canada) Limited

PRINTED IN THE UNITED STATES OF AMERICA

To
Betty and Phil

Preface

A HEARTFELT SENSE OF INADEQUACY CAN MOVE ONE TO THE MOST EXTRAORdinary compensatory exertions. Wars have been started by short men with weak chins. Athletes have achieved greatness overcoming failure to win a school letter. And books purporting to give the reader the inside view have been produced by writers who spent their childhoods — or so they like to imagine — outside in the snow with their noses pressed to the warm glass.

This writer is in the latter category. During my impressionable years I felt outdistanced and overlooked, if not outright rejected, by my more promising peers. I fancied myself on the outside of something warm and intimate and cohesive — I was not exactly sure just what — destined for my many remaining years to be in the cold looking wistfully in. This work, these companion volumes of inside dope on that *something* up here (or there) to the north and east of Boston, are the result; this is my contribution to the literature of overcompensation.

First *Boston's North Shore,* now *Boston's Gold Coast* — and at last it is all out of my system. *I* have been *inside,* I *am* inside, where everybody knows everybody, my nose pressed to the glass. How cold the glass is! How fulfillingly inadequate I feel, peering out at you all in the great world where life is lived so freely and fully and dangerously, where men are men and can stand in the snow for hours without flinching! Now I am truly deovercompensated.

The Orwellian apocalypse is three years hence. Although we have just launched a space shuttle and brought it safely back to the desert, our sense of personal worth — that mark of civilized man — is less lofty than it was in the days when the spirit of the historian John Lothrop Motley soared and he rejoiced in all the amusement he needed on a summer's day at Nahant, musing and chatting and building castles in the clouds, lolling on the piazza, climbing over the cliffs at sunset and galloping full tilt along the beach.

In these times of spectatorism and consumerism and effluent affluence (for some), the eccentricities of wealth that once drew envious gasps are rightfully met with yawns. Be advised that along this coast all that glisters is *not* necessarily gold, because there is more to be learned from how we spend our money (and our leisure) — or used to — than from how we made it.

Boston's Gold Coast is even more myopic and even less informative (though I hope no less instructive) than *Boston's North Shore* and more reflective of my likes and dislikes as events accelerate toward their unclear (never nuclear, God forbid) and present impasse. This volume is even more idiosyncratic than its forerunner. Frequently I have put emphasis on times, places, people, events as the result of a chance encounter with one or another backwash in the stream of history, or simply because something struck my fancy and something else did not. There is a creeping bias toward Eastern Point for which I offer no apology.

As its title announces, this sequel is narrower, or at least more focused, borrowing the price tag Admiral Morison pinned on the poshest portion of the shore between Beverly Cove and Eastern Point, the "Gold Coast" bought up three generations ago for song upon song by well-to-do but modest Boston men of whom he wrote in his *Maritime History of Massachusetts:* "It was not the fault of these newcomers that the North Shore eventually became a millionaires' club. They only asked to be let alone in their simple pleasure of boating and fishing, and driving along the twisty lanes of Essex County."

The Gold Coast — the North Shore — is no longer a millionaires' club, and in that fortunate fact (thanks to the redistribution of some of the land to the worthy gentry . . . within reason, of course!) lurks the salvation of its charm and beauty, let us (we gentry) prayerfully hope.

Yet, as it has been since the day the Nahant Hotel opened wide to the sea breeze a century and a half ago, the Shore is still a land of airs, and heiresses, one of which was put on by one of whom one morning not long ago, a typical staunch, horse-visaged, hoarse-voiced gentlewoman of the Old School who was overheard to ask her Magnolia hairdresser if she had any *aunts*.

"Well yes, two."

"Are they black?"

(Pause.) "Why, uh, no."

"Mine are." (Pause.) "They're coming up in the kitchen."

"Oh, you mean *ants!*"

"No, *aunts*. I *never* use the *short* a."

And herein we *never* — well, *almost* never — use the *broad* a.

You see — the address notwithstanding (the native returned to the soil of his ancestors) — this is not really an inside job . . . or is it?

J. E. G.

"Black Bess"
Eastern Point
April 15, 1981

Acknowledgments

IT WOULD BE AS IMPOSSIBLE TO EMBARK SERIOUSLY UPON SUCH LEVITY AS A summery account of America's first resort without the superb regional library of the venerable Essex Institute in Salem as it would be to navigate the sociological shoals of the North Shore without a favorable *Breeze* — indeed, forty volumes of it at the ready in the Institute.

The Essex Institute has been the silent co-author of eight of my books, and my co-editor in two more. As was the case with *Boston's North Shore,* I particularly appreciate the constant assistance and tireless patience of that bibliographic dynamo, Mrs. Irene Norton, the reference librarian, the amiable permission of Bryant F. Tolles, Jr., director and librarian, once again to make free with the Institute's extensive picture files, and the always friendly cooperation of the other members of the staff. For twenty years this apparently bottomless well sunk through the intriguing strata of Essex County's past has been arousing and slaking my curiosity by turns.

As the reader must have remarked from the start of this second volume of coastal lore, the *North Shore Breeze* breathes life into every other page. An amusing twist that a native Newfoundlander, "a herring choker from down home" out of a small college in Maine, should have dreamed up such an *in* sheet targeted for as closed and socially egocentric readership as the North Shore summer crowd.

But J. Alexander Lodge (no local Lodge, he) pulled it off brilliantly. During the decade between his first issue in 1904 and the Great War, he had so thoroughly captured his market that advertisers were cram-

ming his attractively designed magazine-sized periodical to as many
as eighty pages a week. Subscribers pressed equally as hard for inclusion
between the boards of his companion production, *Who's Who Along
the North Shore: Being a Register of the Noteworthy, Fashionable &
Wealthy Residents on the North Shore of Massachusetts Bay for the
Summer of _____.*

Nary a breath of scandal in the *Breeze,* ever, and hardly a suspicion
of satire. The editor played the game by the rules. He knew his readers better than they knew themselves. Perhaps a hint of the sardonic
now and again, and more frequently — as the years rolled comfortably
along and J. Alex clearly had ensconced himself — brief editorials in-
dulging in "healthy" colonial self-criticism. The very ingenuousness of
the articles and editorials and comments and asides in the *Breeze* —
the assumption that one might write as freely as one pleased for (one
might almost say, *to*) one's peers within the bounds of taste — makes
them one-way windows of utter transparency from the outside in. And
thank heaven for the ever-striving urge toward upward mobility, the
compulsion to discreet and not-so-discreet one-upmanship, the naive
joy in the mention of one's house, one's garden, one's pink-cheeked children, one's hat, one's horse, one's motor car, one's yacht, one's club,
one's crowd and one's guests in the columns of the *Breeze* . . . and if
accompanied by a photograph, sheer bliss!

Resuming publication after his patriotic suspension of it during the
First War, Lodge was producing summertime editions, issued weekly
during the season and monthly in the off, of up to ninety-six pages,
still at ten cents, in the Twenties. In 1930 he reported that 80 percent
of the summer population of the North Shore wintered in the Boston
area and that Bostonians summering on the Massachusetts coast preferred the North Shore to the South three to one.

Somehow the editor kept his *Breeze* alive through the Depression on
a reduced basis. More serious self-examination and, frequently, self-
doubt crept in — articles like "Mental Aberrations of a Deb" and "It's
Smart to be Poor." In 1935 the bank foreclosed, but the *Breeze* strug-
gled on, getting thinner and more disconsolate every year. In 1939 the
founder died at the age of fifty-nine. His widow carried on. But the old
North Shore establishment of the heyday was dying off too, the war
was on, and in 1942 the *North Shore Breeze* was again suspended, this

time for keeps after thirty-eight years of a kind of social chronicling so lacking in self-consciousness that it must be unique in American regional journalism.

Quite as unique in cameo form is that engaging and neighborly chronicle of the "pillbox colony," *Upon the Road Argilla,* by the late Sidney N. Shurcliff. My Ipswich chapter owes its inspiration to this charming little classic, and I am indebted to his family for permission to rely on it materially and pictorially as extensively as I have, and to my good neighbor, David L. Richardson, childhood Argilla Roader, for his comments.

To those readers who have looked in vain for a sequel to the yachting chapters in *Boston's North Shore* I express my regrets. As I was about to sail into the subject I lost my old Blackburn sloop *Cruising Club,* driven ashore from her mooring and wrecked before my very eyes in the unexpectedly hard gale of October 26, 1980, and had not the heart for the task.

Blanche Butler Lane, the late Florence Cunningham and the late Frances E. Cunningham provided vignettes of bygone summers in colorful correspondence. Andrew Gray provided flashes of mordant insight into his favorite *belle époque* with his accustomed wit. My uncle, Philip H. Lewis, savored the sauce with the salt of the North Shore native, and his wife, beloved by us all, the late Elizabeth Garland Lewis, kept it stirred.

Frances L. Burnett, Peter McCauley and Calantha Sears provided priceless photographs of Manchester, Revere Beach and Nahant, as they did for *Boston's North Shore.* They were joined in brightening the pages of *Boston's Gold Coast* most particularly among others by Phyllis Tuckerman Cutler and Major General George S. Patton IV (U.S. Army, retired), who opened up their family albums for rare shots of the Prince of Wales, and the Pattons and the Ayers; and by Paul Harling with his collection of trolley car photographs.

Others to whom I am indebted in many ways include Gordon Abbott, Jr., Thomas E. Babson, William R. Brush, Dorothy Buhler, Ruth Bolger, Peter Denghausen, Frank B. Duveneck, Barbara Erkkila, Helen Patch Gray, James C. Heigham, William D. Hoyt, Steve Howard, Frederick Holdsworth, Jr., Herbert A. Kenny, George C. Lodge, Augustus P. Loring, Donald and Lila Monell, Harry Martin, James F.

O'Gorman, Grace Schrafft Perry, Janice G. Pulsifer, Robert Rapp, Lila Leonard Swift, Alice Shurcliff, Charles S. Tapley, Thomas Townsend, Philip S. Weld and Everett Wilkinson.

This work would not have been possible without the resources and assistance of the following institutions and staff members or officers: Beverly Historical Society (Mrs. Arthur Webber), Cape Ann Historical Association (Mrs. James B. Benham and Deborah Goodwin), Essex County Registry of Deeds, Essex Institute (Marylou Birchmore, John Knight and Bettina A. Norton), Hammond Castle Museum (Naomi Reed Kline), Lynn Public Library (Rita E. Riess), Manchester Historical Association (Sally M. Loring), Nahant Historical Society (Calantha Sears), Nahant Public Library, Newton Public Library, Peabody Museum of Salem, Sawyer Free Library of Gloucester (Stillman Hilton, librarian, and Elizabeth Roland, reference librarian), Swampscott Historical Society (David Callahan), Swampscott Public Library, and Trustees of Reservations (Mary E. Hensel).

To the succession of editors who have inherited me I am grateful for friendship, advice and backing: Llewellyn Howland III, instigator; Robert E. Ginna, Jr., expediter; Mary E. Tondorf-Dick, final implementer of this long project; and Elisabeth Gleason Humez, grinder, buffer and polisher of both volumes.

And to H. R. B., thanks for everything.

Contents

BOSTON'S GOLD COAST

The Wooing and the Winning

ON ONE OF THE INFREQUENT OCCASIONS IN HIS LONG LIFE WHEN HE AP-
pears to have had nothing more ulterior in mind than exposing a
sickly grandchild to the balm of the salt sea air, Colonel Thomas
Handasyd Perkins built the first summer home northeast of Boston
on the breezy peninsula of Nahant.

The year was 1820. We had recently settled the encore of our differ-
ences with the Mother Country. Our ships at last were free to roam the
seven seas in search of commerce. The trades pushed them westward,
and the riches of the Orient pulled. Under the tutelage of the formidable colonel, who looked, talked and acted like, and indeed was, an
archetypal founder of American capitalism, Boston was raising to perfection the practice of buying cheap in one East and selling dear in
another. Untold profits (some untold because they were skimmed off
the odious opium traffic) caressed the Puritan conscience with the
prospect of well-deserved leisure . . . if not entirely well-earned, then
certainly well-spent.

A season of solace from the heat of the town was enough to persuade
Colonel Perkins that he really ought to share his find with his suffering neighbors back in Boston. A proper distance from his cool stone
cottage, he opened the cool stone Nahant Hotel on June 26, 1823, and
without any terribly imperial intentions at the time laid claim to the
north shore of Massachusetts Bay, from which the diminutive demi-isle
of Nahant hung into the Atlantic by the thinnest mile of beach imaginable, as the first summer resort in America.

The drawing rooms of Boston emptied as if vacuumed. Overnight this treeless, rather desolate and almost unpopulated square mile of pasture and bluff became absolutely the place to go. Everyone who *was* anyone with a jot of curiosity or a tittle of pretense to fashion flocked to the wily financier's piazzas and ballrooms, dining halls, billiard parlors, bedchambers and marine hippodromes all set up there so cool above the shining sea. It was an entrepreneurial triumph: the opening coincided with the inauguration of regular steamship service out of Boston, to Nahant of all places, that cut hours of jolting misery from the land route . . . and with the sworn-to reappearance in local waters of the famous sea serpent (named *Scoliophis Atlanticus* by the unrelentingly solemn Linnaean Society of New England); the frolics of His Snakeship, as the papers dubbed the apparition, were just as solemnly attested to from their porch by witnesses of no less probity than the colonel's own family.

Enchanted by the Gothic beauty of this newly blossomed "Floure of Souvenance" — so one romanticist ecstasized over Nahant — Beacon Street rapidly relieved the few natives of the choicest of their landed holdings (*they,* poor souls, were relieved to be rid of such unproductive property), erected cottages above the cliffs and settled into an annual summer sojourn that consisted of shooing the cows out of the garden, hiking over the zephyr-swept moors, chowdering down on the rocks, sailboating in the bay and waving to the family clippers squaring off out of Boston Harbor for the westward and the replenishment of the family coffers. As a matter of course these pioneers packed their Puritan consciences with their trunks and put up a Spartan summer school for their children to keep them out of mischief, and a summer church likewise for themselves that gave rise to the male tradition of bathing in the buff off Cupid's Rock after Sunday services. Thus by preachment and practice did Boston's Best cultivate in this Emersonian setting the sense of rootedness in the New England seaside that some call class-consciousness and others pride; whichever, it would be the peculiar stamp of the North Shore for a hundred and fifty years and quite possibly longer.

The gentle poet Longfellow and a piazzaful of kindred deities from Boston's literary Olympus, including his fat but feisty brother-in-law

Thomas Gold Appleton, summered at Nahant; Tom could not resist hanging the cognomen *Cold Roast Boston* on his close little colony where everybody not only knew everybody but, stuffier still, was related as well. More Boston, if that were possible, than Boston itself, Nahant remained unchallenged the nation's prime watering spot until 1846, year of manifest destiny, when the Ocean House opened at Newport and the Big Spenders from Park Avenue turned that other and bigger peninsula on Narragansett Bay (peninsulas have the advantage of a built-in barrier against the world) into the glistering, gold-plated pot at the end of the American rainbow.

The Hub of the Universe (coinage of another seasonal Nahanter, Dr. Oliver Wendell Holmes) scorned free spending and display, and relinquished its place with its usual grace. "You Newport folks," the Olympian editor James Russell Lowell reprimanded a female correspondent from his North Shore retreat, "always seem a little (I must go to my Yankee) *stuck up,* as if Newport were all the world, and you the saints that had inherited it."

If its rival was stuck up, Nahant was filled up by the 1840s and hadn't enough land left for a fraction of the Bostonians desperate to escape the insufferable effects of another Perkins contrivance, the Milldam. This offal miscalculation was the westerly extension of Beacon Street across the mud flats of the Charles River's Back Bay, designed to provide water power for factories that never materialized. What the Milldam did, when completed in 1821, was to isolate the Back Bay from the tidal flushing of the river, leaving it a vast cesspool that doubled as everyone's handiest dump. Such an unforeseen outcome did not sit well with Beacon Streeters whose own foresight had fallen short of a retreat at Nahant. Each spring they faced, or faced away from, with deepening disgust, another summer of emanations from the trapped effluent borne through their windows on the suffocating southwest wind, when there was one . . . trapped between the impossibility of buying into the town's only resort and the impossibly tortuous and torturing overland road to the mainland North Shore so barricaded from Boston by harbor, river, marsh, wilderness and rocky hill as to be a *terra* more *incognita* than the old colonel's China itself.

And then still another old aborted Perkins scheme, now arisen like the Phoenix, came puffing to the rescue. Or was this a Trojan horse, as some suspicious country people saw it? Whichever, in 1838 the Eastern Railroad ferried its first passengers across the harbor from the city to East Boston, where they boarded the coughing rattlers for Lynn and Salem. The North Shore was finally and forever breached by land. The rails pushed on through Beverly, Wenham and Hamilton to Ipswich and eventually to New Hampshire; the Gloucester Branch in 1847 split off from Beverly through Manchester to Cape Ann; seven more years and the overland link with the city was forged, the ferry was abandoned, and it was Boston to Gloucester in a single hour. "That giant," as one native grumbled, had "stretched forth its arm, and laid, literally, a hand of iron upon the bosom of Essex County." And down those iron fingers dripped and trickled and then poured the summer deluge of discoverers.

Sleepy Swampscott and the Beverly shore — the Cove, the Farms and Pride's Crossing — Manchester "by-the-Sea," Magnolia Point, the choicest coast of the old fishing port of Gloucester "by-the-Smell," Rockport's rocky Pigeon Cove, and finally the holdout, Marblehead Neck, fell to the city's dollars. And Winthrop too, and the gleaming miles of Revere Beach, so remote that they were bypassed by the Eastern, only to be plugged with wonderful directness into the heart of the city by the cleverest scheme of all, the Narrow Gauge Railway — the Boston, Revere Beach and Lynn — and an alphabet of progeny.

Down from the trains, from one end of the North Shore to the other, swung the openhanded Boston men, pushing for all it was worth the myth of their innocence when it came to the utter worthlessness of shore property. Sowing the merest chaff from their bank accounts among the knowing natives, they reaped mile after priceless mile a harvest of salt water farms regarded by father unto son of shrewd Yankee owners as so many worked-out birthrights that looked out on nothing more promising or profitable than the heaving emptiness of the Atlantic Ocean.

The wooing and the winning, not to say the seduction, of that virginal coast between Boston Harbor and Cape Ann followed the railroad as surely as did the opening of the West. Within the lifetime of the first summer residents this upper boundary of Massachusetts Bay had been so thoroughly Bostonized that the sobriquet *The North*

Shore was sufficient the civilized world over to identify America's most civilized resort.

As Victoria and her century neared their end, and another generation settled more comfortably than ever into the family's summer seat by the seaside, yawns were audible. Was the roast so cold, had the shore so out-towned the town, that it had all become just too boringly Boston? Tom Appleton was not the first to spread such heresy, nor the last. Back in 1827 the colonel's hotel had hardly opened before the anonymous creator of *Nahant, or "The Floure of Souvenance"* was groaning "behold, here are the same violins, the same drums, and the same waiters that I thought I had left behind me; the very paraphernalia of a Beacon Street drawing room."

By the end of the century the North Shore was Boston's Riviera, a settled and mature summer society, and in the view of one prominent insider, the Nahant syndrome — marked by the sameness of violins and faces winter and summer due to everybody's knowing everybody — had laid its torpid grip upon the bosom of the whole resort . . . the whole, that is, as defined from the inside — rather like Jonah describing the whale. The Jonah in this case was a Harvard overseer and Suffolk County judge of probate, Robert Grant, better known in his day as a novelist, and the boyhood summer chum of Henry Cabot Lodge at Nahant. Judge Grant in 1894 published a pleasantly patronizing inside story on *The* North Shore, which in his book was the "fringe of aristocracy" that held down the coast from Nahant and Swampscott as far as Cape Ann — since "civilization properly ceases before you come to Gloucester."

With its unique advantages, wondered novelist Grant (not the least of which was "its freedom from either democratic or plutocratic crowds"), why hadn't *his* Shore attracted more than a handful of summer residents from elsewhere than Boston? "Perhaps the reason is to be found in the argument that it is too near Boston, which is a polite way of expressing reluctance to invade the sacred precincts of the most critical society in America for fear of not pleasing. If such be the case, this attitude of caution acts as a two-edged sword, for if there is any plea to be urged against the attractiveness of the North Shore it is that the society is so exclusively Bostonese. The families from a distance are almost to be numbered on the fingers of one hand, and you meet in your walks and drives and social intercourse the self-same people with whom you have dined and slummed, or whom you have seen at the Symphony concerts all winter."

Having so said, the judge retreated to his literary chambers whence he issued the opinion that dissidents who found *his* Shore dull and in need of awakening were limited to a few of the younger matrons. (As for himself, perhaps he resorted to peopling *his* world with the characters in his novels.)

Robert Grant accurately reflected the proprietary attitude of Boston's upper crust toward its North Shore: that is, the Gold Coast from Nahant to Magnolia, in contrast to Newport, Lenox and Bar Harbor, was a summer suburb for the city's busy business and professional men of means who wanted nothing more for themselves than a breezy verandah on which to loll away their late afternoons and evenings, sans cravat, with maybe some sailing, golf and riding, and for their wives and daughters, respite from the rigid, frigid social season in the city.

The jurist was at once oblique and pointed in his allusion to the rise of social barriers along with fences, walls and hedges on the coast: "Those who regard the continued individual ownership of large tracts of land, or even of an acreage sufficient to keep one's neighbor at a respectful distance, as inconsistent with true democratic development, will be likely to look askance at the beautiful estates along the North Shore. It may be that in a few generations we shall all live cheek by jowl with one another in houses built and painted after a stereotyped model. [This was 1894!] . . . Such a period may become necessary in the process of giving all men an opportunity to enjoy equally the fruits of the earth and the fullness thereof. But whatever the dim future may bring to pass in this regard by dint of positive law or ethical argument, there is no doubt that, at present, the beautiful seaside estates . . . are among the most precious of human possession, and that the class of people seeking them is increasing in direct ratio to the growth of refined civilization over the country."

Ever the defender of property rights (why else a judge of probate?), Judge Grant thirty years later was on the three-member review commission that concluded that the anarchists Nicola Sacco and Bartolomeo Vanzetti had been given a fair trial, were fairly convicted, and

Caustic commentary from the pen of Myopia huntsman Otis F. Brown of Hamilton. Essex Institute

Twins John and Edward Motley, nephews of the historian John Lothrop Motley, who summered at Nahant, on the grounds of the Nahant Club about 1890. The Motley family, Nahant Public Library

Picnicking at Magnolia, July 1894. Manchester Historical Society

should be fairly executed for murder . . . which they were, fair or not.

Along the North Shore thus narrowly defined by the new owners who had acquired it, if not for a steal then practically for a giveaway, there was by the 1890s a definite defensiveness tinged, as Judge Grant's conscience betrayed, with a faint streak of Victorian guilt.

No longer now did the leading guidebook to the Shore invite the curious outsider to rubberneck along the private drives between Pride's Crossing and Beverly Farms, with a caution not to pick the flowers or trample the lawns but like his English cousin (note the ethnic assumption) venturing on the turf of the local lord, to be "thankful that his more favored fellow being shares with him thus much."

Indeed, the post–Civil War epidemic among the wealthy of using summer residency to dodge city taxes encouraged a few audacious separationists to hazard putting together entirely new tax havens out of various contiguous North Shore towns by amputation and anastomosis, beyond the reach of the Boston assessors and the encroachments of hoi polloi–ridden horsecars. They failed, but the resentments of natives remained.

Everywhere along Grant's North Shore, as the century wound down, the barriers rose. Some were as visible as the fences and walls — the posting of estates, individually and collectively, behind gatekeepers and constables, the shrinkage of beaches once considered accessible to all, and the yacht clubs, hunt clubs, country clubs, garden clubs, kennel clubs, outing clubs, golf clubs, tennis clubs and beach clubs.

Other curtains against the prying eye such as *The North Shore Breeze* were of mere paper, yet as revealing of their readers as the emperor's new clothes. Rocklike in this seasonal stream of Comings, Doings and Goings stood *The North Shore Blue Book and Social Register,* more inclusive geographically than Judge Grant's close-drawn sanctum sanctorum, but exclusive enough to raise and maintain for the foreseeable future a buffering clamor of *outs* wanting *in.* As if one such *Burke's Peerage* were not enough protection for such a brief fringe of coastline, the *Blue Book* was joined in discreet competition in a few years by *Who's Who Along the North Shore: Being a Register of the Noteworthy, Fashionable & Wealthy Residents on the North Shore of*

Massachusetts Bay. Predictably, *Who's Who* allowed another thousand or so outs in.

If Boston's North Shore had remained by definition Beacon Street's — geographically, economically, socially and exclusively — Judge Grant's dismissal of the rest of the so much more inclusive resort that is the subject of this chronicle would have sufficed for the epitaph for *his,* because he wrote: "More and more do we realize that a residence at a summer watering place hotel is apt to leave soul, mind and body jaded, and that to bang about in the hot weather at fashionable beaches and promiscuous springs may amuse for a fortnight, but suggests by the close of the season the atmosphere of the *corps de ballet* or a circus. We are learning as a nation to rest in the summer, instead of to gad, and those who have been the fortunate pioneers in the movement are indeed to be envied, for though the sands of the sea are said to be unnumbered, the coast of New England has its limitations."

From the spectator's vantage, though, gadding has it all over resting, and as the Victorian era waned, banging about in the hot weather waxed along the greater North Shore. Cold Roast Nahant and Phillips Beach, Marblehead Neck, Beverly Cove and Eastern Point could hear only too well the sounds of the circus on a midsummer night when the wind was right, and blink at the garish lights of the promiscuous parks at Bass Point, Revere Beach, Salem Willows and Stage Fort. For the barricaded ones knew there was another and overwhelmingly larger world out there, pressing in by land and sea, swarming the trains and horsecars and electric trolleys, the excursion steamers, the buggies and the bicycles (hordes of them), and toward the tag end of the century, those queer and so obviously ephemeral contrivances, the motor cars.

Were it not for this steamrolling revolution in mass transportation, so fresh and foolish in the innocence of its infancy, the North Shore and the other beautiful places might have remained the placid preserves of the privileged pictured by Judge Grant. Fortunately for all involved, the energy and the frustration of a city baking in the oven of August could not be contained. The celluloid-collar workers and the brawny blue collars and their crinolined wives and chattering children, the Catholics, the Protestants and the Jews, the Irish and the Yanks, the Italians, Swedes, Greeks, Germans, Poles, Russians and the rest of

Boston's sweltering melting pot poured forth along the rails and roads and seaways to the beaches and meccas of merriment with their nickels and dimes. The freshly rich from New York and Chicago, Detroit, St. Louis, Pittsburgh and Cleveland glided in aboard their private Pullmans with their millions, clamoring for a piece of those "sacred precincts of the most critical society in America." The beach extravaganzas, the extravagant hotels, the marbled mansions rose ever higher as this last great wave of American exuberance approached its crest along the North Shore . . . and so did the dikes of exclusiveness.

It was the most delightful of eras, this fleeting dream of a single generation in time that plunged with such seeming suddenness into the nightmare of the worst of wars — the most superficial, the most impossibly nostalgic, the most susceptible to sentimental stereotype, and the most revealing.

Nowhere was the *style* of our belle époque, with its relaxing patresfamilias, its delicious little girls in their bonnets and ginghams, its full-blown Edwardians, its incredible tycoons, its beachgoers, its climbers and its plungers, played out in more kaleidoscopic tableau than along the North Shore of Massachusetts Bay, in the afterglow of Boston's Golden Age as most self-assuredly the Athens of America.

2

Each Night When I Call on My Sweetie

THE RICH DO GET RICHER, AND JUDGE GRANT'S DEMOGRAPHIC DEFINITION of *The* North Shore was by the 1890s outclassing both the democratic and the geographic. Nahant and the Gold Coast — the Beverly, Manchester and Magnolia shores — were by their own admission the exclusive turf of Boston's Best. Hamilton and Wenham, though as dryshod as Des Moines, were probationary candidates. Certain salty stretches of Swampscott and Marblehead were being permitted to apply. In all of Gloucester improper, Eastern Point alone dared even dream . . . or, as one Beverly Farms–bound train passenger versed in such distinctions was overheard to sniff, "Only the riffraff go beyond Magnolia."

Still, every dog will have his day, and on the dog days even the riffraff — especially the riffraff — deserve, demand, a cooling-off . . . or, as Baedeker warned the North Shore–bound traveler from abroad, Revere Beach was a popular resort frequented by "Boston's lower classes." Yes, like Nantasket Beach, its counterpart at the beginning of the South Shore, Revere Beach was an unattached but captive sandbox for the sweating masses of Boston, safely quarantined from the verandahed summer properties beyond the narrow-gauge reach of the railroad that piped them out from their tenements and three-deckers in the morning and back that night, sunburned and satiated.

In former times, before they separated from the mother town, the all but deserted beach, bluff and marshland of Revere and Winthrop were the remotest reaches of old Chelsea, Boston's poor and indeed only relative in Suffolk County. Then in 1875 the slim track of the Boston, Revere Beach and Lynn penetrated like an irrigation ditch this forgotten appendage of the lower North Shore that had been by-passed disdainfully for thirty-five years by the main-line Eastern Railroad in its dash for Lynn and Salem and the green seaside estates of Essex County beyond.

Winthrop turned quietly to middle-class suburbanhood. But Revere was ruled by its beach, the real objective of the smart operators who pushed the Narrow Gauge through in order to sell off at a smart profit the thousands of acres they had bought for a song and to water the bizarre crop of amusements that sprang up along the miles of sands in the wake of their spindly tracks.

After only twenty summers of the freest enterprise, unrestrained by zoning law, building code or health ordinance, enjoyed every day and abandoned every night by sixty or seventy thousand escapees from urban suffocation, a Boston guidebook found Revere Beach in the mid-1890s "a queer colony . . . a place of low-browed, cheap, unlovely structures, in a crowded row on either side of the tracks, with narrow promenade, protected from them by wire fences. It was picturesque, if shabby, and, packed with its unconventional summer population, not uninteresting to the social philosopher. These structures were summer boarding-houses, 'hotels' and shops for trade and barter, seaside refreshments, bathing-shanties of various sizes and grades, and photographic 'saloons.' Prices ruled at the lowest, and all its ways were democratic."

And they all dispensed their trash and sewage with an equal abandon that advertised Revere Beach to the world, with the help of the mid-summer sun.

Here was much for the raking, strewn in the path of that juggernaut of environmental reform, the metropolitan planning movement just then marshaling behind the lead of the pioneer landscape architect Frederick Law Olmsted, who had already turned the Back Bay into the wondrous Charles River Fens park when the impressed state legislature in 1889 connected with thirty-three communities of Greater Boston together through the Metropolitan Sewerage Commission; three years later the Metropolitan Parks Commission was created.

After the Back Bay, the most culpable candidate for the Bostonian utopia foreseen in *Looking Backward* by Edward Bellamy, the re-formers' leading ideologist, was Revere Beach. The voters of Revere accepted the Parks Act in 1894 with relief, and the new Commission moved in with the new broom. A correspondent for the *Boston Evening Transcript* was mildly excited by the prospects: "The sights are many though not edifying, but it is easy for one to see what this beach was 20 years ago, and what it is soon to be again under the State park control. The project is to remove all the unsightly pasteboard structures from the beach, to move the railroads back and to construct a boulevard on what is now the roadbed of the narrow gauge line, the reservation to include the entire sweep of the sands from the Pines to Beachmont. Many will hail the coming of that happy day with delight. It is difficult to realize today that this was once a favorite shore resort for the best class of people. The sands alone, purified by the scouring tides, retain the freshness of those old days."

By 1896 every trace of shantytown between the Great Ocean Pier, which was the southern anchor of blue-collar respectability, and the former white-collar bastion of the Point of Pines — now descended to more proletarian pleasures — had been swept clean away. As if by a tidal wave, Revere Beach had been purified, and in the small station of the newly recruited Metropolitan Parks Police the Commission installed as its first keeper of its peace a local cop and champion weight thrower, Herbert G. West, six foot five inches and 267 pounds.

In former days some of the "bathing shanties" that rented swimming togs sold liquor under the counter. "Business was good," according to one source, "even when the ocean water was too cold for bathing and many of the suits were returned as dry as when given out." Unsteady patrons bent on getting wet outside as well had to dodge the trains hurtling along from both directions to gain the beach; the moving back of the tracks and the banishment of the shanties by the Parks Commission took care of that. In their place the MPC in 1897 put up its own stately brick bathhouse stocked with suits for both sexes and black hose for the ladies, enough for five thousand, and dressing facilities for a thousand at once.

Still, cavorting in the frigid waters of the North Shore was and remains for the intrepid. While the metropolitan planners dreamed of a model seaside park spread above the beach, the hundreds of thousands of bored and superheated refugees who flocked there from Greater

Boston were less interested in immersion than in diversion, and the more spectacular the better. Well, the Barnums were waiting, plans in hand, direct from Coney Island, some of them, and not for a moment fazed by the MPC's supposedly farsighted regulations that banned stables, factories and rooftop clotheslines on the cleared land, while restricting wooden structures to three stories, brick or stone to five, and refusing the display of signs without permission and the sale of liquor without license.

Overnight a new shantytown-in-the-making arose on the sands from which the old had just been stripped. By 1901 Crescent Gardens, the largest open-air dance hall in New England, and its rival, the Casino, had opened. The heart-stopping Loop-the-Loop had been added to the roller coaster's sickening third of a mile (one female passenger fainted on the maiden run and cut her head; luckily she was strapped in). For beachgoers who enjoyed watching others risk their necks there was a motorcycle racetrack, and for those who cared for neither, Hurley's Hurdlers, billed as the world's most elaborate carousel. The Hurley brothers, John and Frederick, were among the earliest barkers on the strip, of which the ingenious Fred (who once bootlegged fresh water to the thirsty, clandestinely tapped from the town supply, at a penny a glass) eventually owned a third.

America was on the move, and each colossal new attraction had to outdo the last. The summer of 1902 opened to a miniature scenic railway, an elaborate coaching parade that turned into an annual event, and the Steeple Chase, a sort of do-it-yourself circus with "Walk the Rope," "Bumpty-Bump," trick mirrors, a cageful of monkeys, and dancing. The sensation of the season was a water ride inside an enormous wood and tarpaper structure called The Old Mill that went up in roaring flames after only two seasons; the customers escaped simply by pushing out through the tarpaper walls. The wettest shows, for some reason, burned the best: The Johnstown Flood was a macabre recreation of the dam burst that drowned 2,009 in that Pennsylvania mining town in 1889; it opened in 1903 on the biggest stage in the Boston area, with a thousand seats, and was in ashes in 1905.

The summit of silliness in those early years of recrudescence was scaled in the summer of 1904 when the management of the Point of Pines Hotel and associated amusements proposed to celebrate the

Fourth with the head-on collision of two antiquated steam locomotives. So great was the public excitement that crashers stormed the gates, there was a riot involving forty thousand, and the promoters refused to let the show go on, whereupon a mob tried to get the engines moving, in vain. Six weeks later the Great Bash was restaged, but the crews who were supposed to leap from their cabs at the last second apparently lost their nerve and applied the brakes; the locomotives merely stopped and hissed at each other.

It happened that Revere and Nantasket beaches were just then engaged in a hissing contest across Boston Harbor. Senior to Revere in the ways of the playtime world, Nantasket was wiser, and wickeder. For years, notes its historian William M. Bergan, the South Shore's longest sandbar was the only liquor oasis between Boston and Provincetown, wide open under the eye of a local political machine run by boss John Smith, with gambling, confidence games, pickpockets and prostitution. After newspaper exposés pushed the legislature into an encore of its Revere Beach cleanup, the Metropolitan Parks Commission in 1899 and 1900 wiped out a mile of the worst, preparing the way for a new era of laundered amusements under the umbrella of the projected Paragon Park. By cutting Boss Smith in, Paragon's promoters assured its construction, and the Park opened for the season of 1905. The centerpiece was a lagoon with gondolas, a palm garden and an "Electric Tower," and around the periphery an assortment of Oriental mysteries, a Wild West show, shoot-the-chute, a zoo of sorts, and lo and behold, a resurrected "Johnstown Flood."

The North Shore's devastating reply was Wonderland Park, the all-time Revere Beach extravaganza, a super version of Paragon. It opened in 1906, admission one dime. Both were straight steals from Coney Island, and in the case of Wonderland's mammoth shoot-the-chutes ending in a mighty splash and glide over the lagoon, from the St. Louis Exposition of 1904 as well. Wild Bill Kennedy's Wild West Show and Indian Congress with a hundred genuine cowboys and Indians, forty horses, a tent camp, a raid, stage holdup and buffalo hunt every half hour. "The real thing without doubt," enthused one reporter; makes you "want to mount a pony and go careering across the plains, care free and soul untrammeled."

As if the beach hadn't fires enough, "Fighting the Flames" was

staged daily before a grandstand seating 3,500, with a cast of 350, a
twelve-piece ladder company and thirty horses — "a marvelously real-
istic and soul-stirring reproduction of the conflagration in a city
block," and quite enough to satisfy, or inspire, the most ardent firebug.
And all kinds of miscellaneous novelties such as circuses, Oriental
villages, a display of "Infant Incubators" described as "a genuinely
scientific, philanthropic, life-saving institution," and an intriguing
spectator-participation gimmick called Love's Journey, "an electrical
illusion, in which anyone in the audience who sees fit may become a
skeleton guest at a wedding feast." Or, as a popular song beckoned:

> *Wonderland, Wonderland, that's the place to be!*
> *Each night when I call on my sweetie, she says to me:*
> *"Let's take a trolley ride to the oceanside*
> *Where the shining lights are grand."*
> *If you want to make good as a true lover should,*
> *Just take her to Wonderland!*

Too many cowboys, Indians, firemen, Oriental villagers, monkeys,
trained horses, wire-walking elephants, high-diving dogs, miniature
railroads and brass bands per thin dime. Attendance peaked, and the
overhead peaked higher. After two sensational years Wonderland
faltered . . . and was reorganized on the brink. Three more seasons
and the entire flamboyant fantasy tottered, midway in time between
Frederick Tudor's Maolis Gardens at Nahant and an animated cartoonist's Disneyland, and collapsed. In 1911 Wonderland Park closed
its gilded doors forever. Twenty-three years later a nearby dog track
appropriated the magic name of Revere Beach's most splendid
achievement, and the site as its parking lot. But the beach had, in fact,
long since gone to the dogs.

Between the fall of shantytown and the rise of honkytonk there were
a few summers at the turn of the century when it looked as if the re-
formers might be on the right track in imagining that their clean-cut
"American Brighton," as it was being hailed, could thrive untainted
under the scant protection of their laissez-faire building regulations.

"The masses of the people," reflected the *New Ocean House Reminder* from behind the portico of the grand summer hotel a safe

distance away at Swampscott, "have the benefit of beautiful out-door surroundings where they are free to enjoy but restrained from any abuse of the attractions, and where manners and morals are required to be on a par with the high character of the scenery and the well kept roads and grounds. Pure air and the open sky do much to inspire the best that is in them, but should any fail to be so inspired there is always at hand the courteous and far-seeing park policeman to remonstrate."

This was the seaward-looking Revere Beach captured by the rainbowed brush of the great impressionist Maurice Prendergast, that shy, moustached bachelor Bostonian who parted his hair gravely in the middle and wore a high collar and cravat even while working . . . that retiring romantic who could see only vastly hatted and petticoated femininity against luminous backdrops of sand and sea and bobbing little sailboats, parks and picnics and pensive pleasure under a summer sun . . . where so many of his peers saw naught but ashcans and fire escapes.

Prendergast was not yet forty, full of the verve of his tour of study in Europe, when in the summer of 1896 he discovered the brilliant bareness of Revere Beach, restored all too briefly to sand and sea by the wrecking crews of the MPC. The miles of glaring whiteness were populated, judging by his sketchbook and watercolors of that summer and the next, entirely by ladies swathed from the sun, wearing hats almost as broad as their parasols, or perky little affairs with flowers, watching in desultory preoccupation over beribboned and sunbonneted young girls lifting their skirts above black-stockinged ankles to tiptoe from rock to rock above the shining tide pools, and by well-behaved boys in striped bathing suits, and by portly autocrats of their supper tables, properly suited and derbied, hands thrust in pants pockets, staring out over the American Sea.

As saving of his purse as he was lavish with his colors, Maurice hiked the four miles from Winchester, where he lived with his brother, to Medford for transportation to the beach, it is said, to save a nickel. How he managed his further excursions to Nantasket and South Boston and along the North Shore as far as Cape Ann, one wonders. On each of the seaside resorts of Boston, the artist, still under the spell of

Paris, gazed with the midsummer dreaminess of the lovesick swain, as if he were in love with love, entranced by the glimpse of a faintly sunburnt face, half-hidden in the shade of a coquettishly tilted parasol.

Nowhere else, though, did Prendergast catch the fleeting life of a place, and the transience of an American era . . . both gone forever . . . as during his flirtation with Revere Beach, where the most exquisitely feminine of the frequenters would wring from him the bashful compliment, "She is just like one of those French girls!" Ah, les jeunes filles . . .

Too soon the artist's dreamy models and their unruffled plots of sand were overwhelmed by the crowds the metropolitan-minded were drawing to the beach by the hundreds of thousands. Promoting a descending denominator of taste, the proprietors of the amusement park vied to provide the cheapest thrills, the most mindless spectacles. Fires followed Roman circus, and Roman circus, fires, and it was downhill most of the way after the failure of Wonderland Park in 1911, bottoming out (with extraordinary flair, it must be admitted) in 1927 with the Great Marine Bonfire.

The authors of this maddest of mayhems anchored a decrepit three-masted schooner off the beach, loaded her with wood scraps and a thousand old railroad ties, hung her with fireworks, drenched the sails with oil, dumped gunpowder on the decks, torched her off and abandoned ship. They said a million suckers came to gape, jamming the roads for miles. Two hundred thousand couldn't get out afterward and had to spend the night on the beach. A helluva spectacle all right, but the old hulk declined to burn below the waterline for some strange reason, and it cost the promoters $20,000 to clean up the mess.

As mass entertainment, Revere Beach never outgrew its own pimply adolescence, never had a chance against the insinuations of the motor car and the onslaughts of the motion pictures, not to mention television. It remained a hand-cranked thirty-ring circus and tried resourcefully, God knows, to hang on to the sunburnt, roller-coasting, dance-marathoning, hotdogging, love-tunneling, gum-chewing, Kewpie doll–winning trade, into an age of diversion packaged for the passive, into its own sorry, shambling, silly senility.

In its raucous heyday, though, the Beach really was the most outrageous, extravagant symbol around of American energy, restlessness, passion for action and, perhaps most of all, unquenchable optimism.

Farther along the coast, by contrast, the traditional public place of resort on Salem Neck known as the Willows was as much *of* the North Shore as *on* it. The grove of drooping willows had been planted in 1801; the gnarled trunk of the greatest was nearly twenty feet in girth. Salem adopted the thirty-five acres as a park in 1858. In 1877 the Naumkeag Street Railway ran out the first horsecars, three years later hung a carrot in front of Dobbin in the shape of perhaps the first amusement park in America built by a traction company for the purpose of generating traffic.

Virtually overnight, live wire replaced horseflesh, and the trolley car swept across the landscape like a bolt of lightning. In 1885 Leo Daft had run his queer electric trams above Revere Beach, so it was wildly appropriate that one of the first trolleys anywhere in regular service should rattle along the beach at thirty miles an hour on the second of June, 1888. In two months Naumkeag electrified its Salem Willows line. When the owners of Boston's sprawling West End Railroad fired their horses, the rush was on; by 1899 two hundred systems were operating or under construction.

The speed with which the trolley lines spun their web across the face of the North Shore was a phenomenon in itself. Within two years of its first run to Revere Beach in 1891, the Lynn and Boston Electric Railway had plugged into the West End network at Scollay Square in Boston (five cents and forty-five minutes to Revere Beach), inland as far as Woburn and down the North Shore to Hamilton, letting riders off at a dozen and a half resorts and parks on the way. In two more years it connected with the independent Gloucester trolleys running to Rocky Neck and Annisquam since 1890.

Few would take exception to the Lynn and Boston's enthusiastic guidebook boast that "in its annual mission of taking thousands from the heated cities, into the pure, refreshing scenes of the country and seashore, the electric car has proved itself one of the greatest blessings mankind has ever known. It is the universal vehicle, as comfortable and convenient for the well-to-do as it is economical and available for the less fortunate."

By 1899 the Lynn and Boston was the biggest spider in Essex County and ready for the eating by a bigger one, the Massachusetts Electric Company, which in its turn was swallowed in 1901 by the Boston and Northern, a combine of twenty-three independents north of Boston. That was the nadir of expansion for the electrics. The screeching, swaying, sparking, clanging, careening little trolley cars were creating suburbanism and metropolitanism and interurbanism, providing every-body with wheels to everywhere for pocket change. Round trip by trolley car from Scollay Square to Gloucester and all the way around the Cape Ann shore and back to Boston, for instance, consumed nine and a half hours and one dollar.

Ultimately their very success was their undoing. Speculation spurred expansion until the tracks, and costs, were outrunning the riders, and the farther from the city and the deeper into the country, the faster. Then began a period of consolidation. The Boston and Northern on the North Shore and the Old Colony network on the South Shore trumpeted in their joint guidebook of 1910 that the electric railway "carries the banner of progress far in advance . . . makes it possible to snap one's fingers at the gasoline tank, the turbine steamer or the soft-coal, choking steam engine." Next year the two merged as the Bay State Street Railway, claiming to be the biggest in the world, seventy-two former independent lines with 938 miles of track, much of it deficit-producing.

There were demurrers. The *North Shore Breeze* condemned the Salem-Gloucester stretch as "the roughest that we have ever ridden over . . . bump, bump, bump all the way there and back. . . . The run-ning schedule is followed — well, it is followed, but they seldom catch up with it." The arrival of Dr. Holmes's "broomstick train" in sleepy Essex was lamented in the *Boston Herald:* "But once let the street railroad get its clutches on a town and its own peculiar and distin-guishing air seems to disappear with marvellous rapidity. . . . Very many travel simply for pleasure, and wherever people go for their pleasure, there they are apt to spend more money and leave a deeper impression." Manchester did something about it: jealous for their narrow streets and skittery horses, influential summer residents got the legislature to ban the trolley altogether from most of the western section of the town.

For the popular amusement parks, though, the street railways were the conduits of the custom and a particular reliance of Salem Willows after the summer of 1904, when General Grant's Civil War dispatch boat *Monohansett* smashed her old bones ashore between the Misery Islands in a thick-o'-fog. Thus ended seven seasons of excursion steamers from Boston, reinvigorating the North Shore insularity of the Willows and the park's dependence on the street railway that created it.

Salem Willows was an intimate (what is more intimate than a holiday crowd of twenty thousand?), cool, shaded but in no way shady, provincial (locally owned and properly policed), refined (rough-housers were expelled) picnic and play ground featuring a lively, more or less yokel-oriented amusementt park. No beach to speak of, hence no mass bathing, and no liquor. Jake Alpert offered seventeen kinds of temperance drinks to parched bicyclers. Just the destination for an amorous foray.

> *You don't mind the trolley because you can jolly*
> *The nice little girls by your side.*
> *On moonlight nights, Gee! it is dandy,*
> *And on Sundays it's simply divine.*
> *You can have all your "Coneys,"*
> *To me they're all phoneys,*
> *But Salem Willows for mine — it's mine.*

Leafing through the *Salem Willows Budget,* a seasonal weekly published from 1897 until the eve of the First World War, one gets the feeling of North Shore boys and girls (and a few up-the-liners) on a summer spree.

The most sensational crowd-catcher of 1897 (though not enough to pay its own way for more than a couple of seasons) was a shoot-the-chute ten years in advance of Wonderland's that hauled the car-boats up a funicular tramway, then loosed them down the long slide with their shrieking cargoes to surf through a lagoon that is now the junction of Fort and Columbus avenues.

The most durable crowd-pleaser that year was Joe Brown's steam-driven "Flying Horses," one of the oldest and certainly most colorful merry-go-rounds in the United States. His carved steeds were vintage

Holt's Pier, Revere Beach, built in 1910 after the Great Ocean Pier burned. Alongside is the Boston-Nahant steamer, probably the General Lincoln. *McCauley collection*

Bathers, Revere Beach. McCauley collection

The Mountain Railway,
Revere Beach, Mass.

Men made mountains in the peak days of the Beach. McCauley collection

*The Lightning Roller Coaster at Revere claimed speeds of a mile a minute.
McCauley collection*

The poster hardly does justice to the extravaganzas of Wonderland Park during its brief glory. McCauley collection

Wonderland's "fire department" is drawn up in full battle array before the block fronts that belched the flames and smoke seen in the right of the poster for the spectacle "Fighting the Flames." McCauley collection

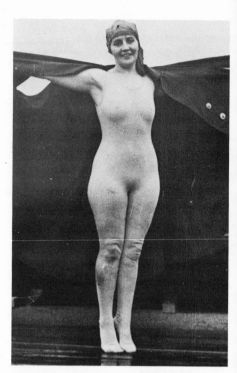

Annette Kellerman, the distance swimmer, poses at Revere Beach in the one-piece suit she made famous with her arrest therein a minute or two later for overexposure. McCauley collection

Bathing beauties not so daring. McCauley collection

Shoot-the-chute at Salem Willows, 1896–1906, in what is today the triangle of Fort and Columbus avenues and Dustin Street. Essex Institute

John W. Gorman's summer theatre at Salem Willows, August 1902, Tenor Richard J. Jose, Miss Lizzie Otto at the piano. Essex Institute

The excursion steamer Cape Ann *churns into Gloucester from Boston, summer of 1913. Eben Parsons photo*

Gloucester, Mass. The Pavilion,
Long Beach, Cape Ann.

LONG BEACH PAVILION.

The rollicking open-air trolley car arrives at the Pavilion behind Rockport's Long Beach with a freight of day-trippers from Gloucester. Paul Harling collection

A wet landing off Revere between Nahant and Winthrop. McCauley collection

The Bass Point House dresses up for Nahant's fiftieth anniversary in 1903. Nahant Public Library

examples of the art, some of them sculptures of famous racehorses. Music for the "over a mile in every ride" was provided by a twenty-four-piece mechanical orchestra. Mr. Brown's chef d'oeuvre after he electrified the drive was his "automatic village" in the hole of his whirling doughnut, with houses, church, gristmill, swan pond, fort, lighthouse, miniature trains, merry-go-round and circus parade, all going to beat the band.

The most elevating crowd-thrillers of '97 were Professor Bonette and his family, who arose above the willows in twin hot-air balloons to an altitude of 6,000 feet, then parachute-raced back to earth. Thirteen years after that, to celebrate the Fourth in his own unique fashion, the iron-jawed Professor Ullven's "Slide for Life" (all true daredevils in those days were "professors") had all agape as he scorched down a tightwire strung from the top of the Pavilion tower to the stone beacon off the steamship pier, hanging from a traveling block by nothing but his teeth.

Or you could pay your penny and catch Edison's Kinetoscope, a primitive motion-picture peepshow featuring "The Seminary Girls' Pillow Fight" and "The Irwin Kiss," or buy a basket from the Indians ("genuine Micmacs") and get your fortune told, or gawk at that party of kite-flying Chinese who "caused much merriment by their queer antics."

As one Century of Progress gave way to an Even Greater One, the *Budget* recorded vaudeville shows in Gorman's Theatre, rousing concerts by the Salem Cadet Band, the arrival of the roller skating craze, jackass rides for the kiddies, and the twenty-eighth year at his usual stand of Pat Kennealley, inventor of the world-famed double-jointed peanut. And all kinds of ways of turning an extra buck. Harry Esbach, the tintype photographer, was attracting custom with his tank of live alligators that he brought up from his Florida winter quarters, while F. J. Tree taught ballroom dancing and on the side ran a soft-drink stand that he called "The Only Poplar Tree at the Willows."

For customers overwhelmed by the glorious victories of the Spanish War, a Salem department store jingoistically prescribed: "Be Patriotic — Ask for a bottle of our smelling salts shaped like a projectile in Dewey's Rapid Fire Guns." And just in case (from a *Budget* military expert watching a squad of "boy soldiers" drilling every evening): "Not a Spaniard, Cuban or Filipino could land at Juniper Point alive, while they are around."

Over it all watched the sleepless keepers of the quiet. Midsummer of 1905: "Tommy Hyde, the Willows cop, had a good taste of rough house with a party of young men under the influence of the ardent fluid, Saturday evening last. It is needless to say that Tommy came out on top although he was presented with a beauty upper cut which nearly knocked him out." A few nights later: "The roughs 'wid der loidy friens' who visited the Willows on Wednesday evening last didn't find our blue coated guardians of the peace such 'easy marks' as they expected. They were on the contrary rushed away from here about 11 o'clock while the Willows assembly piped out in chorus 'Good Bye My Blue Bells.' " Aha! warned the *Budget*. It will be "Skidoo 23" for any more roughhousers who try to take over our Willows.

What makes the world go round, on the other hand, was less summarily dealt with by the blue-coated guardians, as on one Sunday evening in August of 1906: "A spooning match was held on the oval opposite the band stand. Two couples, old enough to know better, took a prominent place to show their affection. The course of events was as usual, the end coming when all four were stretched out on the ground as snug as a bug in a rug. The attention of the bystanders was attracted to the bandstand, where Master Hudson Williams was singing. During this period the match ended by the appearance of one of the park police. The attention of the officer was called and walking over in front of them he threw his 'bug' light on the faces of the quartette. This did not shame them, but simply served to bring the bold visitors to their senses. They gathered up their traps and went on their way, leaving behind them sounds of laughter. Perhaps if the Charles River 'sit-up' law were enforced at the Willows, the conditions would be improved for the visitors who do not care to run into such surroundings."

The *Budget* leaned to the view that the bully boys, if not the spooners, followed the tracks into the Willows. In 1910 it fingered trolley parties from Chelsea for their "hoodlum reputation." In fact, for a few dollars any group could hire an open car with side curtains in case of a shower, motorman included, and go practically anywhere the tracks and the switches led. From near and far they screeched into the Willows for the fish dinners, the amusements, the concerts, the dancing, the spooning or a brush with the boys in blue — Hose Company Number 4 from Melrose in a car decorated with bunting and sunflowers, a bunch calling themselves the "Top Knots" from Gloucester, and all the way from Philadelphia in 1906 a trolley party with the reassuring word that they had passed through few cities and towns where connections were not easily made.

That same year of 1906, ominously for the bouncing electrics, the *Budget* reported that "a big array of 'buzz wagons' commonly known as automobiles were here." In 1908 less speed from "these gasolene-driven demons" was demanded, followed by a call in 1910 for a speed limit of eight miles an hour. Not until America entered the First War, however, was there a big enough array of buzz wagons to threaten the trolleys. When peacetime mass automobile production took off after the Armistice, trolley operating profits plummeted, and the street railway industry suddenly simply collapsed with the dawn of the twenties.

Although originally but a carrot for the horsecars, Salem Willows adapted. The trolley era came and went, and the park whose first amusement was a gala hanging in 1772 (the crowd brought box lunches) found room for four thousand gasolene-driven demons. Like the last of the willows, two or three attractions hang on. The breezes still caress, and Salem Neck welcomes strollers as always, and spooners.

Down on Cape Ann, at the Gloucester end of Rockport's Long Beach, a midway in miniature was so completely the creation of the local street railway that when the one died, the other died too. The company in 1895 had built a trestle across the dunes behind Little Good Harbor Beach and put up a pavilion, dance hall, vaudeville theatre, Ferris wheel, photo studio and bowling alley. The single-truck open cars, wrote historian Thomas E. Babson, "had the habit of galloping like a horse. Guard bars were let down on both sides before crossing the trestle. . . . Even so, a careless passenger was occasionally tossed off into the dunes." One day the breeze took Ada Merchant's hat; the motorman stopped the car, climbed down off the trestle and retrieved it for her.

The trolleys inspired a small hotel, and a long boardwalk above the tide, bordered soon by a lengthening row of small summer cottages. Folks would arrive at Gloucester for the day from Boston on the snow-white excursion steamer *Cape Ann* and grab the electrics for a shore dinner and a gambol (and a gamble, some said) at the Long Beach Pavilion, encouraged, perhaps, by reassurances that North Shore trolley parks were "kept free from objectionable characters and anything that might offend ladies and children who might visit these places unaccompanied." For twenty-five years the little beach park within reach of the salt sea spray paid its way until it fell victim to its sire's bankruptcy in 1920.

At nearly the other end of the North Shore, Nahant's popular park at Bass Point basked happily in the glare from Revere Beach reflected across Lynn Bay and did its damnedest to echo the blare, to the rising dismay of Nahanters who would tear this distressingly democratic viper from the breast of their fair peninsula if they could and actually succeeded for almost fifty years in fending off the threatened incursions of mass transportation and all that implied.

Time and again mainlanders exhorted the town for permission to extend steam, horse or electric railway tracks from Lynn along the sliver of beach to the Shore's oldest and most hidebound resort. Always the natives and summer people alike, with long memories of the crowds drawn to Ice King Frederic Tudor's primeval amusement park, Maolis Gardens, and its oddities that infested the heart of the town, demurred, more than content with the controllable influx of foreigners rationed by the Boston steamer and Nahant's peculiar, indigenous, horse-drawn "barges." Outmaneuvered for a change in 1905, they gave the Nahant and Lynn Street Railroad a grudging go-ahead, and in a few months the trolleys were clanging out the causeway. Then a spur was looped to the Relay House on Bass Point, and the worst, as far as Cold Roast was concerned, had come to pass.

The trouble was that both the Relay House and the Bass Point House had built wharves in the mid-1890s for steamers to disgorge the overflow of proletariat from Revere Beach's Great Ocean Pier and Lynn, and that meant dance halls, vaudeville, brass bands in the middle of the night and the usual other attractions for the unruly, including barrooms. The very real and present presence of the amusement park and its ancillary activities endangered proximate land values. First a tent city of impecunious summerers, then shanties, then camps, then a few small cottages built or bought, as town father and historian Fred Wilson wrote between clenched teeth, "by people of Irish nativity or descent." And the horrid prospect of the blight spreading . . . and the fires . . . and the insurance rates!

Bass Point was a thorn in the side of proper Nahant, no question. Some summer Sundays, between the steamers and the trolleys and the automobiles there were forty thousand souls over on the other shore from Spouting Horn . . . and how they carried on a southwest wind! But the boat service was scuttled by the First War, and the trolleys quit, and the amusements folded, and that was that — to the relief of all Nahant — except for some unpleasantness with bootleggers and bad women around the dance halls during Prohibition.

Through it all, somehow, the reliable old Relay House, which had been the bastion of Bass Point since 1862, retained a touch of class. Witness the traditional opening in June:

"Just as the shades of night begin to fall bewitching music fills the air, coming from the ladies orchestra in a cozy corner of the first piazza; singing follows, and a speech by some leading citizen, who, in his peroration gives a signal which calls for the unfurling of our country's flag, then the multitude relieve themselves by cheers, and all the while fireworks illuminate the sky and the grounds surrounding the hotel. After this the banquet is in order, and the best the house affords is freely served to half a thousand guests, while high class singing and the orchestra entertain. When all is over in the house the flag is taken down for the night, slowly taken down and furled, while twenty-one guns thunder the national salute. There is no cheering now; but all is silent through respect; yet rich, red, patriotic blood flows stronger through the veins, and all are better Americans as the result of the patriotic teachings and the true American principles instilled at each opening of the summer season at the Relay House, Nahant."

Another perspective was adopted by the *New Ocean House Reminder,* which one July week in 1906 reminded guests who were disposed to go forth slumming in their motor cars from the swellest summer hotel in Swampscott that "in these days of aims for raising the ideals of the masses, one should not neglect to see, at Bass Point, the attractions that appeal to the people at large."

3

Arks That Pass in the Night

"The fog has gone!" the bell hop cried:
The guests ran out the door.
One fleeting glimpse of blue they spied:
The fog had gone — for more.
— North Shore Breeze

IN ITS DAY, WHICH WAS A LONG ONE, THE NEW OCEAN HOUSE AT SWAMP-scott was possibly the most disagreeably exclusive of the important summer arks on the North Shore. George Stacy's Hawthorne Inn at East Gloucester may have been more disagreeable (his guests loved him for it), and George Upton's magnificent Oceanside at Magnolia more exclusive (and how his guests loved *him!*). But the turned-up-nose prize went to the New Ocean House, thumbs down.

The oldest Ocean House was opened on Phillips Point in 1836 and was the Shore's senior summer hostelry behind the Nahant Hotel. It burned during the Civil War, reopened above Whale Beach, burned again, was rebuilt as the New Ocean House in 1884 and was sold in 1895 to the owners of the Hamilton in Bermuda. They dropped the "New," wired all 175 rooms with electric call bells, installed a telephone and an elevator and promised prospective guests: "As the patrons of the house are among the best families in the country, the society is second to none."

Not unexpectedly, after a few years there was another fire. Two hotel men, Allen Ainslie and Edward R. Grabow, bought in, pumped

$100,000 into remodeling and enlarging and in 1902 opened as, once again, the New Ocean House. With growing prosperity they added an orchestra, subscription concerts, balls, recitations, juvenile vaudeville, bagatelle, whist, clock golf and tennis tournaments, imported the English equestrian Arthur S. Sankey to teach riding, jumping and hunting, and started up a weekly house organ of gossip and self-admiration, the *New Ocean House Reminder*.

Ainslie and Grabow may have sounded like a vaudeville team, but they waltzed offstage with four hotels in Jamaica and the Tuileries, Empire and Lenox in Boston, besides the Ocean House. They knew their custom, and at Swampscott they knew how to stroke the snob. One of the *Reminder*'s early editorial campaigns, for example, was to have the *p* eliminated from Swampscott. The real gripe, however, soon emerged: "the outside element." Happily, the hotel was free of it, but it was something to be watched out for, as in 1906: "No disturbing outside element . . . no objectionable parties. . . . Even on the Fourth of July, there is none of the annoying confusion that attends the day in some localities." But wait . . . later that season, concerning a block of sixteen tenements noxiously close to the hotel, known locally as "The Acre": "Why do not our people get together and look after the Italian quarter, which is certainly a disgrace to Swampscott? It is a pity that that portion of the town should not be made into a beautiful park when so little stands in the way of doing it."

Elitism was selling so well that by 1907 it was the *North Shore Reminder,* distributed from Nahant to Marblehead, published by the Ainslie and Grabow Press and puffing not one but all the hotel holdings of the owners. How grateful its guests were reminded to be that the New Ocean House had a buffer of land next the highway, "thus preventing the approach of any outside element. . . . When a management has had long experience with an exclusive and wealthy line of patrons, it knows what to do to confirm those patrons in their predilection for a certain resort. This, in the case of the New Ocean House, is especially true. And its guests, to an unusual degree, express a thorough appreciation of the efforts so generously put forth to further their comfort and pleasure. . . . To the several exclusive resort hotels within its borders Swampscott owes that immunity from all objectionable summer patronage, which has always been one of its special claims for the select and refined class of people who seek a summer home along its cool and lovely beaches."

The New Ocean House eventually succumbed to its enemy of sorts — not the outside element but the fiery one. Chief among the others to which Swampscott owed its immunity from objectionable patronage were the Lincoln House and the Hotel Preston. The latter dominated Beach Bluff with spreading piazzas and stately porte cochere through which clip-clopped turnouts spic and span, and glided silently electric automobiles periodically rejuvenated at the hotel's own charging station. The elk's head surveyed the lobby with glassy gaze from above the main fireplace, every room had its own India rubber plant, and an ensemble of Boston Symphony players gave morning and evening concerts to the staccato obbligato of the smartly struck croquet ball upon the Preston's rolling lawn.

Proceeding down the Shore, Marblehead had a few of these breezy piles of lumber, nothing in the grand style. Beverly was shoulder-to-shoulder in private estates, and so was Manchester with the solitary and memorable exception of the Masconomo, named after a local Indian sachem of former days. This was the sprawling dog that the actors Junius Brutus Booth, Jr., and his wife Agnes had attached to the tail of their summer cottage above Singing Beach in 1878, when their neighbors were fellow theatre people, and not many of them, and none disposed to mutter an *et tu, Brute* over the presence of such a captive audience in their midst.

Eleven foreign ambassadors were summering in Manchester in 1904, from which one may infer that the Masconomo's vaunted "immunity from malaria" — certainly no hazard on the North Shore — was a redundant come-on directed to the diplomatic corps. Among them was the envoy of the Czar, and it was said that the Russo-Japanese War might have ended in the Booths' octagonal hall the next summer, except that it was not large enough for all the delegates, with the result that the peace stage-managed by President Theodore Roosevelt was consummated in the larger Wentworth at Portsmouth, New Hampshire.

Manchester-by-the-Sea tolerated the Masconomo and the close colony of actors and actresses from which it sprang in the post–Civil War era, and who lent the town interest and liveliness, though the hotel had obviously been snuck in. By 1908 it was being publicly and quite huffily dismissed by the *Breeze* as run-down and third class. Junius had long since joined his more famous and infamous acting brothers. Aggie, remarried, leased it out, and things began to look up until September of 1909, when her new manager, leaving a score of employees and a $1,600 unpaid payroll behind, was last seen running toward Smith's Point, where he allegedly put to sea in a motor boat owned by the son of his financial backer, the convicted New York "policy king" Al Adams. When Aggie Booth died soon after, her third husband, Boston theatre owner John B. Schoeffel, bought the Masconomo from the executors for old times' sake. The once colorful old hotel enjoyed a brief revival during the First War, but in 1920 most of it was torn down.

Kettle Cove and its Crescent Beach separated Manchester's Coolidge Point and Gloucester's Knowlton's Point, and still do, except that when the Knowltons started selling off their pasture for summer boardinghouses in 1867, some romantic renamed the fishing hamlet of Kettle Cove and their farm, Magnolia and Magnolia Point, after the exotic flowering shrub found only in the north in the sylvan swamp out back. Rapidly Magnolia was adopted by Manchester, which owned most of the intervening beach, as a convenient guest colony for its summer overflow . . . so convenient that in 1877 Gloucester had to beat back a seditious attempt by the Knowltons to get Manchester to annex its major share of Magnolia.

Gloucester's union, nominally anyway, was preserved. In 1879 George A. Upton acquired one of these bucolic boardinghouses, the Oceanside. Here was no mere dispenser of bathing suits and blueberry muffins. The man was a veritable Noah of the business; he foresaw the flood of fashion in resorts even then, and he swore to all the creatures of the summer that he and they would be borne upon it. His house grew to arklike proportions, and as if a craft alive, sprouted and swallowed lesser arks until it tumbled and spread eastward — from the summit of Lexington Avenue down over Magnolia Point toward the sea. Deck upon bay-windowed deck, bridge over shingled bridge, bow unto stern of grandeur rode with profound and yet playful majesty over a vast and undulating groundswell of lawn, and one day as the century turned, engraved in the annals of verandahdom, the proud proprietor surveyed this most cosmopolitan collection of lumber ever assembled on the coast north of Boston, perambulated his piazzas with a measuring tape, and discovered to his and the world's amazement that he had 881 feet of them — almost exactly one sixth of a mile.

But George Upton's imagination could be encompassed by neither piazzas nor statistics. Who knows how many rocking chairs he owned? Certainly not he. His main dining saloon was forty-five feet wide and a hundred and fifty long, half the length of a football field, enclosed within a tenth of an acre of plate glass windows and sea-green walls. The Oceanside casino . . . why, it was of such horizon as to support a perfect firmament of fleecy clouds drifting across a cerulean ceiling from which starlike electric lights twinkled and beamed upon the swaying dancers below.

By 1908, when this sagacious Noah sold his ark for a half a million dollars after clearing upward of sixty thousand a season for the past ten, he had gathered in ten arklets and 600 rooms. The momentum of fashion surged on. In 1912 the Oceanside gobbled up the rival Hesperus on the west side of Lexington Avenue . . . the mammoth parent structure, twenty-two cottages by then, 750 rooms . . . the biggest summer hotel in New England.

And the classiest.

George Upton was a strong temperance man, with interesting standards: he accorded his guests storage privileges under the control of his cellarman. "The single violation of the accepted rules of courtesy and politeness," shuddered John W. Black, Jr., who worked there in the Upton era, "ended the career of any employee who came in contact with the guests." That was class.

And the twenty-piece orchestra playing from on top of the porte cochere every afternoon, and Sunday evenings when the concerts were serious, if not deadly, and "absolute silence was required and obtained." That was class, and so was the rousing rendition of his own marches when that annual habitué, John Philip Sousa, annually borrowed the baton. And the Chinese princess dressed all in silks, with feet bound, riding the elevator in 1903 and in Black's memory for the next fifty-three years . . . class. And his mental picture of walking down the path to "Highland Cottage" behind the ramrod figure of young Major Douglas MacArthur, visiting his aunts. And glimpses of William Dean Howells and Mrs. Ulysses S. Grant, Alice Roosevelt Longworth and Mrs. J. P. Morgan, and the Turkish ambassador, and the Chilean ambassador and the Uruguayan ambassador, just drops in the buckets of ambassadors who poured into the Oceanside or rented summer mansions as nearby as they could get. Very classy.

The Ketchup King, Henry J. Heinz of Pittsburgh, brought his family to the Oceanside, fell for Magnolia and in 1904 built a $240,000 mansion on the shore there. They had to sell out after the 1929 Crash; eventually the Heinz site sprouted wings of hostelry as the Magnolia Manor, but since then, between fire and foreclosure, glory in all its fifty-eight varieties has fled forever.

The Biscuit Baron of Chicago, Jacob L. Loose, had for his houseguest for most of the summer of 1906, probably in one of the Oceanside cottages that the rich rented by the season, cigar-chomping Joseph G. (Foul-mouthed Joe) Cannon, the uncouth boss of the House of Representatives, one of its less distinguished Speakers. Smitten like Heinz, the senior partner in the Loose Wiles Biscuit Company built a mansion on the ocean side of Gloucester's Eastern Point in 1916. And like the Heinzes, the Looses suffered relative deprivation in the Crash. They had always supported the local Episcopal church, but when their summer neighbor, Bishop Philip M. Rhinelander, visited Mrs. Loose during his annual "Dough Sunday" rounds on its behalf, she apologized . . . ahem . . . but did dig up the dough, well baked in a steady supply of biscuits — communion wafers, perchance? — for the next two years.

And there was the Silent Partner, the slight and seemingly unassuming Colonel (by decree of his political pal, Governor Hogg of Texas) Edward M. House. Heir to a plantation fortune and astute enough in his own right, Colonel House was already the kingmaker of Texas politics when he discovered Magnolia in 1901. He brought his family there regularly thereafter, usually if not invariably to the Oceanside, where they were fixtures at least until 1910, often in "Breakers Cottage." House and his king of kings, Woodrow Wilson, were not to meet until 1911, although the then president of Princeton had sojourned the summer of 1903 in East Gloucester, separated by the mere length of the harbor from the man whom fate destined to be the greatest influence in his life.

And clearly it was the Oceanside with which Episcopal Bishop William Lawrence (a Nahant summerer himself) enjoyed illustrating the social provincialism of the Harvard academic community. Upon their return to Cambridge one autumn, a dean inquired of the fabled three Palfrey sisters, all spinsters of determination and renown, what sort of season they had. Replied one: "We have had a delightful summer. We stayed at a great hotel in Magnolia, and met a number of really intelligent and agreeable people of whom we had never before heard." Though they had traveled far and wide abroad, Cleveland Amory claimed in a similar version of the story, it was the only occasion in this country that they had been farther from home than Nahant. Actually, according to Amory, they referred to themselves as "retired Boston gentlewomen sleeping in Cambridge."

Summering diplomats, most likely, dreamed up the truly outrageous sporting events called gymkhanas that were held for five years on Crescent Beach beginning in 1905, mainly under the aegis of the Oceanside, which concluded each one with its grand banquet and ball of the season. The word is a bastard, claiming some Hindu parentage, originating among bored English officers in India and covering a miscellany of equally bastardized athletic activities involving men and horses.

The long and smoothly curving beach was the perfect arena for such goings-on, which attracted thousands of the North Shore's elite in yachts by sea and by land in a flood of carriages and motor cars, swarming the boardwalk and the bathhouse and piling into the boxes and reserved seats in the pavilion. The high point of the 1908 gymkhana, to give sufficient flavor of the antics, was the eight-mile horseback race for men requiring the contestants to dash along the beach from start to finish, dismount, toss off a bottle of ginger ale (so the *Breeze* had it, anyway), remount, gallop back to the starting line, remove coats and put them back on inside out, and charge back to the finish.

The gymkhanas ceased in 1910, perhaps because the center of Crescent Beach was being quarantined by the Manchester Bath and Tennis

GUESTS OF THE NEW OCEAN HOUSE IN THEIR MOTOR CARS

The initial skepticism of the New Ocean House management toward the new motor car had given way to enthusiasm by 1911. Essex Institute

Porch, and rockers, as far as the eye can see. New Ocean House, 1908. Essex Institute

Dining room and foyer of the New Ocean House, 1908. Essex Institute

The massive Colonial Arms commands the Eastern Point shore of Gloucester Harbor, 1905. The Niles farmhouse is barely visible under the service wing at left. Ernest Blatchford photo

Porch upon pilaster, George Stacy's crowning (though soon dethroned) achievement, the Colonial Arms, climbs above its porte cochere. Ernest Blatchford photo

Club, which opened in 1912, soon to be fashionable with its pool, courts and dining room overlooking the cove and the ocean.

The crowning ball, however, continued as the apotheosis of Oceanside class and the social pinnacle of the season before the clouds of war o'erspread the great dining room ceiling. John Black worked five of them, and in his bedazzled memory, Mrs. John Hays Hammond, Sr., was "undisputed queen, indescribably beautifully gowned and jeweled, especially the glorious diamond tiara she wore." And why not? Her husband and Cecil Rhodes had been partners.

Doings at the Oceanside by 1912 dominated the extensive hotel news in the *Breeze,* which duly documented arrivals and departures of private railroad cars at the Magnolia station on the one side, and the Magnolia Horse Show replacing the gymkhana on Crescent Beach and managed by its riding master, Harry Coulter, on the other. The summer weekly, toward the end of one rather stormy July, observed that the lobby, "on an afternoon or evening, when the ladies are at whist and the gentlemen are talking politics or wrapped in revery behind good Havanas, furnishes a spectacle that does one's heart good. There, seated about, are distinguished representatives of every civilized nation of pretension throughout the world. Spanish senoras exchange compliments with English noble-women, and Frenchmen of noble blood discuss finance with South American ministers. Yet they seem like one great family."

The Oceanside's tennis and golf tournaments, water carnivals, marshmallow toasts down on the rocks, chaperoned automobile parties to Revere Beach ("the comic-relief in the North Shore summer drama for the younger set") all fluttered through the pages of the *Breeze,* none with such abandon as the mania that struck in 1913: "If it is true that the North Shore is dance mad, then the central asylum is Magnolia, for everybody goes there."

Ah, the afternoon *thé dansant* at the Oceanside featuring the Castle Walk, the Trot, the Maxixe, the Texas Tommy and the Aeroplane Glide . . . the Wednesday night hop . . . and the Saturday evening ball when, in the "sophis" patter of the *Breeze* correspondent, "fashion merrily cracks its whip. . . . The orchestra begins! A gaily gathered crowd in amazing Paris frocks trots, promenades the veranda, chats and gossips. Others are arriving and leaving by familiar motor sounds.

Some are chaperoning in pleasant groups from exchange and veranda. Some are just listening to the music and still some others are using the ensemble as an accompaniment to the ever-lasting fascination of the card table. The charm of youth and the brilliancy of maturity in shadow lace and brocade, many colored chiffons and all the materials de soir, with the inevitable wide-winding girdle, with the sparkle of jewels and the prance of cut-steel-buckled slippers, dance to the rhythm of ragtime chimes, through the many variations of one-step and trots, and the maxixe, and hesitations. It is a spectacle that repays attention."

Yes, John Black, you were right: "This establishment spelled *class*." And war and taxes and automobiles and changing patterns of summer life killed and buried it. And though Bill Tilden and Paul Whiteman graced court and casino in the Twenties, the old grandeur reigned over by the Natalie Hays Hammonds of the North Shore died with them. On December 11, 1958, the magnificent Oceanside burned to the ground. George Upton had been in his grave for thirty-nine years, that Noah who, when his beloved ark one time was damaged by fire, refused to accept the award of the insurance adjuster because he thought it was too high. Now *that* was class.

As Magnolia whirled around the Oceanside, so East Gloucester wandered around the Hawthorne. The two Georges, Upton and Stacy, held decidedly different views regarding the accommodation of guests.

The brusque and, when it suited him, genial son of a Gloucester insurance man, George Stacy learned the hotel business from the front desk back. In 1891, at thirty-one, he built the foundation of his empire on Wonson's Point, facing Ten Pound Island across the water, and called it the Hawthorne Inn after his favorite author. As if infected with Oceansiditis, cottages sprouted until his overgrown main house, bulging with casinos, ells and other useful excrescences, was the helter of a skelter of structures named out of his idol's various works and fashioned, nay plagiarized, from the secondhand building materials he so dearly loved, Gloucester-fashion, to glean from here and there — nearly thirty in all when you counted in a derelict lumber schooner he converted into a houseboat — bedding down 450 guests in all, in delighted discomfort.

Mrs. Blanche Butler Lane first came to the Hawthorne from New

York with her mother, grandmother and nursemaid in 1902 when she was two. Her earliest memory is of an early arrival from the Gloucester depot over the dusty road by carriage after a sooty train ride down from Boston behind the coughing steam locomotive. No clean towels in their rooms, a mild remonstrance that met with much muttering from Proprietor Stacy.

An uncertain symbol of status among the guests was the number of trunks the delivery wagon delivered from the depot for the hotel's faithful man Jim Thompson to lug in. The popular Hawthorne had a permanent waiting list, and the only way in was said to be in the wake of a hearse. And at that, neither baggage nor seniority was a guarantee of admission in the face of inheritance, if Stacy liked the family.

Once in, the initiate was at the mercy of a singularly nigh host. "The food was mediocre," Mrs. Lane recalls fondly. "We had *one* bathtub and toilet to a cottage — wash basin, pitcher, slop jar in each room. We put the pitcher outside the door at night and had hot water in the morning. We put another small pitcher out and received ice water at night." The single tub dictated a rigid ritual. In the evening the first guest in, presumably the senior occupant of the cottage, drew the water, bathed, drained and scrubbed the tub and refilled it for the next, being allowed exactly thirty minutes from start to finish, with the result that the new visitor was lucky to be in bed before midnight.

Evidently an engaging child, Blanche was adopted as a sort of mascot by Mr. Stacy and every Fourth of July was boosted up on top of the piano and waved a little flag while five hundred or so guests sang the national anthem. This tradition endured "until we were nearly thrown out when I damn near burned the place down, leading my gang through in a game of Hare and Hounds with *live matches* as the hare's trail. Another time we played Follow the Leader, which took us up one of the old so-called fire escapes to the roof, where we all pranced across, much to the horror of the assembled guests below."

Speaking of matches, it used to be said that they were made not in heaven, but at the Hawthorne Inn.

Of his older guests, George Stacy was not always so tolerant. One courageous soul informed him at breakfast that the coffee was vile, to which he replied airily, "Yes, it is. I *never* drink it when I'm here."

Another dared to complain that the ceiling leaked over her bed. "Can't have that," said he — and had the bed moved. To a third dissident he joshed: "This is a third-class hotel run for first-class people."

But a fourth habitual griper tried the Stacy patience too far: "You are very unhappy here, so Jim will put your trunk on the baggage truck at three in time for you to take the four o'clock train home."

Half sea, half country, East Gloucester and its appending Rocky Neck had their especially picturesque charm for the summer visitor, and the cantankerous Hawthorne, which actually sprawled on the grounds of the first home in the area opened to boarders in 1843, commanded a fanatical following. Eastern Point and Bass Rocks, the ocean-clad tail and backsides of the peninsula that gave Gloucester Harbor its lee, had been captured by the wealthy summer residents, but East Gloucester remained the stronghold of the independent native fishermen/lobstermen/farmers, removed from the hustle of the inner waterfront and at least some of its smell, tolerating the summer folks and a growing art colony with some amusement, and no doubt a few imprecations on Captain Frank Foster for ever leaving the sea and converting his wife's homestead into the Rockaway House — which was in a fair way of doing just that when its rocking-chair brigade commandeered the piazzas in aged array.

The smart hotelkeeper, like W. P. Osborne, who operated the Harbor View at the foot of Patch's Hill on Wonson's Cove, advertised that his environment allowed him to provide all the essential amenities of a large hotel at half the price: "But of one thing a prospective visitor [to East Gloucester] should be warned. . . . There are many who have become so enthusiastic over the charms of the place they forget that when they first came they were disappointed. The reason for this is that the resort is different from every other and its attractions are not showy but grow on one until it is a matter of affection, if not something like a passion. . . . The Harbor View is the same sort of house that East Gloucester is a resort. It is quaint, rambling, different, but it is comfortable and has many staunch friends."

Among those friends was the great American impressionist painter, John Henry Twachtman, who breathed his last while staying at the Harbor View in 1902, and Princeton professor Stockton Axson, host there during the following summer to his sister, Ellen, and his close friend, her husband, the new head of the university, Woodrow Wilson. It was a bright artistic and literary salon, almost, that the future President of the United States found there, and he joined in publishing a clever little periodical for the occasion, *The Trifler,* which naturally had to have an editorial policy: "In politics it is strictly independent but with the firm conviction that the Democratic Party is right in every particular."

Farther along the road to Eastern Point the old Fairview crowned the crest of Patch's Hill, older (1842) and no less quaint. Louisa May Alcott occupied the best third-floor room in 1868 and 1871; the father-and-son artists Stephen and Maxfield Parrish went off with their sketching kits from here in the 1880s; and for several weeks during the summers of 1895 and 1896 Rudyard Kipling and his American wife holed in while he dug into the fishing lore of Gloucester for his classic novel of the life, *Captains Courageous,* in which he wrote whimsically of the place: "A strange establishment, managed apparently by the boarders, where the table-cloths were red-and-white-checkered, and the population, who seemed to have known one another intimately for years, rose up at midnight to make Welsh rarebits if it felt hungry."

For all his infamous frugality, George Stacy was a man with a large view. Five seasons with the Hawthorne Inn staked him to the first sizable summer hotel on the Atlantic Ocean side of the East Gloucester pastures at Bass Rocks, where he had apprenticed at the Bass Rocks House as a young man. In 1896 he went partners with Edward P. Parsons in building the 300-guest Moorland on the site of the smaller burned-out Pebbly Beach Hotel.

A hotelier of large view, Stacy, and a dreamer, and it was as if all his parsimony, all his vile coffee and his pitchers of hot water and his secondhand lumber had been hoarded against the grand, effulgent splurge of his life that proceeded to blossom upon the supposedly strictly private landscape of Eastern Point in the summer of 1903.

Doubtless on the qt, George had gathered unto himself several parcels of prime harbor frontage on either side of the old Niles farmhouse beyond the southerly end of Niles Beach, land from which, like the rest of the Point, commercial construction was banned until 1917 unless by special permission of the owners' syndicate, the Eastern Point Associates. How he got around the hardheaded businessmen and lawyers who were so determined to keep the public off their private preserve is a mystery.

But George Stacy built in the inner sanctum, and for the North Shore, on an incredible scale. His Colonial Arms opened on June 25, 1904. The 175 rooms and three and a half stories first announced had swollen to 300, and five, with living quarters for 125 employees. The massive, wooden, colonial–Greek Revival anarkronism spread towering mansard wings joined by splendid, high-columned porticoes and a superelegant porte cochere from which emanated tier upon tier of breezy porch. Three hundred feet long and sixty deep, rising full-blown from the stark ledge at water's edge, dominating all of Gloucester's glorious outer harbor, the Colonial Arms was the greatest, grandest hotel, winter or summer, ever conceived in a single stroke north of Boston.

No, Stacy the summer hotel man did not spare the horses. The Arms cost him $230,000 in 1904 money. A tremendous, lofty center lobby opening to a stunning view of the harbor, a resplendent dining room in the east wing, a beatific ballroom in the west . . . adjectives simply fail . . . a morning room, fireplaces and antiques, and professional decor everywhere, and reading and writing and reference rooms, and toilet parlors and suites with their own baths and seventy-five shared bathrooms besides (no pitchers outside the door here), and an elevator, and a six-piece orchestra (three concerts a day), and a wharf for the Colonial's own steam launch to ferry guests back and forth into Gloucester (touching at the Hawthorne on the way, of course), and a great garage for the enthusiastic new automobilists.

Well! And to launch it all with the biggest possible bang, the annual outing of the Essex County Republican Club, assembled to get the word from its velvet-gloved boss, Senator Henry Cabot Lodge of Nahant.

Booked solid for four seasons . . . until the night of New Year's, 1908, when fire unaccountably broke out somewhere in the extreme end of the deserted hotel that was almost within spitting distance of the cottage that Henry Davis Sleeper was building on the next lot. By the time the steam pumpers came flying over the frozen road from Gloucester behind their steaming horses, a half a gale of wind from the southwest had swept the flames through the whole gigantic works, and in three and a half hours, while a great crowd watched in awe, George Stacy's dream of a lifetime, fifteen thousand square feet in area, resolved itself — or was resolved — into a smoking ruin. They said you could read the classified ads of the newspaper by the light of it two miles away.

There was talk that sparks from the chimney of Sleeper's cottage, where fires had been lit to dry plaster, might have been carried by the wind to the roof of the hotel, but his mason said only space heaters were in use. Whatever the *machina,* the *deus ex* must have been perfectly satisfactory to the young interior decorator, just then enclosing the nucleus of his fabulous "Beauport" in the shadow of his neighbor's manic monolith. And could it have been effect following cause that within three months of the utter destruction of his closest competition, George Upton across the harbor in Magnolia sold the Oceanside?

George Stacy's name is immortalized, not over the flung-open doors of a period piece of resort architecture, however grand in sweep and view, but in the graceful arc of boulevard for which he was responsible and which gives Gloucester Harbor its Bay of Naples air. The New Ocean House, the Masconomo, the Oceanside, the Hawthorne, the Colonial Arms, all the great ones, are gone in flames, or torn down, or shrunk to nothing worth remembering.

The great summer hotels, the arks, when the citified family was content to take a packaged vacation in immobility on the shore, invited their own destruction, and the end of a way of living, when they welcomed through their shaded portes cocheres those first gents in their goggles and ladies in their dusters in those first roaring touring cars and runabouts that put the wheels under the second American Revolution.

4

Horsepower versus Horse Power

THE SUMMER OF 1901, A PIONEER-IN-REVERSE NAMED F. M. AYERS, SEIZED with the spirit of the forefathers, chugged off from Indianapolis, Indiana, for Magnolia, Massachusetts, in a carriage powered by a gasoline engine. He got as far as Albany, New York, where the abominable roads at last broke the spirit of his Winton phaeton. Not too daunted, he abandoned the useless vehicle and continued on to his sophisticated seaside destination over the reliable rails of the New York Central.

Unfazed by failure and urged on by the cheerful Scot who had invented his conveyance, the intrepid Mr. Ayers embarked again the next summer on the nearly trackless trail of the fathers with two companions in a Winton touring car pulled by the power of fifteen horses, again for Magnolia. This time he made it, in nine and a half days, declaring with justifiable self-congratulation to the gentleman from the *Boston Evening Transcript* (so newsworthy was the astonishing feat) that over the entire 900-odd miles they hadn't provoked a single horse to bolt or caused a single accident to another traveler. The dimensions of the achievement may be judged from the fact that Alexander Winton was the first of the American gasoline automobile manufacturers of any durability and had been in production in Cleveland only since 1898.

For his objective Ayers could not have picked a more fertile testing ground for the infant industry. Eleven years later, in a backward look that may not be all hyperbole, the *North Shore Breeze* had this to say: "When the motor car was yet in its infancy and wealthy people from all over the country gathered on the North Shore to spend their summers, there were more cars here during the warm weather months than in any other equal territory in the country."

The North Shore summer people had the cash and the leisure (primitive automobiling was, after all, a sport — albeit with the masochistic overtones of mountaineering and distance running — for who other than doctors would undertake errands of mercy or business by such uncomfortable and unreliable means?). And Essex County had the Yankee tinkerers — more per square yard, possibly, than any other equal territory in the country. Amesbury was already the Detroit of the carriage trade when horse was king; the town up in the north of the county just naturally turned to automobile bodies in those pre–mass production days, and in the years before the Great War, according to Essex County antique car historian Hayden Shepley, turned out more of them than any other place in the world.

Shepley has dusted off some fifty individuals and firms inventing and producing one or more motor cars in Essex County before 1915, beginning with the steam tricycle assembled by Andrew Philbrick in Beverly in 1886. The most prolific, oddly, was the General Electric Company at Lynn, with a variety of electric, steam and gasoline vehicles inspired by its guiding engineering genius, Elihu Thomson of Swampscott.

The most influential of all, undoubtedly, was the combination passenger and baggage body of wood that a Beverly buggy firm introduced around 1918 as a custom option for a Model T Ford chassis that turned it into a "Beverly wagon," the first beach, or station, wagon. The Beverly was adapted from the original horse-drawn rig with bench seats, leather side curtains, slatted canvas top, and varnished side panels fancied for carrying the family to church and fair. The motorized Beverly in its early days was relegated to the servants. It was elegant Lucius Beebe's first car: "Only families or individuals possessed of an ample stable of other motorcars would dream of having a Beverly Wagon, and it was a sort of luxury item in the garages of the rural or suburban aristocracy." The proper beach wagon was not complete without the owner's monogram tastefully painted and varnished over on the side panel of the driver's door, or perhaps the name (the more cryptic the better) of his estate. In their old age, subjected to years of damp salt air, the wooden door frames of the author's mother's beach wagon sprouted modest crops of tree fungus that had to be harvested regularly to maintain headroom for the passengers.

In those early days, though, the motor cars that invoked really reckless enthusiasm in owners, if not in passengers, on the North Shore were not at first of parochial manufacture. Many were imports or truly custom jobs, quite, and sometimes outrageously, expensive.

One who fell in a big way was Henry Perkins Benson of Salem, who bought his first, an electric, in 1898. "I believe," he wrote, "I was sane, normal and conservative in my sporting life as I was in business. I sailed and raced twenty-one-foot yachts out of Marblehead, played golf and tennis, and for indoor sports, billiards was my favorite. But motors did something to me. With them I was not calm or cautious or level headed. I fell for them in the most extraordinary manner."

Over the next fifty years Benson suffered through dozens of such love affairs. Nothing of course ever matched his early *mésalliances,* typical of the unrequited love that the founding generation of car nuts seemed to thrive on and which are now part of the lore.

The roads with which the Hoosier Ayers chose so happily to contend raised clouds of dust in dry weather (hence the goggles and dusters of automobilists exposed entirely to the elements) or turned into miasmas of mud slipperier than sheer ice or unfathomable bodies of murky water concealing somewhere, anywhere, potholes invariably two inches deeper than the hubcaps. The foolish consequences are too thoroughly documented to require repeating here . . . slithering slides ending in turnovers, unexpected obstacles, met at ten miles an hour, such as tethered cows that had wandered across the road in the middle of the night (as befell the author's father once; the cow fetched up on the hood). There were inglorious bottomings-out in downpours, ingloriously pulled out by leering horsepower, busted springs, snapped steering gear, boiling radiators, burned-out clutches, much camaraderie among the fraternity, horselaughing farmers, and flat tires, endlessly, as remembered with classic pain by H. P. Benson:

"Jacking up the car was perhaps easier as they were lighter in weight but the rest of the process was almost beyond the power of the English language to describe adequately. Indeed these repairs were seldom executed without involving abuses of said language as recognized in polite society. With two stout tire irons we pried the shoe off the rim, removed the damaged tube and by that time we were pretty weary but the job was only half done. To insert a spare tube and pry the shoe back on the rim without pinching the tube was the most difficult part of the operation. Then after a short rest pressure was pumped in with a hand pump, the car lowered off the jack, and pump, jack, tools and the old tube stowed away and the trip resumed."

It is told of Bishop Lawrence, probably apocryphally, that he happened one day upon a frustrated driver of these years somewhere along a North Shore road, swearing profusely as he tried to pry the flat tire off the rim. "Have you tried prayer, my good man?" gently inquired the bishop — upon which the poor fellow, in the desperation of his plight, fell to his knees, clasped his hands and lifted his eyes heavenward. He then picked up the iron, inserted it, and off popped the tire. "Well, I'll be Goddamned!" exclaimed the bishop.

Henry Benson moved from electric (equipped by the absentminded manufacturer with a buggy-whip socket; Benson used the whip to keep dogs from the front wheels) to steam to gasoline, ever more powerful and faster; but he never forgot the pioneer days when "at a top speed of fifteen miles per hour one of my older guests, on leaving the car muttered 'terrible experience.' . . . In contrast, my young daughter three years old, when asked if I was driving too fast at twenty miles per hour, just lisped 'fwow poke.' "

Sensible North Shore summer people with the means hired a chauffeur; equal to his ability behind the wheel, he must be a specialist in the internal medicine of his steed. Such a one was Henry Williams, a machinist for the company that built a Cleveland purchased in 1906 by Edward Williams, no relation but the son-in-law of Mrs. Emma Raymond, who reigned over Eastern Point's reigning "Ramparts." Henry was loaned by the firm for a week to teach the new owner how to drive the car, then for another week to accustom the ladies to riding in it . . . and stayed with the paint manufacturer's family until his death sixty-three years later.

Chauffeurs tended to be a happy-go-lucky lot when given their rein (the French imports were happier and luckier than all the rest), and they were continually getting their employers in trouble with the law, which had never concerned itself with anything more hazardous to the public safety on the roads than a runaway horse. In 1904 the law was confounded by an epidemic of chauffeurs accidentally smearing their number plates with oil, which made them illegible under a coat of road dust. Next year one who nevertheless did not escape the toils was fined ten dollars for going twenty-one miles an hour in Gloucester, where he drove for a family staying at the Hawthorne . . . notwithstanding his objection that his passenger was an old lady of seventy-six and he'd hardly be "running wild with such a freight."

The limit in Beverly and Manchester was first set at eight miles an hour within the town limits and twelve outside, almost to no avail. An angry Manchester resident complained to the *Breeze* that the road hogs had so clogged the town in August that the electric trolleys might have to be admitted in self-defense — an alternative worse than almost anything to the forces of exclusiveness-by-the-sea.

How to catch these speeders? At first, a cop could sometimes do it on a horse. One day in the fall of 1902 Edward Parsons, the genial manager of the Moorland Hotel at Bass Rocks, drove to Boston to visit a friend. "On Commonwealth Avenue," the *Gloucester Times* reported with glee, "in endeavoring to pass a team, Mr. Parsons threw open the lever and the machine forged ahead. It had not gone far when Mr. Parsons noticed that a burly policeman on horseback was on his trail. Consequently he slowed up the auto and the guardian of the peace came up and placed Gloucester's leading practical joker under arrest, charged with traveling at a rate greater than eight miles an hour." Jailed, bailed and fined twenty dollars.

Marty Larkin, Nahant's chief, finally nabbed a Lynn scofflaw after a series of heroic chases on his bicycle. To the prototypical motorists a speed limit was an infringement on their liberties and was keenly resented. Fred Wilson told of the day the Nahant police hired a couple of the newfangled motor cars as a lark for an outing. Autos were topless then, and as they drove home above Lynn Beach a thundershower overtook them. "An attempt to hurry the driver was met with the reply, 'I can't do it. My father was fined for driving faster than fifteen miles an hour on this road.' He put the car in low gear and the party was drenched."

An early chronicler of the antics of the automobilists was young J. Alexander Lodge, a native Newfoundlander who was graduated from Bates College in 1902. He cut his journalistic teeth on the *Boston Journal* before founding the *North Shore Breeze* in May 1904 in Beverly, moving it after two years to his adopted home town of Manchester. The editor started right off with a novel feature, "Auto Notes," remarking that just about everybody had some kind of machine and was joining the new North Shore Automobile Club.

Lodge snooped around and learned that Eben D. Jordan, owner of the Boston department store Jordan Marsh and of an Elizabethan manor on the water at West Manchester, had been seen in his $10,000 Napier with canopy top and glass windshield. And an oddity, a woman — Frances Stotesbury — behind the wheel of a twelve-horsepower Panhard, "which she drives with the skill and daring of the most experienced chauffeur." Fannie was the younger daughter of the Philadelphia parvenu banker Edward Townsend Stotesbury, Drexel and Morgan partner and sometime North Shore summer visitor, who when she married J. Kearsley Mitchell III, of Philadelphia, a few years later gave her a check for a million dollars and a diamond tiara and necklace and rope of pearls that set him back another half a million . . . small price for entrée.

Fannie Stotesbury was way ahead of her day, for it was not until 1912 that Salem's Henry Benson observed the ladies in the front-seat driver's seat in any numbers, "thus adding a new and intriguing peril to the sport. The foot that rocked the cradle sometimes wrecked the car. Without presuming to understand their signals we gave them all the road room possible and they soon became as proficient as we were."

A year after Benson's cautious tribute the *Breeze* was raving about "chic little girls in their debutante years driving big six-cylinders with the command of a seasoned captain of a yacht, the quick decisions and proper judgments, the control of clutch and brake and gas and all the rest of it, would never have been associated with the hoop-skirt era. . . . The poise alone that it requires is a special tribute to the astonishingly clever American girl."

The big, tony watering places were natural oases and meccas for the automobilists, who frequently traveled in caravans for mutual morale and rescue, packs like the Glidden tours rediscovering America from atop a snorting monster, no mean adventure in the days of carriage roads. The hotelmen, entirely geared as they were to the sedate carriage trade, and many of the more conservative on the Shore, of whom there have always been not a few, were of two minds about the furious fad and the infernal influx.

The first wave of the mania struck Swampscott's New Ocean House in the summer of 1906, when its house organ, the *Reminder,* noted the presence on the grounds, among many others, of Miss Shearer's Columbia three-horse electric (the hotel was keen enough to install a battery charging station), Colonel Wood's forty-horse Napier, a multinomial Charion, Garardon and Voigt, two Winton Model Ks, a couple of Stevens Duryeas, a Pope-Hartford, a Cleveland, a Stanley Steamer, a Rambler, a Rainier, a Pope-Toledo, a Packard, a Peerless, an Oldsmobile and a Locomobile.

Wonderful for business, but the *Reminder* had its doubts: "The terror which a puffing, dust-raising, bad-odored automobile inspires in an aged man or woman wending a slow way along the familiar road, lost perhaps in thoughts of days that were happier when walking was less difficult, can never be dreamed of by the cheerful, care-free party who so enjoy flying through space. They only laugh at the queer antics of the frightened country people and dash on to the next adventure."

This was Puritan Road, which winds along above the Swampscott shore. It was the access to the driveways of the New Ocean House, and as splendid a promenade for high-stepping equipages as could be found anywhere. One needed look no farther for proof that this was *the* Turf than to the stables of J. Chancellor Crafts of Boston, who leased the Haskell estate on Puritan Road in 1907 and 1908 and stunned every connoisseur of horseflesh along the way with his knockout English Unicorn hitch (one horse leading two), his prancing tandem, and his pair drawing a London phaeton, coachman and footman up.

Although the afterglow lingered on, how fast the Victorian sun had been knocked down by the Wintons of the world! The mid-Nineties were merely yesterday afternoon, alive sixty years later in the memory of the North Shore historian and Boston publisher James Duncan Phillips, when every returning commuter train was met by "two or three spanking pairs attached to Victorias or Landaulets with coachmen in full livery on the box and a footman at the horses' heads, in which sat tightly laced dowagers under beautiful lace parasols. Surprisingly dowdy looking old gentlemen usually got into these smart vehicles and dumped some paper parcels down on the floor. A smart little trap or two might be in waiting driven by a lovely bride who prided herself on her horsemanship as much as on her young and handsome husband. The basket-work pony cart full of children and driven by the eldest was the happiest of the vehicles, especially when it was evident that father's return was the most joyous event of the day for all."

In certain elegant and old-style precincts of the North Shore the motor car was a damnation. On the Manchester road one July afternoon of 1906, as an example, Robert C. Hooper's groom was exercising the master's steeplechaser "Land of Clover," reputed to be the fastest in America and worth $50,000. Passing a Lewandos laundry wagon, he was struck by the automobile of C. S. Houghton of Coolidge Point. Clover had to be shot. His bereaved owner ordered his forehoofs cut off and made into inkstands, and for good measure saved his tail.

This was the sort of encounter between old ways and new ways that fired the ardor of Colonel William D. Sohier of Burgess Point in Beverly, and the conscience of Walter D. Denègre of West Manchester.

Years before the first one-cylinder gasoline motor shattered the serenity of the Shore, Colonel Sohier had taken up the post of watchdog over the privately owned forests and woods roads of Beverly and Manchester. The role of Cerberus fell naturally to the doughty State Street lawyer: during the winter season in Boston he served Society as the "self-appointed major-domo for all First Family debuts," according to Cleveland Amory in *The Proper Bostonians,* and was "the all-time terror of the Boston press."

On the thirty or so miles of private roads over which Colonel Sohier eventually presided, the motor car was strictly *machina non grata,* a total ban whose implementation was paradoxically assisted by the North Shore Automobile Club, of which lawyer Denègre was a founder and president in those first days of uneasy standoff between horse and horselessness.

The auto club was started about ten years earlier, if a 1913 article in the *Breeze* can be given credence, expressly to cordon off the inner close of the North Shore from the obnoxious invasion perhaps not so much of members as of nonmember outsiders. It posted Sohier's pri-

About to start an adventurous motor trip to New Hampshire in 1906, Dr. Francis B. Harrington sits in the front seat of his Pierce Arrow at the door of his Ipswich summer cottage with others in his party, which includes his begoggled chauffeur, standing, and Fred Lord's green Napier. Upon the Road Argilla

Breakdown on a dirt road, somewhere. The men tussle with the Napier, while the ladies, well protected from all but the mosquitoes, wait it out around the Pierce Arrow, which is silently plotting its own revenge. Upon the Road Argilla

Conserve Your Energy in Summer

You can, literally, get "recreation"—be "made over" again, when your physical self is rested, your energy and your strength conserved by the use of this Ford Runabout.

Simplicity and good taste are embodied in the lines and appointments of this popular car. Uninterrupted use is insured by nation-wide, "around-the-corner" Ford service. Better get your order in *now!*

Ford Motor Company
Detroit, Michigan

Touring Car $295   Coupe $525   Tudor Sedan $590   Fordor Sedan $685
All prices f. o. b. Detroit

SEE THE NEAREST AUTHORIZED FORD DEALER

The Runabout
$265
F. O. B. Detroit
Demountable Rims
and Starter $85 extra

Ford
THE UNIVERSAL CAR

You can buy any model by making a small down-payment and arranging easy terms for the balance. Or you can buy on the Ford Weekly Purchase Plan. The Ford dealer in your neighborhood will gladly explain both plans in detail

The price of a Model T bottomed out with the Runabout in 1924, as advertised in the North Shore Breeze.

You can ride high-style, as "Judge" Moore does in his "gray-and-four" at Myopia Hunt, about 1909. Essex Institute

Or you can ride high-style, as these happy guys and gals do, to a picnic on the Back Shore of Eastern Point in one of Tom Reed-the-teamster's wagons, Fourth of July, 1913. Eben Parsons photo

Pa Baker takes the girls for a smooth and almost silent spin in his sedate 1905 (?) Stanley Steamer. Manchester, 1912. Manchester Historical Society

An equally proud father takes his girls for a trot in a genuine surrey with a fringe on top at Revere Beach, about the same time. Mr. and Mrs. Henry Nicolas

vate roads off limits to motor cars. "The biggest thing the club ever did was to adopt a system of 'tagging' [presumably numberplating] cars, which system grew and was later taken up by the state and by other states and has developed into the numbering system now used all over the country."

The swellest thing the North Shore Auto Club ever did was to elect Denègre president, commodore or whatever, considering the flagship he designed and had delivered in time to take on a European tour in 1907. The body was fashioned by Quinzler of Boston on a Packard chassis, in black, with family monogram on the door, wheels in English vermilion. There was an enclosure for the driver, who received his instructions through a megaphone speaking tube. The servants rode in the rear compartment, which was fitted with a revolving back step. The interior was illuminated electrically, a great luxury, and fixtures were finished in gunmetal. The seats were upholstered in imported black goatskin.

By that summer of 1907, the *Breeze,* always on the lookout for trends, pronounced the North Shore auto-nutty. Motoring parties were the rage, and every evening all evening the talk in every hotel lobby and on every cottage verandah was of machines and their merits and speeds. By 1909 there were noticeably fewer horses on the roads. "In fact it is unattractive to use a horse-drawn pleasure vehicle having once used a car. Time, speed, reliability and control are in favor of the motor car and the cost of operation is against the horse."

Ah, but the wherewithal and the timewithal are what set the horseman and the yachtsman apart! It was back in 1878 that Colonel Henry Lee and Charles H. Dalton built the first private woods road on the North Shore from Preston Place north of Beverly Farms winding through the wilderness surrounding Gravelly, Round and Beck ponds and Chebacco Lake in Hamilton and Essex, then asked Colonel Sohier to take over the project of preserving the privacy of this primeval hinterland of the Shore. Sohier secured rights-of-way and raised money to insinuate a network of private dirt roads through the Beverly, Manchester, Hamilton, Wenham, Magnolia, West Gloucester and Essex backwoods, in some cases improving ancient ways such as the old stage road between Manchester and Essex, and Hesperus Avenue above the west shore of Gloucester Harbor.

The colonel's inroads were originally ten or twelve feet wide and cost about twenty-five cents a running foot. With increased traffic they were widened gradually to eighteen at a dollar a foot by 1914, thirty miles of them, open to all but automobiles as a "haven of safety," amidst the influx of motor cars, for those who still clung to the saddle and the surrey seat.

Alarmed by an infestation of gypsy moths in 1908, Colonel Sohier and his committee set out to raise a control fund; by 1911 they had sprayed 3,300 acres of woods at a cost of $54,500, half public, half subscribed by summer residents. By 1914 they had cleared, sprayed and creosoted a strip of woods 200 feet wide along the entire thirty miles in cooperation with the state forester and with funding assistance from Beverly and Manchester, but not Gloucester, which for two years had refused a dime and hence lost the benefit of this innovative public-private conservation project in Magnolia.

Colonel Sohier was still at it in 1921, when he reflected that over a period of twenty-five years the summer people of the Shore had contributed $125,000 toward moth control and another quarter of a million for road construction and maintenance. Not a bad record of privately financed public works, perhaps topped only by the $30,000 private bridge built by the residents over the railroad tracks to Norton's Point in Manchester in 1912, the largest concrete highway bridge in Massachusetts, 387 feet long, with graceful arches and balustrades, at $77.52 a foot.

Colonel Sohier's anathematization of the motor car, if not the gypsy moth, from the thirty miles of roads and woods he ruled held sway into the Twenties. But he was a Canute, and his only footprint above the tide today is Sohier Road in Beverly. The wave of the future lapped not the woods but, from inland, the shore itself, to which, the state legislature had declared, the mass of people should have access to bathe, sun or frolic by whatever means were at hand to get there.

Once there, however, they were encountering another wave, brought from who knows whence, of sewage. That tide is still rising. In Swampscott as late as 1893 the "honey bin men" were dumping cesspool night soil on the beaches for the tides to take care of, in defiance of local ordinance. In 1910 Shore summer residents retained a sanitary engineer in their efforts to prevent Beverly from installing an outfall that would diffuse along the contiguous beaches already strewn with sewage and garbage dumped from Lynn, Salem, Marblehead and as far away as Boston.

A Los Angeles man in 1914 asked the *Boston Herald* why so many wealthy people chose a resort where "at times, the shore from Glouces-ter to Beverly is strewn with decomposing fish, which, together with the odor of sewerage, is nauseating in the extreme." Truer than ever today, and Gloucester persists in disgorging its offal, the "Bubbler," into the middle of its beautiful harbor.

One rich Manchesterite provided his own solution, as it were. Gardi-ner M. Lane in 1912 spent $100,000 to install a private filtration plant to render the entire sewage from his house and stables into liquid fertilizer for the benefit of his extensive gardens via an intricate net-work of underground pipes.

Holding its collective nose, the Metropolitan Parks Commission, after it wiped out the shantytown that soiled the skirts of Revere Beach in 1896, seized the rest of the prime shorefront from King's Beach in Swampscott to Winthrop and built roadways of access for city dwellers who chose to spurn the Narrow Gauge Railroad and the five-cent trolley.

Revere Beach Boulevard was the first, and in all the planning for a grand, continuous ocean drive, the automobile was a mere mad nov-elty: witness the sensation created during the 1901 season at the beach by Kilpatrick and his daring ride up and down a 170-foot incline. Yet within three years motor cars were seen as a serious problem on the new boulevard; the MPC police were being trained to ride motorcycles, and on one April day in 1905 (preseason, mind you) six drivers were haled into Chelsea court charged with exceeding the ten-mile-an-hour limit at the beach.

But the revolution would not be denied. The craze was on. The bridge over the Saugus River linking Revere Beach and the Point of Pines to Lynn and the Lynnway was completed in 1906, and the day the Lynnway was opened to the public in July, they counted 1,271 pe-destrians, 881 carriages, 581 automobiles and 409 bicycles passing over . . . the horse the winner still, but for how long?

Such a menace had the motor car developed into by 1910 that on July 1 a Sunday ban against its presence on Revere Beach Boulevard went into effect, a ban ten thousand times overturned three days later, in the eyes of the cheering throng anyway, when President Taft, the nation's Chief Automobilist, rolled along it in his big black open touring car on a drive from the Summer White House in Beverly.

Half the world was already bleeding to death when the *Breeze* looked back on the 1916 season as the best in years. All hail the motor car, which had brought countless tourists from the Midwest and even the West Coast for their first taste of the North Shore!

5

A Tale of Two Islands

OF THE NORTH SHORE'S THIRTY OR SO VEGETATIVE ROCKS AND SANDBARS flattered by the sometimes capricious cartographer as islands, hardly more than half are even marginally habitable. Of those capable of sustaining a human toehold, if not a very tenacious one, six have been umbilicated by thoroughfares, including Deer, which is a Boston prison colony, Winter, which is Salem's hoary chowder and marching ground, and Five Pound, literally swallowed up by Gloucester's state fish pier. Lighthouses no longer tended serve the solitary purpose of four more.

Among the remainder, only on the twin sentinels of the Salem ship channel, Baker's and Misery, has chance favored the spontaneous generation of a bona fide summer colony bearing any semblance of social organization; and that on Baker's alone has survived. With few exceptions, islands of the North Shore unlucky enough to stand in the way of the Atlantic swells are inhospitable to all but the sea birds and stray seals.

The happy outcome for the smaller and more barren Baker's — the self-fulfilling fate of ill-named Misery — afford a study in what makes islands, and men, work. Great Misery, eighty-nine acres, with Little Misery snuggled under its southern shore, is half a mile from Beverly's West Beach. Offshore another three quarters of a mile across the main ship channel out of Salem Bay lies Baker's, shy of sixty acres, beset to the south and west by a wretched maze of rocks and ledge and shoal that makes the passage to Salem (absentee tax collector for both islands), Beverly and Marblehead a tricky trial in fog or dark, and sometimes in broad daylight too, as the author once learned to his chagrin.

Baker's is not so elevated but commands the bay as Misery can't, so its north shore was the logical vantage in 1798 for a pair of lighthouses that for the next century and a quarter were familiarly addressed as Ma and Pa Baker until Ma, the shorter, was gracelessly dismantled in 1926. Vantage, too, from which the Salem pilots scanned the horizon for vessels wanting guidance through the twisty channel; east of the lights they built their lookout shack with bunks, and peepholes facing out to sea. Any island with both a lighthouse and a pilothouse is off to a good start. Misery, poor Misery, had neither, nor even a clue to the origin of such a prejudicial name.

Once timbered, stormswept Baker's never recovered from colonial cutting and went to pasture, good forage for the farmers of Salem who ferried their stock out for the summer, and themselves and their families back and forth for picnics. In the late 1870s Thomas Gilbert ran the only farm on the island, kept hens, geese, ducks, a couple of dozen cows and a bull that had the brass one day to charge no less a personage than George Dewey, the lighthouse inspector who had rowed out in his skiff in the line of duty. "Kill that bull!" the hero-to-be of Manila screamed at keeper Walter Rogers, leaping back in his boat. "I'd rather go into an engagement any day than face that beast!"

Bracing sea air, good food and ample exercise keeping clear of his bull had worked wonders for keeper Rogers, who set foot on Baker's feeling poorly and weighing 101 pounds, and retired back to the mainland at 226. The same ameliorative conditions weighed as heavily with Dr. Nathan R. Morse of Salem, induced by a patient who owned one of the ten squatters' cottages to join him in the summer of 1882. Dr. Morse was recovering from an accident and mended so miraculously that he returned the following summer with a tent, then bought one of the pilots' shacks, built his own cottage in 1885, bought the entire island except the lighthouse reservation from its Marblehead owner in 1887.

The Salem doctor's grand plan unfolded in 1888 with the opening of the "Winne-egan" (Indian, supposedly, for "beautiful expanse of water"), a health spa that he announced as "a most delightful place of retirement from the heat of summers, the annoyance of mosquitoes, the cares of business and a sure tonic and a perfect panacea for the tired and worn-out nervous system, *neurasthenia,* so common nowadays to a large proportion of our American business men and women."

In fact, the enthusiastic Dr. Morse was a homeopathic physician, professor of the diseases of women and children at the Boston University School of Medicine, which a decade earlier he had helped to institutionalize in the name of infinitesimal dosage out of the old New England Female Medical College in Boston's South End. His latest venture must have been influenced by the success on smaller Cat Island, a mile and a half toward Marblehead Neck, of the Children's Island Sanatorium, formerly the Lowell Island House when that rock patch of many aliases was the resort of the summer crowd from Lowell.

Joyfully proclaiming that his island air was "highly charged with ozone from the ocean," the jolly homeopathist fed his guests from the island farm, watered them from the well he dug and from the middle of the three ponds which he deepened and walled, cooled their brows with the ice keeper Rogers cut for him in the dead of the island winter, and warmed their souls with Sunday evening "praise meetings." He got the steam ferry service between the electric trolley line at Salem Willows and Beverly and Marblehead extended to the island with six trips a day. Before the first pier was built out from the western beach, passengers hitched themselves over the rail of the ferry into a scow that was hauled to shore by block and tackle, and walked a plank to dry land — exceeding dry, since the deeds for the eighteen cottage lots Dr. Morse sold off during his tenure forbade the sale or even gift of alcoholic drinks on the premises.

In 1892 the doctor turned over the active management of the Winnegan to his son Henry. Before he died in 1897 his pride and joy boasted an addition, seventy-five rooms, a café, a tennis court and a bulging register (1,013 guests in the peak year of 1894) that featured the signatures of former President Benjamin Harrison and actress Lillian Russell in 1893, though certainly *pas en pas de deux.*

For the healthiest drafts of the only stimulant he approved, ozone, Dr. Morse had somehow managed to impose the appearance of a six-hole golf course on terrain whose natural challenges were multiplied by the haphazard croppings and droppings of the livestock pastured thereon. The members of this motley herd shared the special sensibilities to sights and sounds so characteristic of islanders isolated in the middle of the sea and were the bellwethers, in a manner of expression, in protesting when the bureaucracy replaced Ma and Pa Baker's old familiar fog bell in 1907 with a compressed air siren. At the first blast, wrote De Witt D. Wise, the island's historian in *Now, Then, Baker's Island*, "they, with one exception, stuck their tails in the air and headed for the southern part of the island. One cow, intrigued by the bovine-like sounds, thrust her head through the strands of the government fence and answered it — moo for moo — until it stopped."

Taking their cue from their kine, the two-legged islanders and the more wealthy and influential mainland summerers were soon in full moo against the horrid siren themselves. They held meetings and hired a lawyer to harass the government to take it away and to hell with fogbound mariners—a hue and cry reminiscent of the success of Miss Elizabeth Stuart Phelps, the extrasensitive authoress, in getting her friends and admirers in Washington to have the Eastern Point whistling buoy lifted every summer in the 1880s . . . and of Nahanters years later in having removed from near Old Sunk Ledge a bell buoy whose "infernal irregularity," in Fred Wilson's unappreciative words, "threatened to depopulate the town." Sure enough, by the end of the season Baker's fog siren had been aimed out to sea through a tremendous megaphone, to the relief of animal and man.

Unfortunately for Henry Morse's efforts to beef up his offerings with Saturday night hops and a darkroom for "fiends" of the new Kodak, the ferry *Surf City* was returning to Beverly from the island on the Fourth of July, 1898, after disembarking passengers at Salem Willows, when she was struck by one of those savage squalls that erupt so unexpectedly across Salem Bay; she swamped and sank like a stone. Though in less than seven feet of water, eight of the sixty aboard — all women and children — were trapped in the cabin and drowned.

Henry Morse's career as a summer hotel proprietor ended as abruptly one chilly day in the early spring of 1906 when his man fired up one of the stoves and then fell asleep. The room caught, the barking of his faithful dog roused the careless caretaker, and he fled, but the Winneegan, after eighteen interesting seasons, went up in flames.

Burned out, Henry sold out in 1909 to his brother, Dr. Charles Morse, who collaborated with their uncle, Dr. Martin van Buren Morse, and the latter's wife in further subdivision of the family's holdings that resulted in a final building boom of twenty more cottages before America entered the First War. Martin was a homeopathist too, and he and Clara made enough money at a dollar a bottle with their home-made "Syrup of Hypophosphites" to buy themselves a grape-fruit plantation down south, which they sold to pay off the Baker's Island mortgage.

The loss of the Winne-egan and sale of most of the Morse holdings left the cottage owners momentarily without the catalyst that had at-tracted them to the island in the first place. The hotel had been the social and religious center for a fun-loving but God-fearing summer colony, and the Morses got things done. Faced with languishing ferry service and a rotting pier, the islanders in 1914 organized the Baker's Island Association to advance their social welfare and reestablish Sunday re-ligious services. Their object was self-government, since about all they got from the city of Salem was receipts for their taxes — and for that they had to supply their own post office, namely the old pilots' shack, "Driftwood," which had been moved hither and yon about the island behind a Model T Ford, finally coming to rest as their combination mail drop, shop, library and social center.

As the years passed, the Association saw to it that there were reliable ferry and divine services, provided fire protection, kept up the roads, held up the pier, ran the store, chaperoned social events, and once, when the pond looked alarmingly low during a drought in the early 1960s, wondered about tapping a supposed subterranean stream that someone claimed ran from Rowley to Milton by way of Baker's Island Under — the questionable evidence being that the levels of the island's reservoir and Wenham Lake seemed to correspond.

By the mid-1920s there were fifty-eight snug cottages and 170 con-genial summer souls on Baker's, a census, and a consensus, virtually unchanged fifty-five years later. A happy and unpretentious island, an island that works, a tight little island — but a dry one — officially — as Dr. Nathan Morse had wisely decreed by word and deed.

The origin of Misery Island's name is as miserably obscure but as probably associated with some dire shipwreck of colonial times as that of Norman's Woe, the stark hunk of rock five miles down the coast on which Longfellow cast up his mythical *Hesperus*. Because the island is rough and gouged by a shallow valley cradling a small pond, Salem leased it out for nothing better than pasturage as early as 1628. In 1705 smallpox victims were banished there during an epidemic that swept the mainland. Several generations of the Dodge family of Wenham owned Misery, carrying on with what by then appears to have become the traditional practice of rowing the spring calf out from West Beach for a free ride in the dory, letting the fatted heifer swim back astern in the fall.

Daniel Neville, an Irish immigrant who made his living quarrying stone from the islands of Boston Harbor, bought Misery in 1849 and after a while settled there with his family to farm and fish. Robert Rantoul, the Salem historian, described Neville as the affable "Lord of the Isles," who regaled visitors one and all with the hospitality of his farm. Chief among them was Chief Justice Salmon P. Chase of the United States Supreme Court, who arrived in the west cove on July 26, 1865, aboard the revenue boat *Excelsior* with his friend the state treasurer, General Henry K. Oliver, for a chowder party on the island. The jurist was a large man indeed, and his transfer to land dry-shod was in some doubt until General Oliver, who was nothing if not a classicist, supporting Justice Chase on the one side, carried the day on the other with the assistance of Plutarch: *"Ne time quicquam! Caesarem* [he pronounced it "Chaserem"] *vehis!"* meaning roughly, "You have nothing to fear! You travel with Caesar" (or, in this case, Chase)!

A more recent chronicler of the Miseries, however, Reed Harwood, had it from a descendant that Lord Neville in truth spent much of his time chasing the less distinguished off his domain.

Whatever his disposition, Daniel Neville died in 1885. His farmhouse burned ten years later. In 1897 his widow followed him, and in 1900 Great Misery was sold by her executors for ten times its valuation of $6,000 to a Newton man, who sold it to a group of speculative enthusiasts, whose bites, it would all too soon turn out, were much too big for their bellies. Under the banner of Charles Stedman Hanks and Thomas W. Peirce, Boston and North Shore, the Misery Island Syndicate had hardly entered its deed in the Salem registry that spring when the members were floating out to their new holdings, blueprints in hand, on a $100,000 mortgage.

At the same time Hanks *et al.* organized the Misery Island Club with himself as president. They issued a membership call at $25 per annum to the select of the Shore, bought a pair of naphtha launches, *Josephine* of thirty feet and *Lizzie* of eighteen, and built a pier on the west shore of the cove opposite Beverly Farms, the idea being that a member could be ferried to the mainland, walk the five minutes to the Farms depot and be in Boston within an hour.

The Syndicate dammed a portion of the cove to make a salt water swimming pool, erected the "Custom House" at the head of the pier and converted into a bathhouse an existing cottage moved from the west side of the island, dug a well and raised a water tower. Guest cottages materialized, "The Governor's Palace" and "The Castle," and servants' quarters. A clubhouse rose above the west shore of the cove. A trap-shooting range appeared, and a tennis court. An old boathouse was resurrected as a caddie house and locker room, and to go with it, a nine-hole golf course of 2,610 well-bent yards was squeezed with the greatest ingenuity out of the Neville pastures. Finally, to complete the almost all-round sporting picture, another old cottage was rolled down to the cove as the Misery Island Station of the Manchester Yacht Club, and a regatta committee was appointed.

The speed of the promotion was exceeded only by its dazzle. Late that same spring of 1900 the Misery Island Club published a snazzy book bound in red and green, with its hurriedly conceived pennant imprinted in gold on the cover — a seahorse on a folded anchor — and the motto (Misery loved Latin, too, as we have seen): *Te salutamus miseria comitatum amat.* The first invitational golf tournament came off on June 30, with thirty-seven clubs represented. Thirty boats competed in the first three-day regatta a month later. By the end of the first season more than 260 of the better-known figures of Boston and the Shore were intrigued enough by the bizarre island setup to sign on the line.

The Misery Island Club's second season got off to a rouser of a start with the combined reunions in June of the Harvard classes of 1886 and 1891. They marched boisterously up and down the new carriage road behind their band, shared an *al fresco* luncheon, had an unsteady round of golf and wound up the day with a chorus of college songs to the presumed delight of the mainlanders, for, in Rantoul's words, "the wind happened to favor the shore that day, so that the music lost nothing when wafted across the water."

And yet, within a week, President Hanks was most disingenuously informing a reporter: "Here we are isolated and run little risk of intrusion. There is no temptation for display, as people cannot exhibit their expensive equipages [then why the expensive carriage road?], and those who wear expensive clothes will ruin them. There are no servants in livery or any similar indications of formal life. It is a place to rest in, and nature has done what she could to the island to make this possible. Here one finds liberty and privacy, things most desired in modern civilization," But nary a word about solvency from the president, who neglected to mention that back in January the first disagreeable dissent had been raised: the contractor who built the new clubhouse filed a lien against them for $782.87 in unpaid bills.

Nevertheless, the 1901 roster swelled to 350. Regular steam ferry service to West Beach was arranged. A second golf meet was managed, and a second regatta, with ten classes, and the Salem Cadet Band.

But 'twas all puff. The Misery Island Club survived its third season, 1902, at the end of which the city of Salem demanded $685.20 in back taxes. So it expired — golf, regattas, trapshoots, brass bands, cool July evening galas, gilded seahorse and all. For that was but the iceberg's tip; the Syndicate, it seemed, owed $35,000 in notes and $45,000 in bills. For two years the corpse was clobbered. Salem auctioned it off twice for taxes, and the bank foreclosed and sold the island for $5,000 to the trustees for the bondholders, who got rid of three one-acre lots for $5,000 each, with plans for more subdivision, and turned the clubhouse into the euphemistically named "Beverly Farms Island Inn."

Rumors that certain creditors wanted to buy the island and make another Revere Beach of it caused a frightful stir on the porches of Beverly, which was not at all quieted by an alternative suggestion from Senator Winthrop Murray Crane, a figure to be reckoned with in Washington, that Misery be acquired for the construction of a national leper hospital.

With the deflation of the Syndicate's bubble from a puffed-up sportsmen's paradise to the manageable proportions of a compact summer colony gathering around the warm social nucleus of a modest inn, the

The Winne-egan, Baker's Island's only summer hotel, and its proprietor, Dr. Nathan R. Morse. Essex Institute

Veranda Cottage, Great Misery Island. Little Misery tags along behind. Beyond is Baker's, the islanders' pier on the right, the lighthouses "Ma and Pa Baker" on the extreme left, 1912. Misery Islands album, The Trustees of Reservations

The Misery Island Club piazza, from the club booklet, 1900. Essex Institute

Madam takes aim on the Misery Island shooting range. Club booklet, 1900.
Essex Institute

The "Mystery" Island Casino and landing, probably 1912. Misery Islands album, The Trustees of Reservations

The Hollander cottage with its unusual thatched roof. Misery Islands album, The Trustees of Reservations

fortunes of Misery again rose. A few more summer cottage lots were sold. John H. Harwood of Brookline bought one on the west shore in 1909 and built a large double-winged bungalow in the spirit of the island, "Bleak House." Here his son Reed, who after fifty years wrote nostalgically and bitterly of the island's history and fate, spent the happiest summers of his childhood with his brothers and buddies.

The leading shareholder and figure in the renewed try at making Misery pay was Jacob Rogers, one of the original syndicators. Rogers put up a cottage and strove to put across the Casino, as they decided, unfortunately, to call the former club. He plumped doggedly and without success to get the island's equally invidious name changed officially to "Mystery" — even pushing a quixotic petition in 1911 to persuade the legislature to incorporate "Mystery Islands" and its dozen summer cottages as a separate town, since they got nothing from Salem for their taxes.

Jake Rogers survived in Reed Harwood's mind's eye as "a dapper man dressed in a blue serge jacket and white flannels, with a stiff straw hat" — hardly the type to promote, one suspects, another abortive scheme that surfaced alongside secession. This was the proposal of the Pride's Crossing contractor Daniel Linehan to erect barracks on Misery Island for his foreign-born laborers, mainly Italians and Poles, making of it a sort of private Ellis Island to which these necessary undesirables would be ferried every night after work, out of prideful sight and smell.

Still, these were the happiest of Misery's years. The island had a summer population of a hundred. The men took the ferry or their own motorboats to the West Beach landing, walked up to the Farms depot and commuted weekdays to their offices in Boston. Gus Rengman, the Swedish caretaker, kept an eye on the Casino, ran the engine that pumped fresh water from the well up into the tank, and delivered ice to the cottagers that he had cut from the pond during the winter. When heavy supplies were wanted on the island, he towed them over behind his launch in a scow.

Stemming the unstemmable tide, the Casino rocked with gaity and parties as the Great War rolled across the Atlantic. Ominously, at the end of the 1915 season the trust mortgaged its seventy-seven acres against $15,000 in debts, and the Casino opened in 1916 as usual.

But when 1917 dawned like thunder, the property again changed hands, new money was found, and the summer was spent adding an annex to sleep the expected overflow that never flowed. There was a war on, and we were in it. The Casino, alias the Mystery Island Inn, alias the Beverly Farms Island Inn, née the Misery Island Club, never again opened its doors. The foreclosure in 1918 locked the lid. Even the concrete hangar that Godfrey Cabot had built on the west shore for his experiments with refueling seaplanes in flight was abandoned when he entered active service in 1917.

A litany of miscalculation, bad luck and failure, as Dr. Harwood ruefully reviewed it. Misery had a bad name to begin with, and the shady connotations of the Casino didn't help. The carriage road was a waste of money, the golf course couldn't pay for itself, the telephone was an unreliable party line, there was no electricity, a new steam launch blew up at its mooring, and the 3,500-foot fresh-water pipe laid all the way from Pride's Crossing in 1913 cracked somewhere between the shore and the island and delivered seawater to the storage tank. But least forgivably, the founding syndicate overcapitalized by far what was essentially a relatively inaccessible seasonal weekend operation, overestimating by far its revenue potential.

The final demise of the Casino left the seven or eight families remaining on Misery Island in 1917 the sole beneficiaries of the prized liberty and privacy Charles Stedman Hanks had so hoped to share with 350 kindred spirits from the mainland sixteen years earlier. The golf course returned to nature, the ocean reclaimed the swimming pool, crabgrass recaptured the tennis court, and rabbits reproduced with abandon in the cool spaces beneath the deserted clubhouse. Ironically, the privacy got to be too much of a good thing for most of the cottagers, and none but the Harwoods returned for the 1919 season.

And now the three "Bleak House" boys had the whole domain of Misery from shore to shore to themselves — and the rabbits and Gus Rengman. They worked the Harwood victory garden, raised chickens, fished and lobstered, rowed the family maids to the mainland for mass at Beverly Farms, and pitted their wits against the caretaker's, successfully enough to break into the shuttered cottages for games of hide-and-seek and pillow fights.

Their last year was 1920. Mrs. Harwood had had enough of the loneliness, and the family never returned. Gus was left Lord of the Isles. On May 7, 1926, the Casino with all its cottages, the barn, the water tower and one of the private houses burned to the foundations when a brush fire ran out of control. The rabbits panicked, bounded into the sea and drowned.

Again Misery was sold. Years passed, and in 1935 a Beverly oil dealer wanted to erect storage tanks for twelve million gallons of oil on the island. The Salem city council turned him down after a howl arose up and down the Shore. This time an alarmed group of citizens chipped in and once more bought most of Misery and gave it to the Trustees of Public Reservations for perpetuity.

Vandals with less than pillow fights on their empty minds invaded, and one cottage after another succumbed to neglect, destruction and fire, until all were gone, even Godfrey Cabot's concrete hydroplane hangar, demolished . . . all save one. Joseph B. Henderson, possibly inspired by the example of Mrs. Evans in dismantling her mansion on Woodbury Point, cut his in half too and moved it by lighter, as she had, to Marblehead, where he rejoined it to his satisfaction.

Today Baker's thrives, and Misery . . . well, Misery loves company, unrequited.

Thus ends our tale of two islands.

6

Thank God for the Greenheads

IPSWICH, WITH ITS SALT MARSHES AND SAND DUNES, HAS ALWAYS BEEN A place unto itself, regarded by hardly a soul, native or otherwise, as having anything to do with the North Shore. Until 1881, that is. In that year, comparable in local annals to 1620, the authors of a guidebook to the North Shore discovered poor Ipswich, and with presumptuous enthusiasm announced its inclusion within Boston's summer orbit.

"There can be no question as to the future of this place," proclaimed Messrs. Hills and Nevins. "It cannot possibly remain unoccupied much longer." Unoccupied? Well, this surrogate invitation to the speculators did not appear in next year's edition, and in 1883 all mention of the town from the guide to the North Shore had been expunged. Had some rustic but influential *un*occupant who desired it to stay that way persuaded the authors that Ipswich wasn't there after all? If so, to only temporary avail, as we shall see.

Geographically and geologically there is almost nothing North Shorish about Ipswich. But generically and in a cousinly sort of way genealogically, though past the ledges of Cape Ann and host to its own bay, Ipswich is the farthest fringe of Boston's North Shore, farthest from Boston and last colonized, thanks to distance, to too little water for much yachting, to too much heat and humidity for a little comfort, to too many mosquitoes, and to the most voracious of all the winged beasties of summer, the greenhead fly.

"Thank God for the greenheads," grinned one bite-scarred veteran

of many a season on the Ipswich marsh's edge who regarded their in-
discriminate guardianship as a small price for his privacy.

Ipswich is the softer variety of Essex County farmland drifting off
into lowlands riddled with creeks, lowlands into marshlands, mile after
mile of knee-high salt grass erupting offshore in rounded islands and
necks of sand as dazzling as snow, piled up by the swirling currents
into a dune-backed beach clean-cut and surf-smoothed for as far as the
eye can squint.

Castle Hill lords it over the estuary. Ancient Appleton Farms sits
nobly astride rural Ipswich, a pastoral duchy of a thousand acres, the
lesser part in Hamilton, granted to Samuel, the First of the Appletons,
by Charles the First of England in 1638, the oldest farm continuously
in one family in America, they say. Continuously renewing themselves,
the Appletons extended their business and professional connections to
Boston and New York and beyond, always returning and retiring to
the Ipswich seat, summer and winter, to survey their fields, mend their
fences, oversee their herds and herdsmen, gathering in their children
and their in-laws, and their horses quite as well bred, true country
squires to the last of the male line unto the ninth generation, who was
Francis R. Appleton, Jr., presiding when he died in 1974 at eighty-nine
over one of the last of the patriarchies of old.

Uncommon land indeed. Not so Jeffrey's Neck (or Great Neck) and
its Little Neck, protected from the smashing Atlantic by the barrier
bar of Plum Island; common land, so Ipswichians supposed, since the
days of the colony. Then along came Alexander B. Clark in the 1890s,
buying up the old shares of Jeffrey's Neck, which he sold off for summer cottages, running the road through to Little Neck. The town followed with water mains and leased out a whole colony, all to the liti-
gious bewilderment of feoffees, squatters, summer folk, natives and
title-searchers, but not to lawyers from up the line the like of Charles P.
Searle of Boston. No dealer in postage-stamp lots of dubious ancestry,
Searle consolidated sweeping tracts of marsh and uplands along the
Ipswich River on the way to Jeffrey's Neck and nailed them down in
1906 with a mansion designed after the famous Florentine Villa Bel-
riposa. Some box for a town of saltboxes.

Here a farm, there a farm, and soon old MacDonald had no farm, to the dismay of the Ipswich correspondent who awoke one morning to find "their rapid transfer to out-of-town parties quite appalling."

North of the Ipswich River, Jeffrey's Neck, on the south, Castle Neck, like Plum Island to the east and Coffin's Beach to the west, roughly, a pile of sand carried along the coast by the slant of the Atlantic swells and laid down before the breakwater of Cape Ann. In the lee of these tremendous sandbars the broad marshes stretching from West Glouces-ter to Newbury and beyond used to yield good money crops of salt hay. While important as wildlife sanctuaries, they are even more so as marine nurseries for the huge crops of ocean fish endangered by any encroachment on their earliest feeding grounds.

It is as insect preserves, however, that the salt marshes have nurtured the generations of blood-starved mosquitoes and carnivorous greenhead flies that imposed a natural selection on the summerization of old Ar-gilla (Latin for hard white clay) Road that takes its time from Ipswich town some four miles along the ridge to Castle Neck. Survival of the fittest along the road produced the Pillbox Colony — not the military kind (the defense against the greenhead has not yet been devised) but the medical — an enclave largely of doctors in escape from their Boston practices.

As Argilla Road saunters around Heartbreak Hill and over Labor-in-Vain Creek toward the sea, it affords pleasing vistas of the marshes quilted with the long-abandoned haycutters' drainage ditches and of the hump of Hog Island. Skirting Castle Hill, the road crosses the dunes to the Ipswich lighthouse, the only structure along the nearly five miles of Castle Neck's incredible beach, which on the chart looks like an ill-fitting sock.

All around here were the 250 acres of Castle Hill Farm, which since 1843 belonged to Manasseh Brown, upon whose death near the end of the century it passed to his son, John Burnham Brown. The new owner had made it in railroading in Chicago and now returned to his native Ipswich to turn the farm into his country estate. At the same time he bought Town Hill near the center with the notion of building some kind of railroad institute on its summit. Litigation, it is said, did a job on his fortune, and when J. B. Brown died in 1908 his dreams were only partly realized.

All along the road then was farmland and meadow, few trees, for the drumlins were kept cropped by the livestock. J. B. made roads and added buildings, landscaped and planted thousands of trees in his ambitions for Castle Hill Farm. Simultaneously, by coincidence, the Bostonization of Argilla Road got off to a quite different start, as related in Sidney N. Shurcliff's amusing and nostalgic account of the Pillbox Colony's first twenty-five years, *Upon the Road Argilla.*

The first to own summer property, the nominal founder of the colony, was not a pill-pusher but a Boston insurance man who commuted from Salem, George Patterson. In 1897 he bought a speck of an island in the marsh south of Castle Hill and downgraded its one small and flimsy house to a gunning camp, where he retreated with his shooting pals, the most notable of whom was the artist Frank S. Benson. Here Patterson gave vent to his inner self — Yankee tinkerer whose masterpiece was a complex of hanging basins and mini-aqueducts for the interior consolidation and collection of roof leaks — Yankee dreamer who one summer imported a cowpoke from Oklahoma to teach him western-style riding, rope tricks and gunslinging.

Actually, the preliminary medical reconnaissance, diagnosis and prognosis of Argilla had already occurred in the late 1880s when Eugene A. Crockett, Mark W. Richardson, Charles W. Townsend, Herman F. Vickery, Francis B. Harrington and Joseph L. Goodale took to vacationing in various combinations and at various times at Smith's boardinghouse about halfway out the road. All were graduates within a thirteen-year span of Harvard Medical School, or were finishing there. Most had trained and were on the staff at the Massachusetts General Hospital, and all practiced in Boston. All would be outstanding in their specialties. All were unpretentious spirits, not all Boston-born or Brahmins by any means. For all, the simple saltwater farm life and setting of Argilla Road were antidote to the demands of patients and the pressures of teaching within the inner circle of a great medical center.

And what a setting to which to rusticate their growing families for the summer, the ambience and privacy of it all fortified by the common bond of epidermal durability required to endure the absence of the cooling southwester in August and the insect life with which the colony existed in such strange symbiosis! Amos Everett Jewett, writing of his youthful summers "marshing" thereabouts, reminisced painfully on the season of the greenhead fly: "While they lasted they were probably the cause of more profanity than was anything else, although I have mowed in a cove, where there was no air, when mosquitoes and midgets made it quite entertaining. The greenhead drew blood with every bite, and if there were those who did not indulge in profanity, at least they felt like the old man in Rowley, who, when he met with an accident and some one asked him if he swore, replied 'No! but I had very profane thoughts.' "

In 1898, only a year after Patterson acquired Seeby's Island, Crockett bought the Trojan house of Smith by which the doctors had insinuated themselves. He got married in London soon after, with the red tape–cutting help of the American ambassador, the formidable Joseph Hodges Choate. Back in Ipswich, the newlyweds heard that the great man was in Boston. Wishing to gesture thanks, they offered to ferry him out to Hog Island, otherwise known as Choate Island, to inspect the ancestral farmhouse where his quite as famous elder cousin, Senator Rufus Choate, was born.

To the young couple's alarm, the ambassador arrived for the voyage, which was to be by rowboat, as if for an audience with His Majesty, right up to the stovepipe hat. They rowed him out anyway. Unfortunately, the Great Man enjoyed himself so much wandering about the island that the tide had preceded them at departure time, leaving their boat high and dry. Mrs. Crockett told Sidney Shurcliff "how Mr. Choate sat stiffly and regally in the rowboat while she and Dr. Crockett jumped over the side and pulled the boat with its distinguished freight over hundreds of yards of slimy mud to deep water." Some time after, Choate again visited the family island and exclaimed, as he surveyed the view from the heights, "I would rather be governor of Hog Island than of all of Massachusetts!"

Dr. Crockett showed up with the first automobile on Argilla Road, a 1903 Stanley Steamer that did not seriously seduce his colleagues who settled after him away from their bicycles, the colony's summer transport of choice to and from the Ipswich railroad depot. His purchase of the Smith house forced the other boarders out, and the same year, 1898, doctors Richardson and Townsend picked up some land and built a summer house they occupied with their families until 1902, when Richardson built his own, and a boathouse down on the Castle Neck River that served as the community landing for almost fifty years.

Charles Wendell Townsend was thirty-nine when he settled upon the road in 1898. He was already settling into the Goldsmithian mold: a respected physician who pursued his avocational passion, which in the bald and blackbearded Townsend's case was natural history, to the gradual abandonment of his profession. In his calm book about the region around his farm, *Beach Grass,* published in 1923, he expressed the dilemma of such duality: "The ornithologist in particular or the naturalist in general, the greater part of whose life is spent in the busy haunts of men, leads a double life of which his acquaintances know nothing, which is indeed a sealed book even to his intimate friends, if they are destitute of similar tastes and knowledge."

Dr. Townsend called his twelve acres "Merula Farm" after *Merula migratoria,* his favorite bird, the robin. One acre he planted with saplings that grew into his "Forest," where he hammered together a lean-to from which to observe the wild life attracted there. Here the Franciscan physician invented the "cricket thermometer." To arrive at the temperature, count the chirps in a quarter of a minute (crickets chirp faster as it gets warmer) and add thirty-nine.

Townsend and his first wife had four children and were great hikers and outdoor people. A few years after her death in 1917 he married her sister, but she too died soon after. His first Ipswich book was *Sand Dunes and Salt Marshes* in 1913; he wrote another on *The Birds of Essex County,* and three more about the natural history of Labrador, once walking all the way around the Gaspé Peninsula.

As an ornithologist Charles Townsend was internationally known. As a lover of the Ipswich salt marshes, beaches, dunes and drumlins, he was an observer with a magical eye and ear, the insights of the medical clinician, the pen of the poet, writing in *Beach Grass* of a night spent alone on a dune above the Ipswich beach: "The laughing cry of the loon comes to his ears from the sea and the noisy clamor of a great company of herring gulls, gossiping with each other as they settle down for a night on the shore. Sandpipers and plovers whistle as they fly over, and the lisping notes of warblers, migrating from the sterile cold of the north, drop from above. Forming a continuous background to these voices is the boom and the crash of the waves on the sea beach."

After Townsend, Dr. Goodale succumbed, buying in 1900 an 1815 farmhouse and much acreage, to which in 1920 he added another house and the well-known apple orchard that has passed into other hands but retains his name. Dr. Vickery got a house and 130 acres in 1902 and the next year sold off enough to Dr. Harrington for his purposes.

Still more of the Harvard medical fraternity followed, until 1907, when a rare but congenial breach occurred. Dr. William B. Robbins and his close friend Arthur A. Shurtleff (who in 1929 changed the family name to Shurcliff), a most original and inventive young Boston landscape architect, bought a drumlin and a large field on the water side of Argilla Road, called by the natives Skim Milk Hill because it was such thin pasturage. The new owners divided, and Dr. Robbins won the toss for the lot with the ocean view. Both built summer cottages on the heights, found well water at the bottom of their hill. But how to get it up to the house?

The handsome physician was one of the most popular in Boston's Back Bay, so much in demand that the routine answer to phone calls in Ipswich was "Doctor's taking a bath." To fill the tub, he had his water pumped up by an old one-lunger gasoline engine.

Not so Arthur Shurtleff, who was a greater tinkerer even than George Patterson. Wind power he would harness, but not with an ugly high farm windmill on an iron tower such as some of his neighbors employed. Shurtleff reproduced a picturesque old-timer in the Dutch style he had seen flailing away on Nantucket, and from this he strung wires all the way down the hill to the arm of a hand pump at the well. Occasionally this rig worked and lifted a trickle of water into the tank in the house. Conveniently he departed for the office and left his wife in command. A niece of the sculptor Augustus St. Gaudens, Margaret Shurtleff was an excellent tennis player, a feminist, political liberal, civil libertarian, a leading Beacon Hill bell ringer in her later years, and the mother of three boys and three girls. She recalled in her memoirs, *Lively Days,* that when there was no wind the dishes were washed in an emergency supply of rainwater, and the guests, if they insisted, in the creek, "a long walk across the prickly marshes and, unless the tide was high, a slimy descent down a muddy bank."

Tending the windmill, the energetic Mrs. Shurtleff decided, was "more of a responsibility than all the children lumped together. My first duty in the morning was to unfurl the sails on the four arms, push the big wheel that turned the hood of the mill into the wind and wait to see if the wind was strong enough to turn the arms. . . . The wind was not always cooperative. It might change in direction, it might die down or it might speed up and snap off an arm of the mill. In a high wind it was necessary to furl the sail in a hurry, a ticklish job. First the mill must be turned out of the wind, but even then the sails continued revolving at some speed. By catching one moving arm after another I could generally slow the mill down enough to tie the arms and furl the flapping sails."

Arthur Shurtleff's loathing for automobiles was surpassed only by son Sidney's obsession with them, but he was devoted to the bicycle, which he was once inspired to mate with his favorite water conveyance, the kayak. The result was the family "jolly boat," a kayak on wheels stuffed with small children and towed behind a bicycle. All in all, the jolly boat was a greater success than the Icarian glider he built and tried heroically to get aloft on the run from a hilltop.

The glider lasted about as long as the Shurtleff "Self and Family Starter," which he abandoned after ten exciting days of trials. The object was the prevention of a broken wrist cranking up the Ford "banana wagon" the family finally talked him into buying. He welded a tireless baby carriage wheel onto the axle of the crank, wound one end of a length of clothesline around the rim and stationed his wife and the children on the other, tug-o'-war style.

"At a signal from my father," Sidney wrote, "the team would run vigorously away at right angles to the car, thus spinning the wheel and the motor." After a few such dashes, it would usually start. The invention was short-lived, however. A large labor force was required, and, in Mother Shurtleff's words, because they had to run across the highway "we often held up passing cars whose drivers wondered what was going on, causing me no end of embarrassment. A trip from Ipswich to Boston, a distance of 30 miles, took about four hours. And always a spark plug had to be cleaned on the way."

It chanced that in 1908, the year the Shurtleffs crowned Skim Milk Hill with their skim-milk summer house (cost $1,000; no electricity; hot water from a 50-gallon drum heated by a kerosene lamp), John

Burnham Brown died, and after a few months his Castle Hill Farm out at the end of Argilla Road was put up for sale. The following summer President Taft spent on the Beverly shore, and it was persistently rumored that his brother Charles was buying the Brown estate in Ipswich.

It also chanced, that summer of 1909, that the President, having failed to convince his crony and Gloucester summer neighbor, John Hays Hammond, to accept the ambassadorship to China, named Charles R. Crane of Chicago, vice president of the Crane plumbing empire, who had traveled extensively in the Orient and, though a Democrat, supported Taft's Far Eastern policy. En route to his post in China, however, Crane let fly some critical remarks about Japan, was summarily recalled by Secretary of State Philander Knox and resigned.

Charles Crane's younger brother, Richard Teller Crane, Jr., had been renting summer estates in Manchester since 1905 and was on the lookout for a spread he could call his own. Hearing about Castle Hill Farm, he inspected it one day not long after it had been rumored sold to the President's brother, and bought it the next. On January 14, 1910, papers were passed, and for a reported $125,000 the plumbing heir became the new owner of the Castle Hill Farm, all of Castle Neck but the lighthouse, and Cedar Point, eight hundred or so acres.

With a stroke of the pen, a Yale man, class of '95, was possessor of the strategic high ground, most of the approaches by water and lowland, and nearly five miles of beach at the end of Harvard's Argilla Road. Had an Eli stolen a marsh on the Crimson?

Richard Crane, at thirty-six, was really quite an amiable and unpretentious man who carried his family wealth offhandedly enough. And yet the first thing he did was to put the Boston architects Shepley, Rutan and Coolidge to work designing an Italianate mansion of about sixty-five rooms, some one hundred by three hundred feet, on the absolute crown of Castle Hill. Olmsted Brothers, the Boston landscape architects, created a matching Italian garden. Work was pushed with such speed that the next spring the Cranes and their household were able to move into the castle on Castle Hill, suddenly (as all magic castles should be) the lordliest and loftiest summer mansion on the North Shore.

In all this may be detected the hand of Florence Crane, née Higinbotham, whose father, Harlow, rose from farm boy to partnership in Chicago with the mercantile genius Marshall Field and married her off to plumbing and her sister to publishing in the person of Joseph Medill Patterson. The Cranes arrived with their young son, Cornelius, and their daughter, Florence, who also saw every little girl's dream come true and grew up to be the Princess Belosselsky. The children arrived with Catherine Mulvey, who was called by all "N-U-R-S-E," as Corny's new friend Sidney Shurtleff clearly remembered, "in a slow Chicago drawl with a lowering inflection at the end." Luxuriously bearded Grandfather Higinbotham and Uncle Harlow, Jr., and his wife were installed for that and some summers to come in the large J. B. Brown house partway up Castle Hill.

Manifestly under the same infatuation with the clean sweep that had piled up such a tidy family fortune, Richard Crane had to have a clear view in the manner of Charles Greely Loring sixty years earlier, who had never coveted any land in Beverly save his neighbor's. Over the next few years Crane swept up Wigwam, Sagamore and Caverly hills, through Woodbury's Landing, around Hog (Choate) and Patterson's (Seeby's) islands and across another large farm adjoining Labor-in-Vain Creek, always in quick abhorrence tearing down any shacks or sheds that intruded on the Crane view, until he had about 3,500 acres.

The Townsend family and a few friends whiled away August of 1912 in one of those shanties and a spread of tents on the dunes above Castle Neck Beach, and the naturalist described in *Beach Grass* how they dined on fish, clams and blackberries cooked over a driftwood fire, bathed in the tub of the ocean and slept, when they felt like it, under the stars. "The gulls and terns and sandpipers were our constant companions. We lived a free and open-air existence in the sand and in the water, and we were well sunned, sanded, and salted."

Then the squatters were banished and the camps torn down or suffocated under the drifting dunes that even buried most of a nearby grove of trees. Still, better this than the crowds brought to the shore by the electric trolleys and the motor cars, wrote Townsend, where elsewhere he had seen the dunes "covered with summer houses, tin cans and Sunday newspapers, detestable to birds and bird-lovers alike. Fortunate indeed are the birds and bird-lovers who can wander in a

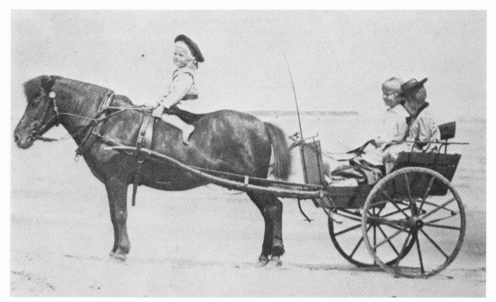

Stella, with Davy Richardson up, draws Dr. Townsend's pony cart along the beach not yet known as Crane's, Ipswich, 1899. From Upon the Road Argilla

Dr. Charles W. Townsend in his new Cadillac at "Merula Farm" July 4, 1908.
Upon the Road Argilla

Landscapist landbound. From the brow of his hill, Arthur Shurtleff awaits the lift that never came during his 1911 glider experiments. Upon the Road Argilla

Father Shurtleff's bicycle trailer, with Bill and Elizabeth, is more successful in 1913. Upon the Road Argilla

Mother Shurtleff is about to take off down the road with a Jolly Boatful of young Shurtleffs in 1913. On the hill are the Shurtleff house and windmill, the Robbins cottage behind the pole. Upon the Road Argilla

The first Shurtleff automobile, a 1916 Model T Ford. The touring car body has been replaced with a beach wagon body. It is late June 1917. Margaret Shurtleff is the driver. Behind her are the family nurse and five of the six children persuaded by their car-hating father to power the "Self and Family Starter." Upon the Road Argilla

The Pillbox Colony's summer circus at the Harrington place invariably featured on the drums Richard Crane, the Plumbing King, standing at left, in straw hat. Dr. James D. Barney is the comic cop. Cornelius Crane is running next to the lady in the funny hat, his mother. N-U-R-S-E sits in white at far right. Around 1912. Upon the Road Argilla

Watching tennis at the Osgood court on Ring's Island, 1913. Upon the Road Argilla

Richard T. Crane at the helm of his yawl Northern Light, *about 1927.* Upon the Road Argilla

The Cranes' first castle on Castle Hill, new in 1911. Deemed "inadequate" by 1925, the Italianate villa was razed and replaced with the present "Great House." Upon the Road Argilla

region unmarred and 'unimproved,' and grateful are they to any one who can order such a state of affairs. May it always remain so!"

All did not at first share Dr. Townsend's farseeing approbation of his neighbor's territorial annexations. The gobbling-up of the five miles of Castle Neck Beach caused the *Ipswich Chronicle* to wonder why the selectmen hadn't been consulted prior to the sale concerning the town's claim of perpetual ownership for the public weal.

The new owner said nothing, but on the first of July of the first season of his tenure invited the entire Ipswich school population of nine hundred to his beach to celebrate Cornelius Crane's birthday. Transportation was provided, and barge and boat rides. During swimming, his men patrolled off the beach in his launch, and just in case, a first aid tent was pitched among the dunes, with doctor and nurses. Music by the United Shoe Machinery Company Band.

The next July, 1912, a thousand came, down the Ipswich River in the excursion steamer *Carlotta* and a fleet of twenty motorboats. After the third such beach party in 1913, an annual tradition now, the *Chronicle* was pleased to report that Mr. Crane's "controversy" with the town was being conducted most amicably, and he had made no effort whatsoever to bar the public from the beach to which he held title, legitimately or otherwise. By 1922, for Corny's seventeenth, fifteen hundred came down the river to, yes, "Crane's Beach" with their lunches; their host provided the ice cream and candy. For the young man's twenty-first his father had the 84-foot schooner *Me Gildis* built in Essex.

After President Taft's withdrawal of his ambassadorship to China in 1909, Charles Crane, in John Hays Hammond's peevish words, "in high dudgeon betook himself and his wealth to the opposing political camp where, through judicious campaign expenditures, he did much damage to his former political associates." The injured plumber first moved as far left in the Republican Party as there was room — to Senator Bob LaFollette and the Progressives — and then, as the 1912 election heated up, instead of bolting to Theodore Roosevelt and the Bull Mooses, leaped back to the Democrats as Wilson's heaviest campaign contributor. It was a dudgeon by which eventually, as Hammond added, in 1920 Charles Crane "reached port" as Wilson's minister to

China, where he served, in the mining engineer's more generous estimate, with distinction.

Richard T. Crane, Sr., the blue-collar machinist who founded the giant company and later branched out to dominate the elevator industry as well, died in 1912 at eighty. Charles succeeded him as president, but in two years, preoccupied with politics and philanthropy, sold out his interests to his younger brother and turned over the pull chain to him — a metaphor that had earlier inspired a heraldist commissioned by the family to come up with a coat of arms (so Cleveland Amory claims in *Who Killed Society?*) which was rejected out of hand: "The shield was divided into four parts, including, in each section, a sink, a bathtub, etc. Over all was a hand gripping the handle of a chain — with the inevitable motto, *'Après moi le déluge.'* "

The Cranes survived the deluge quite handily, but long before the rains descended that dark day of 1929 they had forehandedly equipped themselves with their private Pullman, *Nituna,* in which to arrive, fleets of shining motor cars in which to flee, and, if the waters rose even unto the terraces of Castle Hill, a flotilla of arks (not hotels this time) disguised as yachts.

Along Argilla Road a very few of the Pillbox Colonists couldn't or wouldn't master the new mechanics, though they were adept enough at extracting a gallbladder, and set chauffeurs and even wives behind the wheels of a movable feast of conveyances that kept Sidney Shurcliff in a state of euphoria from one end of his youthful summers to the other — buggylike Stanleys, queer Hupmobiles and Pierce Arrows, a Peerless, a Napier, a Packard or two and even a Cadillac runabout purchased by the usually pedestrian Dr. Townsend, but a predominance of Ford flivvers, as befitted the simple rusticity pictured as the good life by most of the sophisticated yet so very Yankee Boston doctors and the scattering of nonmedical friends they let in.

Huge Renaults, prepossessing Packards, overwhelming Cadillacs, gigantic Chalmerses, indescribable Rolls Royces, and even a Citroën desert half-track, with a top speed of ten miles an hour, that Crane thought would be great for dunes but never used, these were the caravans of the family in the villa on the hill, topped off, in Sidney's expert opinion, by Mrs. Crane's absolutely tremendous maroon Simplex trimmed with German silver and upholstered in moleskin; he and Corny thought this great steed must be terribly fast, but when they snuck it out from under the chauffeur one day they couldn't get it up to fifty.

Mrs. Crane preferred sedateness anyway, to the annoyance of her housekeeper, Mrs. Strahan, who would complain to Sidney and the other children that one faithful family chauffeur, Alvin Johnson, "has only two speeds — DEAD SLOW and STOP!"

The grandeur of the Simplex was in some contrast to the extraordinary arrival of Mrs. Roger Warner at Mrs. Crane's for tea one day. The Warners built a house on the road in 1916 and owned several secondhand foreign cars bought at bargain prices, including an Itala that lacked, for some reason that escaped Sidney, both body and rear fenders. "The chauffeur, in full uniform, sat on a box placed over the gasoline tank . . . and Mrs. Warner, dressed in her afternoon best, sat behind him on a large sand bag with one hand clutching her skirt around her ankles and the other holding on her hat and at the same time gripping her handbag!"

No chauffeur but Richard Crane himself was at the wheel of his Stevens Duryea roadster, emerging from Linebrook Road onto the Newburyport Turnpike one day in late summer of 1915. In the seat beside him was his old Yale classmate Benjamin Stickney Cable, President Taft's Assistant Secretary of Commerce and Labor, who was visiting at Castle Hill.

Suddenly they were struck by a car headed for Boston on the Pike, and overturned. Crane was injured. Cable was killed. The other driver was Dr. David L. Edsall, the six-foot-four Jackson Professor of Clinical Medicine at Harvard Medical School and Chief of the East Medical Service at the Massachusetts General Hospital, who was not seriously hurt although his bride was thrown through the windshield and permanently scarred and lamed. When the case came to court, no blame was fixed, though both men were suspended from driving for six months. But Crane claimed that Edsall was indeed at fault, and there was a great stew in Boston.

In memory of his dead friend Crane built the Cable Memorial Hospital in Ipswich, and never again, according to Shurcliff, took the wheel of a car. The impact on the Pillbox Colony of this tragic confrontation between their neighbor on the hill and their distinguished colleague, shortly to be the most famous dean in their medical school's history, may be judged from Shurcliff's omission of Dr. Edsall's identity from his bare account of the accident in *Upon the Road Argilla.*

In his last major "private work" before World War I rendered such fancies inconsistent with the national interest, Crane had engaged his neighbor Arthur Shurtleff to design a mall dipping down from the mansion on Castle Hill and up slightly over lesser Steep Hill, then tobogganning off into the ocean — a half a mile in length, 160 feet wide, of velvety grass and lined with statuary and four rows of evergreens standing at arms. As the Crane landscape architect, Shurtleff oversaw the creation of what was described in the press as "the most splendid thing of its kind in this or any country" in the fall of 1913.

With the resumption of such extravagences a permissible, enviable, and in some quarters even admirable conversion of surplus value after the Armistice, Crane decided he must have a superintendent, and none but the best. He interviewed Robert Cameron, who had been tending the Harvard Botanic Garden, and revealed to the Scot a bit of himself: "I don't want a man to come to Ipswich and think that I am anything more than any other man. I do not want a man to come to Ipswich that cannot get along with the people there. I want the people of Ipswich to have a kindly feeling towards my family." That understood, Mr. Cameron went to work.

To complement the magnificence of his mall, Shurtleff conceived broad avenues winding up from Argilla Road to the mansion through groves of rare trees, exotic flora and native fauna (for which he created a deer park), a maze, gardens and groves. Super Cameron, his Scots spirit renewed by travels across America and back to Britain inspecting great gardens everywhere at the laird's expense, turned the architect's dreams to reality with exploding vegetable gardens of Eden, a rose garden of six hundred varieties to shame the rosiest fingers of an Atlantic dawn, ponds scalloped from the earth for watering it all, and lawns without end. Crane decreed that one of his farms become the private Labor-in-Vain Golf Course, that a lake-sized swimming pool be scooped out, that there be a casino, a guest house for bachelors, and cottages for Cameron, and his head farmer, and his gamekeeper. And all materialized.

In about 1919 Crane bought up Hog Island and had the dozen or so scanty summer cottages there torn down — all but the almost two-hundred-year-old homestead on Choate Hill and a barn that he carefully preserved. He directed Cameron to provide this bald drumlin on his horizon with a headpiece of a hundred thousand trees. The word, as usual, was father to the deed.

Hog Island is in fact in Essex, which for at least fifty years maintained a town road from the mainland across the marsh, not always above the tide. One elderly lady told Gordon Abbott, Jr., Director of the Trustees of Reservations, to whom the Cranes ultimately gave the island, of the race to get across before the tide set in. One night she was riding back with her father in the buggy when he commanded: "Quick, put your feet up!" The water was then up to the floorboards. Another resourceful summertime Hog Islander, as Abbott tells it, got back and forth to the mainland by means of a canoe, a wheelbarrow and a pair of rubber boots. When the tide was up, he put the boots and the wheelbarrow in the canoe and paddled across. When it was out, he put on the boots, loaded the canoe in the barrow and wheeled across.

In the spring of 1925 the plumbing king was feeling so flush that he ordered his Italianate villa of sixty-five, more or less, rooms torn down. It *was* fourteen years old and was believed by Mr. and Mrs. Crane, so reported the *Boston Evening Transcript,* to be too inadequate to be longer put up with.

Within a few months David Adler, a Chicago architect, was supervising the construction of the replacement. "The Great House" it would be, Georgian in style, of the period of Charles the Second in a fashion that might or might not have elicited an ironic comment from the English satirical artist William Hogarth, whose house in London Crane bought and stripped of four rooms, which he had reassembled in their entirety within the walls of Dutch brick and Ohio limestone atop remote and windy Castle Hill in the simple New England country town of Ipswich, Massachusetts.

"The Great House" was pronounced by one and all, the Cranes included, as quite adequate though it contained only forty-nine rooms. Five years passed, and on November 7, 1931, his fifty-eighth birthday, the son of the machinist died.

Florence, née Higinbotham, daughter of the farmer's son, waited until 1945, when she gave a thousand acres — most of Crane's Beach and Castle Neck — to the Trustees of Public Reservations, as they were then called. This nonprofit institutional device for holding on to the beautiful lands of Massachusetts, hopefully forever, had been the inspiration in 1890 of Charles Eliot, son of the president of Harvard, a young landscape architect who had sat at the feet, as Arthur Shurtleff did, of the father of their profession in America, Frederick Law Olmsted.

Thus were the fears of the Ipswich selectmen put to rest.

When Florence Crane died in 1949 she bequeathed "The Great House" and about three hundred surrounding acres to the Trustees. Having no endowment, they were about to raze it when in 1950 Harold F. Lindergreen founded a summer art school there, and the next year a series of six summer concerts was arranged by Samuel L. M. Barlow, composer and summer resident of Gloucester's Eastern Point. The Castle Hill Foundation has carried on under the jocular impetus of David Crockett, son of the doctor who led the pillbox colonization in the days of windmills and jolly boats.

Fascinated with the Far East like his Uncle Charles, slim, shy Cornelius Crane led an anthropological expedition to the South Pacific with his chum Sidney Shurcliff. In 1955 he married a beautiful and artistic Japanese girl, Mine Sawaraha, in Tokyo. Corny died in 1962 and was buried on the high ground of Hog Island. In 1974 his widow gave the Trustees of Reservations the Cornelius and Mine S. Crane Reservation, another seven hundred acres of marshes, dunes and islands, including Hog.

That double-lived Argilla Roader, Dr. Charles Townsend, had summed it all up in advance in *Beach Grass:* "Growing near the edge of the dunes at the foot of Castle Hill is a willow of great age, a veteran, with split and hollow bole, unable longer to hold up its great branches which rest on the ground. In touching the ground it has renewed its life like Antaeus of old or like the banyan tree, and has taken root and sent up fresh and vigorous willow saplings."

7

King of Clubs

"Get to your places!" shouted the Queen in a voice of thunder, and people began running about in all directions, tumbling up against each other; however, they got settled down in a minute or two, and the game began.

—Alice's Adventures in Wonderland

IF CLUBBISHNESS IS KING ALONG THE NORTH SHORE, AS THE QUEEN MIGHT have roared, then Myopia by uncommon consent must be King of Clubs. The name is as odd as the game, which consists in its most traditional form of pursuing the fox or, for lack of one, a bag called a drag, and no other private club around, few anywhere, can touch the Myopia Hunt for the panache with which its roster dashes faster, ever faster, across the rolling wonderland of Hamilton and environs.

There are other suits too, besides hunting pink, in this sometimes very loaded deck — steeplechasers, polo players, golf addicts, tennis fiends, backgammon nuts, boozers and even a few cards, a deck that has trumped generations of jealous jibesters and thrives behind its own peculiar looking glass as never perhaps before, in scornful defiance of what passes for reality all about.

The October horseman is oft the August helmsman, and the more tightly knit King of Clubs has for a very long time shared the realm of social governance on the North Shore (keeping a rein on the wheel, though, through certain interlocking memberships) with Marblehead's Eastern Yacht Club, Queen of the Waves. Their Jack is the

Essex County (a country) Club of Manchester, whose badges of office are burnished each June by the annual one-day laying-on of hands of Harvard's twenty-fifth reunion class.

All very elite, this clubbishness? A sometimes insufferable yes . . . or slight tilt of the head. Effete? When you tote up the broken collarbones, cracked skulls, aching backsides, burning bursas, torn ligaments, chilblains and nauseated stomachs — hardly. But it is Myopia that practically endows a bed at the Beverly Hospital, and it is to Myopia ("But, oh, Utopia!" as the old toast starts off) to which the North Shore crowd — that "overly uninhibited and rather rowdy fringe" of Proper Boston, in the words of Cleveland Amory — raises its glasses and its social sights.

Myopia began royally enough, not on the North Shore but on the country estate of Frederick O. Prince, a wealthy Boston lawyer, adjoining Wedge Pond in Winchester. The four stalwart Prince scions — Frederick, Gordon, Charles and Morton — reveled in the rural life, rowed and sailed, helped Dr. Jim Dwight of Nahant set up one of the first tennis courts in America on their property, and in July of 1876, while their father was running successfully for mayor of Boston, organized with their friends a baseball team that naturally demanded a name.

The brothers were all nearsighted, a family trait. Hey, how about "Myopia"? And they stitched it on a red banner in black letters. One evening the "Myopians" got up an impromptu tug-o'-war with a celebrated Irish team in a local bowling alley. The Prince gang, in rubber soles, had it all their own way until the last round; unaccountably they couldn't gain an inch, when there was a sudden crash and most of the ceiling came down. The Hibernians had taken a turn around a supporting pillar, with unexpected but predictable results.

Mayor *O'Prince,* as some democratizer tagged him, pulled the table out from under the boys when he decided to summer in Nahant in 1878 and take his kitchen staff with him. His sons countered with a clubhouse on the two hundred Princely acres overlooking Mystic Lake, on what came to be known as Myopia Hill. Next year they incorporated as the Myopia Club, with an almost instant membership of 150 drawn mainly from the rosters of the exclusive Somerset and University clubs of Boston. Among their festivities, fueled by unlimited drafts of Myopia Punch, was the Myopia Landslide, which they pulled on a visiting Englishman one evening at a Lexington hotel by suddenly lifting up one end of the table. Not subtle, but effective. The table was long, and so was the landlord's bill, recalled their first president, Marshall K. Abbott, "as a successful land-slide necessitates the smashing of much crockery."

Britain took her vengeance on Yankee drollery by the device of exporting the recently devised sport of foxhunting in costume, a deviate form of chase that Oscar Wilde twitted as "the unspeakable in full pursuit of the uneatable" but which Fred Prince, Jr., a hard rider like his brothers, who had no time for Wilde, discovered to his delight among Anglophilic friends at Newport and Long Island. In the fall of 1881 Prince infected his brethren o'er the bumpy hills and dales of Winchester behind a borrowed pack of hounds, and forthwith Myopia must have its own. The following spring the club's pioneer pack arrived freight-free on one of member George Warren's Warren Line steamships, purchased from Lord Willoughby de Broke, Master of the South Warwickshire hounds.

The rough and wooded terrain of Winchester did not suit two particularly influential members, Charles H. Dalton, chairman of the Boston Park Commission, and William Appleton, whose ancestral Appleton Farms in Ipswich, spilling over into Hamilton, the Myopians had assayed in 1881. The two persuaded the club to rent the open, rolling acres of the Dodge farm in Hamilton (the pleasant old farmhouse was raised in 1772 by Robert Dodge before he went off to fight in the Revolution) from its owner, John Gibney, a Salem leather manufacturer. Meanwhile, a group of Boston sportsmen that numbered several Myopians organized what they called simply The Country Club at Clyde Park in rural Brookline, a sprawling country town immediately west of the city, just beginning its rise as the richest suburb in the America of its day. These splinterers proposed to absorb within this first of the country clubs the Myopia Club, whose residual identity was salvaged by a simple change of name to Myopia Fox Hounds, designating its narrowed pursuits.

All this was in 1882, and for nearly ten years Milord's hounds and their heirs and assigns bayed after the genuine scent or the evidently as irresistible anise bag dragged ahead by a horseman who thought like a fox, followed at full gallop by the pink-and-canary-coated Yankees of Boston. Hill and dale they traversed, to the singular cry of the Master's horn, through copse and thicket, over fence and stone wall, across field and stream and ditch, and wherever a run of open country presented itself, sometimes upon the invitation of the owner, sometimes not.

Winchester was forsaken in 1883, to the regret of local people who had succumbed in spite of themselves to the color and excitement of it all, but in those early days most of the towns to the west and south of Boston were not yet suburbs, and the shout of Tallyho! and crack of collarbone echoed and reechoed not only through Hamilton, Wenham and Ipswich on the North Shore, but across the meadows and over the hedges of Brookline, Dedham, Westwood, Milton, Newton, Framingham, Southboro, Lexington and doubtless elsewhere.

The pitiful prospect of a frightened fox "turned loose in the suburbs to get away if he can from a pack of intelligent hounds and a rout of empty-headed puppies on horseback" was made to order for the mill of the press, which ground exceeding coarse from such un-American grist as the pink coats, white britches and top boots of "the daring riders," the thundering horses, the hounds baying after the "little fifteen-pound, tame fox, which hasn't the shadow of a chance of escaping, through meadows and lawns to his place of refuge beneath some farmer's woodshed"—or more asinine still, "the agile anise seed bag."

From the loftiness of Nahant, Judge Grant was mildly amused that "the beautiful inland country about Wenham, Hamilton and Topsfield has become a race-course for this hunting element, many of whom do not hesitate to risk life and limb in their almost hysterical enjoyment of the transplanted ancient sport." The farmers, His Honor had heard, "were at first inclined to resent this new invasion of red-coats as undemocratic impertinence and a legal trespass. But well-mannered tact, especially if it go hand-and-glove with liberal indemnity, will mollify the wounded pride even of a New England farmer. By degrees the hard headed countrymen, who sniffed at fox-hunting as mere Anglomania, have become genuinely, though grimly, enthralled by the pomp and excitement of the show."

Among the obdurately unenthralled was Louis Dodge, who prided himself on the evenness of his stone walls, over one of which the overbearing Freddie Prince, introducer of the not-so-ancient sport to the North Shore, was practicing jumps one day with his horses and grooms. Soon the stones were flying. The owner appeared and stood watching, silently and even grimly. "Out of the way, my good man!" shouted Prince as he flew by . . . "And that," said Mrs. Hilda Ayer, "was the end of that!"

To smooth rural feathers, the club in 1882 staged a season's-end ball for its neighbors "at which the wives and daughters of the countryside," Judge Grant wrote, "dance with the master of the hounds and his splendid company, who valiantly, if vainly, endeavor to cut pigeon-wings in emulation of the country swains." Pigeon-wings were no match for swallowtails, however, and the annual Myopia Hunt Ball was increasingly held in Boston with a color and dash not seen, supposedly, since the British occupation. For the neighbors left behind, the club in 1890 set up "Labor Day Sports," in which the swains were allowed limited participation until this event, too, narrowed down to the Myopia Horse Show six years later.

The Hunt Ball, which came to be considered the social highlight of the Boston season, was the source of numerous anecdotes arising from the discriminate mixture of alcohol and arrogance. One will suffice, concerning the Boston cop affably handing out discarded favors to guests departing in the wee hours, who was ordered by a huntsman "to get the hell out of there" or he'd give him a kick that would land him on Boston Common. The outcome, or outgo, is not recorded except, perhaps, on some long-discarded blotter, but can be imagined.

For such valor, not to say foolhardiness, in the bull ring the victor (if the matador) is awarded the ears of the vanquished. At the successful conclusion of the hunt, Reynard was systematically dismembered, and his brush, mask, and pads (that is, his tail, face, and feet) were distributed to those veteran Myopians, male or female (the ladies superbly on side saddle in the early days, including Mrs. Jack Gardner, who would try anything) deemed by the Master to have ridden hardest and best, in descending order; the foxblood, it is said, was smeared on the visages of the initiates.

The bag of anise seed (succeeded in recent years by a foul mixture of animal droppings, mineral oil and hot water) had pretty much replaced Br'er Fox by 1890. The ground was too broken on the inland North Shore (thirty-mile chases are recorded), too often ending with the wily prey losing himself, exhausted but intact, in the miasmic Wenham Swamp.

Owner John Gibney died, and in 1891 the club bought the Dodge farm with its 150 acres from his heirs for $20,000 and remodeled the farmhouse more to its purposes, after almost surrendering to the temptation to accept the offer of the Boston tycoon T. Jefferson Coolidge of his Manchester estate, already hemmed in by shore development, at a rent equal to the town tax.

That was the year polo came to Myopia, and the rivalry with the Dedham Polo and Country Club. The field was rough and the action ragged, and at the conclusion of their first match a Myopia wit commented that the best playing was done by the band. Polo was crashing, bashing madness on horseback (two players locked in combat chased the ball off the field onto the tennis courts one year, and James H. Proctor, an early veteran, proudly displayed in his home a mallet with his two front teeth embedded in it). The King of Sports deserved kingly spectatorship, and in the 1890s the coaches *Myopia* and *Constitution,* behind marvelously matched four-in-hands, leaped and lurched over the dirt roads from Manchester and Pride's Crossing, laden with top-hatted toffs and their dustered ladies, bound for the play at Hamilton.

Presiding over all this tallyho was a succession of masters of fox hounds (MFHs) beginning with Frank Seabury, a ramrod rider of definite stamp who maneuvered his hunt across the farms of the yeomanry with the command of a Washington and the tact of a Franklin. His successor in 1892, Randolph M. (Bud) Appleton of the Ipswich squirearchy, consolidated Seabury's diplomatic conquests (one farmer even planted and harvested his turnips early so the club could range freely across his patches) and handed over the horn in 1901 to George S. Mandell.

Mandell ran the family newspaper, that voice of Brahminism practically from the grave, the *Boston Evening Transcript.* His creed: "We run no prize fights, no scandals, no divorce cases and no debasing sensational matter of any kind. We mention only the weddings and deaths of prominent people." In a day when the numerous Boston papers were widely if not well known for their eccentric informality, the *Transcript* under Mandell was a famously loose ship, or hunt, as the case may be, but, as he said, "it works well."

The decade of Mandell's mastership at Myopia passed serenely, and in 1911 he was succeeded by his predecessor's younger bachelor brother, James W. Appleton — "Mr. Jimmy" — the most popular of all MFHs, and durable, for he served until 1935 with a two-year break for the First War.

While a fox, an anise bag and even a polo ball were considered objects of horseback pursuit worthy of your true Myopian, a lump of gutta-percha, afoot, was not. MFH Bud Appleton encountered derision and dismay when in 1894 he seriously suggested that the club follow his lead (the family had recently put in a crude course on the farm) and lay out nine holes of its own. As Edward Weeks, another journalist-Myopian (but a golfer, not a hunter) tells it in his history of the club, the only other links around, as golf swept the country in the Nineties, were a nine-holer at Pride's Crossing (long since abandoned), a six-holer at the Essex County Club in Manchester and The Country Club's six in Brookline, all opened in 1893.

The derision of the equestrians at such pedestrian sport was exceeded only by their paradoxical dismay that the terrain was too rough for it. But the MFH won the day. The fairways were laid out, and put to sheep, and a few infidels were soon whacking their unfamiliar way toward the greens to the hoots of the watching horsemen.

Fortunately for the future of the game at Myopia, and indeed in America, another of those lifelong (maybe because a birthmark disfigured the left side of his face) Harvard bachelors, Herbert C. Leeds, joined the club in 1896. "Papa" Leeds was a very superior golfer and immediately dominated the sport at Hamilton. In two more years the long faces were proven right: the terrain was rough and tough, so tough that in 1898 the first of many National Open Championships was played there. Land was bought, and more leased, and Papa himself — with a diabolical feel for the game and the terrain — laid out a new eighteen-hole course, which opened in 1900. Brilliantly conceived, Myopia's for years was regarded as among the most challenging in the

Fraternal founders of the Myopia Hunt Club: Gordon Prince on horseback, Charles in the cockpit between his wife and Gordon, Morton lower left, Frederick lower right. Myopia scrapbook, Essex Institute

Polo at Myopia in 1910 occasionally invited, nay compelled, spectator participation. Essex Institute

Herbert (Papa) Leeds, founder of Myopia golf, on the putting green. From Myopia Songs and Waltzes

Monday September 5th

ON ~~AND AFTER JULY~~ 12, 1892,
THE FOUR-HORSE COACH,

"CONSTITUTION"
WILL LEAVE THE
MASCONOMO HOUSE, MANCHESTER,
~~DAILY (SUNDAYS EXCEPTED) AT 3.56 P. M., FOR THE~~
MYOPIA KENNELS, HAMILTON.

Down.			Up.
P. M. *3.30* Leave	**Masconomo House**		Arrive 7.10 P. M.
	Beverly Farms,		
" *4.05* "	*Pride's Crossing,*	"	6.40 "
	Princemere,		
" *5.30* Arrive	**Myopia Kennels,**		Leave 6.05 "
	Change Horses.		

Passengers on the Coach have the privileges of the Ladies' Rooms at the Myopia Club for the time being. On POLO DAYS the Coach goes directly to the Polo Field, not stopping at the kennels.

Fares, Single, $2.00. Return, $3.00.
Box Seat, $1.00 Extra.

BOOKING OFFICES: MASCONOMO HOUSE, MANCHESTER, PRIDE'S CROSSING STATION, HOTEL VENDOME, BOSTON.

Train Connections. DOWN. At Pride's with Flying Fisherman, and 3.20 Down from Boston. UP. At Pride's with 6.46 U train to Boston.

Riding in Style with a capital S. Myopia Scrapbook, Essex Institute

James W. Appleton—"Mr. Jimmy"—Master of Fox Hounds. Myopia scrapbook, Essex Institute

The Myopia clubhouse and stables in Hamilton, 1890s. Myopia Songs and Waltzes

Dinner at the 152 Beacon Street home of the Jack Gardners in Boston before a Myopia Hunt ball, early 1890s. Left to right, Alice Forbes Perkins, Master of Fox Hounds Frank Seabury, Anna Anderson, R. M. Appleton, Mrs. Appleton, Augustus P. Gardner and his aunt, Mrs. Jack Gardner, Francis Peabody, Jr., John L. (Jack) Gardner and Ellen T. Bullard. Myopia scrapbook, Essex Institute

"A Myopia Minuet," Marshall Abbott captioned this otherwise unidentified photograph in his Myopia Songs and Waltzes — but clearly Mrs. Jack and nephew Gussie Gardner, the future congressman, after the table was cleared.

George von Lengerke Meyer, president of Myopia in the 1890s and member of the Roosevelt and Taft cabinets, and his "Rock Maple Farm," one of the rustic showplaces of Hamilton. Essex Institute

BRILLIANT AND BEAUTIFUL PICTURE WAS
THE NORFOLK AND MYOPIA HUNT BALL

The combined 1907 hunt ball at the Somerset Hotel in Boston was attended by 600, the Boston Globe *reported. Myopia scrapbook, Essex Institute*

country, and by the great Bobby Jones as one of the most interesting, and the more charming, as he wrote once, for its absence of artificiality, built "with trust in nature."

Some of the world's best golfers — Scots, many of them — tested Myopia and found it not wanting, and some of the worst. All teed off under the proprietary eye of Papa and his cohorts who held forth on the Male Porch, the altar of the clubhouse on which no female (banned from membership anyway) could set foot, however dainty.

The worst were led or possibly even trailed by that pair of high-stake artists in the larger game, Henry Clay Frick and William H. Moore of Pride's Crossing, who vied in endowing Myopia with this or that (each tipped John Jones, the pro, a thousand every Christmas) and in cozying up to the heaviest hitter of them all, President William Howard Taft, when he was summering in Beverly. The tycoons and the President were bursting with expansive Edwardian egos, but not so John P. Marquand, the novelist, who a quarter of a century later took golf lessons three times a week but remained too intimidated by his fellow members to compete seriously.

Once the britches of the hunt had been breached by golf, tennis was bound to follow, but the game never rose above an indifferent third in the Myopian preference. The most colorful of a clutch of top players was that eccentric Amazon, Eleo Sears of Pride's . . . the classiest of the tennis tourneys those that pitted the best from the Myopia, Essex County and Nahant clubs, clashes invariably topped off with cocktails, lobster Newburg and champagne.

Tales of Myopia lean to the boozy, and not surprisingly, the confrontational. Encounters between man and man, man and horse, man and mallet, man and martini, occasionally even man and woman, are legion and legend . . . of Myopia machismo . . . and once she had topped or tumbled the bars to membership, of his nobby North Shore spouse, who could hold her own with genus Myopius, over the bar or at it.

There was the couple who lingered into the night over the hospitality after the Saturday drag, as Gordon Prince told it, then set out for Beverly Cove and home in their trap, only to reappear at the club in a short while, in a most disheveled and muddy state, on foot. "We've been in an awful accident! As we turned out of the Avenue a great motor truck, with only one headlight, crashed into us, smashing our buggy to bits, hurling us out, and the horse ran away. Lucky we weren't killed!" A reconnaissance party found the horse still in the shafts, the buggy overturned against a great stone post surmounted by an electric light marking the entrance.

And there is Ted Weeks's yarn of the Myopian who got home unexpectedly early after the annual dinner to find that "he had been preceded by a Club mate whose dogcart and horse were parked on the drive. A light on the second floor told him enough. So he shot the horse and went back to the Club."

Just before terminating in the Crash, the Era of Makebelieve culminated in an ugly clash at Myopia that left a bad aftertaste and the question in some minds: Who wins what wars on which playing fields? (Myopian George Patton's soldier-slapping temper tantrum in an army hospital in Sicily was fourteen years in the offing.)

On June 26, 1929, Arthur Mason, a very hard-riding polo player, overtook Fred Prince, the last of the founding brothers, and overrode him with a terrific bump in order to make a back shot. Prince, whose fuse was shorter than ever at the age of sixty-nine, a few minutes later pounded up behind Mason at the bell and whacked him full on the head with his mallet. And when it was all over, in an even worse breach of the game's etiquette, he refused to apologize. Mason came out of it with chronic headaches and double vision, brought suit and was awarded $20,000 damages. Frederick Prince would not budge an inch; he was suspended from the club he helped found and resigned.

The matter was of course a *cause célèbre* and did nothing for Myopia's reputation for nearsightedness, though it was regarded by some as further illustration of its usefulness as a lightning rod for the static of the satirists, allowing the rest of *The* North Shore to go less unbearably about its snobbery.

Furthering the gentler side of the Shore, on the other hand, Myopia in its younger days attracted many Bostonians back to their Essex County roots, as Marshall Abbott observed in 1897, adding, in that time of growing class-consciousness in America: "English country life is a relic of the feudal system; but no such conditions exist in New England. Simplicity is most prominent in Hamilton. Though the leaps from city luxury to Hamiltonian simplicity are wide, all seem to land safely and to enjoy life even more on the 'landing side.'"

Indubitably, thanks in no small part to diplomatic MFHs, and none to the Freddie Princes. And the acquisition of the rolling farms by the leapers (as cheaply as the Lorings and their crowd bought up the coast) has insured — at least during the dynastic sway of the Ayers, Princes, Tuckermans, Searses, Appletons and their cousins, in-laws and friends — the incomparable beauty of Essex County's inland countryside.

Myopia has been an outlet for more, and less, conspicuous consumption of excess wealth and leisure than, say, the Eastern Yacht Club, whose activities, it can be argued — especially the ancient art of coastal cruising — are a genuine extension of the honored seafaring heritage, adopted or handed down, of its practitioners . . . rather more so than chasing the anise bag in pinks and jodhpurs (though Myopians and Easterners are often one and the same, as the season goes!).

Is Myopia Brahminism a trifle awry? Perhaps. Its *rowdy fringe,* as Amory implied. The more wonder that the publisher of the papyral *Transcript* should have been a Master, that the studious Allan Forbes should have penned its early history, that the satirical Marquand should have felt so put down by his fellow members, and that the distinguished editor emeritus of the *Atlantic* should extol its centennial.

Still . . . hmmm . . . there is an awesome arrogance in the hunt, a splendid savagery in the kill, a knight-errantry of sorts on the polo ground, a swagger to the roistering, that compel a grudging wonder in the looker-on. Oh, to be one of *that* crowd! How they *do* carry it off! Après *nous* le déluge!

No use to take Myopians more seriously than they take themselves. A Sears, for instance, constant kibitzer at the regular four o'clock game of hearts in the Polo Room where young Ted Weeks was sometimes permitted by the presiding Mr. Jimmy to join in. The middle-aged Mr. Sears, "immaculate in white ducks and blue serge coat, wearing a straw boater with the Porcellian hatband; he followed the play attentively but would never remove his hat or take a hand."

Porcellian? The absolute, the king, the Myopia of the Harvard undergraduate clubs.

8

Look Out, Mr. Frick's Coming!

THE BOSTON LAWYER CHARLES GREELY LORING BOUGHT HIS FIRST TWENTY-five acres on the ocean at Pride's Crossing in 1844 for $4,000 and built the first summer cottage in Beverly. "I never want any land except the piece next to my own" was his creed, and he left a hundred acres to his heirs.

A long generation elapsed, the industrial revolution succeeded beyond the wildest expectations and fears of Charles Dickens and Karl Marx, the century turned, and a paltry fraction of the original fell into the steel grip of Henry Clay Frick, who erected up above the Loring compound the greatest mansion on the North Shore, behind the longest and costliest ($100,000) fence.

Hoping (and presuming) to improve his situation, the Pittsburgh magnate offered Miss Katharine Peabody Loring one million dollars for her house and land. C. G.'s granddaughter calmly turned her neighbor down, it is reported, with the rejoinder: "Goodness! What in the world would I do with a million dollars?"

The ephemeral Age of the Tycoons — those dinosaurs of finance who made America tremble to their tramples in that thin stratum of time between the invention of the rolled steel rail and the imposition of the rolling income tax — was upon us. Except that Miss Loring did not tremble, nor did the rest of the North Shore that remained Boston's and resisted, or absorbed, every effort of the lesser Vanderbilts to gild the Gold Coast in the reflected gloss of Newport. The mansion whose privacy Frick's bauble of a fence so publicly shielded from pry-

ing eyes is gone, and the barrier remains . . . like the other monu-
ments of the moguls (with the shining exception of Richard Crane's
"Castle Hill"), an antediluvian footstep in stone.

It is commonly supposed that the financiers, industrialists and entre-
preneurs who bankrolled, engineered and commanded the explosive
expansion of the closing quarter of the American century — and their
wives — were buying social status, or thought they were, when they
commenced shoehorning their way between the shingled cottages of
the Shore north of Beacon Hill. They surely were, but their mass
descent, if it can be called that, upon the North Shore between the late
1890s and 1910 suggests that the herding instinct, if anything, was
stronger. Not to mention the scenic attractions, a poor third perhaps,
for a Frick who had to cross Loring land to take a swim in God's
ocean.

Frederick H. Prince, Boston banker and one of the horsy brothers
who founded the Myopia Hunt Club, settled summers at Pride's Crossing in the early 1890s; Prince made it possible for Frick's partner
Andrew Carnegie to buy the railroad that connected Carnegie's Mesabi ore with his Pittsburgh mills. T. Jefferson Coolidge of Coolidge
Point in Manchester was associated with Frick in running the Atchi-
son, Topeka and Santa Fe. Another Boston man, John Greenough,
was a railroad financier and merger expert with the Poors in New York
and had one of the first summer homes on Eastern Point. Plenty more
Boston money that fired the industrial furnace from the Bessemers of
Pittsburgh to the looms of Lawrence was ensconced along the Shore.

No surprise, then, that one of the most powerful Republicans in the
Senate, the Detroit rail and steamship man James McMillan, should
turn up in Manchester in 1895 as the new owner, for $200,000, of the
dramatic Towne estate "Eagle Head." Or that the self-sworn "Judge"
William H. Moore of New York and points west, among the most
brazen and astoundingly successful stock-waterers in American finance, should be found on the Shore in 1897, presumably renting, and
golfing at Myopia. Next year the dapper Cleveland bachelor Henry C.
Rouse, president of thirteen railroads, friend of John Greenough,
bought the decommissioned Civil War fort on the heights of Eastern
Point and built his "Ramparts" inside the earthworks.

In 1902 Moore and Frick, closely associated in the first failed attempt to buy out Carnegie in 1899, purchased land almost cheek by jowl at Pride's Crossing and laid plans for their mansions. In 1904 H. J. Heinz, the Ketchup King, built a house so large that years later it was converted into a famous resort hotel, the Magnolia Manor. In 1906 Richard T. Crane, Jr., Chicago's Prince of Plumbing, discovered the North Shore, renting a Manchester summer estate. Likewise Otto H. Kahn, the New York financier and art patron involved with Moore in the takeover of various western railroads; Kahn rented the Charles Head estate in Manchester for three years at $10,000 a season, brought his horses and carriages in on a special train.

John D. Rockefeller, Jr., tried the North Shore first in 1906 at Otis H. Luke's "Pitch Pine Hall" in Beverly Farms; the family's arrival on the private Pullman *Wyoming* in July with fourteen servants and over forty trunks was duly noted in the press . . . "They will live very quietly and entertain very little." The same year the enormously wealthy and powerful international mining engineer John Hays Hammond bought the Hovey estate overlooking Gloucester's Freshwater Cove for $45,000 for his wife for a birthday present. And Edwin Carleton Swift, the beef packing family's New England man, died at his "Swiftmoore" at Pride's; a special train of eight cars brought the bereaved from all over to the funeral.

Joining Henry Clay Frick at Pride's was Henry Clay Pierce of St. Louis, bank messenger at sixteen, son-in-law of the first refinery owner west of the Mississippi, oil and rail multimillionaire in the Southwest and Mexico, and Washington B. Thomas of Boston, whose fortune was in sugar. J. Harrington Walker, Detroit, whiskey, plonked his Italian-style villa down on the bold shore of Magnolia Point. In 1910 Richard Crane absconded with the jewel of Ipswich, and Hammond, the great engineer, had a fifty-minute audience with Czar Nicholas in St. Petersburg to inform His Imperial Majesty with rare prescience of his plans for the investment of American capital in Russia.

But it was Frick and Moore, the most tyrannosaural of the creatures of capitalism, whose thunderous descent upon Pride's Crossing caused the greatest stir and left, if not the least, certainly among the lesser marks.

The first exposure of Mr. Frick, as he was customarily referred to with a figurative tug of the forelock, to the North Shore may have been

Cleveland rail tycoon Henry C. Rouse, in boots, surveys his baronial "Ramparts" with his summer neighbor, John Greenough, soon after its completion in 1899 behind the reconstructed earthworks of the Civil War fort on the height of Gloucester's Eastern Point. Hilda Raymond Williamson

Chicago stock-waterer William H. Moore's "Rockmarge" at Pride's Crossing.
Essex Institute

"Judge" Moore and his man behind his bay gelding, Burgomaster, about
1912. Essex Institute

Mr. Frick transfixes the photographer on the golf links. Culver Pictures, Inc.

The anarchist Berkman transfixes Mr. Frick during the Homestead strike. The Bettmann Archive

Which is which? Frick's "Eagle Rock" is below, his stable across Hale Street, above. Essex Institute

in the late 1890s in company with "Judge" Moore as *he* was always addressed (judge of horseflesh, *that's* what he was, in a neighbor's view).

In the autumn of 1902 Moore bought lots on Hale Street in Pride's from Francis Lee Higginson, the Boston financier, and (with ocean frontage) Dr. Reginald H. Fitz, world-famed pathologist of Boston, whose most notable contribution was his discovery of the cause of appendicitis in 1886. A month after this, Frick purchased three nearby parcels, one of which provided him with a fifteen-foot right-of-way through the intervening Loring land to a boathouse and bathhouse on the beach, his only access to the Atlantic Ocean. Moore started building his summer mansion and stables almost immediately; Frick rented the Robert S. Bradley estate at Pride's and didn't build until the end of the 1904 season, after tearing down the house of the late George Tyson of Philadelphia, from whose widow he had acquired his principal land surrounding Eagle Rock, so called for the eagles once observed nesting there.

How the paths of Frick and Moore crossed, and then converged on the North Shore, is a story by itself.

Henry Clay Frick was fourteen when he quit school in the farming and coal mining country of Westmoreland County, Pennsylvania, in 1863 to work in his uncle's store. That he had a fast head for figures was soon obvious, and he was made clerk and accountant in the distillery of his maternal grandfather, Abraham Overholt — "Old Overholt," who stares so sternly from the label of every bottle of his rye whiskey. The old man died in 1870 and left a half a million dollars.

A compulsive worker with a fierce ambition for power and wealth, young Frick saw in the underground around him an unlimited potential for the manufacture of coke, with iron ore the basic resource of the steel industry that was then in its infancy in Pittsburgh. Borrowing heavily with the backing of the Pittsburgh banker Judge Thomas Mellon, a family friend with whose son Andrew he grew intimate, he bought up mining land and built coke ovens on it right and left, nothing at all daunted by the panic of 1873, of which he took advantage to buy out his competitors at distress prices. With recovery, the H. C. Frick Coke Company was in the swing spot, the major supplier of coke to the reawakening steel mills. By his thirtieth birthday Henry Clay Frick had made his first million.

Through Andrew Mellon, Frick met Adelaide Childs. And on their wedding trip he consummated another partnership — with Andrew Carnegie, who since the death of his brother Thomas had been looking for some organizational genius to run his steel mills.

In ten more years — by 1892, when 3,800 workers struck their Homestead, Pennsylvania, mill over a relatively minor contract issue — Frick had engineered the acquisition of their chief rival, Duquesne, imposed order on the largest segment of the chaotically mushrooming industry, and established the absolute dominance of the Carnegie Steel Company.

"The Man," Carnegie admiringly called him, and so he was — of medium height, powerfully built, authoritatively handsome, reserved, calm, private — a man who kept his counsel until he was ready to act — and then, watch out. H. C. Frick was as much as any figure of his day the high priest of corporate property rights, in defense of the absolute sanctity of which he beat the union at Homestead when the governor sent in the National Guard after the three hundred armed Pinkerton guards The Man imported were routed by the strikers with heavy casualties on both sides. At the height of it, in his office, Frick was shot twice in the neck and knifed three times by Alexander Berkman, an anarchist who had no connection with the dispute. Swathed in makeshift bandages, Frick coolly returned to his desk after helping wrestle his assailant to the floor.

When Frick managed the purchase of the Oliver ore field in the Mesabi Range, Carnegie tied them into his mills by buying the Pittsburgh, Shenango and Erie Railroad with the aid of Frederick Prince of Boston and Pride's Crossing, who had saved it from bankruptcy. By the century's end Carnegie was ready to sell out and devote the rest of his life to redistributing his immense fortune for the betterment, as he saw it, of humanity.

Enter William H. Moore, who now offered the once-poor Scot $158,000,000 for his holdings in the Carnegie and Frick companies, secured for ninety days with a $1,170,000 deposit, of which $170,000 was put up by Frick himself and Henry Phipps, Jr., another Carnegie associate, with Moore's assurance of a $5,000,000 stake in the deal.

Ten months Frick's junior, Moore came from a Utica, New York, banking family and practiced corporation law with his brother, James, in Chicago until 1887, when with the most astute foresight they decided to concentrate on the new speculative game of "corporate promotion." After reorganizing the Diamond Match Company they moved into the biscuit industry, recouping an initial $4,000,000 loss with a merger in 1898 that created the National Biscuit Company, a 90 percent monopoly.

Somewhere along about this time Moore tagged himself or got tagged "Judge," the sardonic sobriquet he carried for the rest of his life . . . sort of like "Honest John" Jones, the used-car dealer.

Biscuits and matches were mere practice for the big move by the "Moore Gang" (as the brothers and their henchmen were known on Wall Street) to round up strays of steel left in Carnegie's trail until the Gang ranked as one of the industry's Big Four. The Moore methods: stock-watering and overcapitalizing by puffing up all kinds of expectations of future earnings, then selling off or merging at fantastically inflated values. The results, in the words of the *Dictionary of American Biography:* "The creation of monopolistic control, the contrivance of devices to avoid the operation of the anti-trust laws, the reorganization of production and marketing to effect economies, and the retention of control in the hands of a small group."

It was in May of 1899 that the Moore Gang in alliance with Frick made its offer to buy out Andrew Carnegie. But at that moment a transient financial panic intervened; their funding was delayed, Carnegie refused to extend the option and pocketed their $1,170,000, and the deal fell through with a large noise. Already differences had cooled relations between Carnegie and his "Pard," as he sometimes in former times had affectionately addressed his right-hand man. The volatile Scot, whose humanism kept creeping up on his capitalism, chafed increasingly under the younger man's uncompromising attitudes and outspoken nature, while Frick was finding it harder all the time to check his contempt for what he regarded as Carnegie's time-serving, his inconsistencies, his compromise of principle.

Late in 1899 Carnegie forced Frick out as chairman of his board and then bought him out for $15,000,000 after The Man sued The Master for the market value rather than the book value of his holdings.

The Moores went on in 1901 to organize and add the American Can

Company to their other steel properties. When J. Pierpont Morgan finally did buy out Carnegie that year and put together the United States Steel Corporation (with the essential help of Frick, who persuaded John D. Rockefeller, Sr., to sell Morgan his Mesabi holdings), the Moores were included, though Morgan barred them from the management, he mistrusted them so. Moore's share of the new giant made him richer than ever, and so did Frick's, which was $60,000,000 worth.

From steel Moore moved on railroads, and by the time he landed his Pride's Crossing property in 1902 he had wrested control of the Chicago, Rock Island and Pacific, which he proceeded to reorganize in what one observer described almost speechlessly as "the most astounding piece of stock-watering the world has ever seen."

Tall, powerful, handsome, genial, and so glacial that they were soon calling him with less than complete admiration the "Sphinx of the Rock Island," William Moore operated, as avowed by the *Dictionary of American Biography,* with "complete indifference to public sentiment." In the first decade of the new century he would add one railroad after another until his syndicate controlled 15,000 miles of track, and he would be wondered at and feared as "the most daring promoter in American business."

Until the gang moved in, the old management of the Rock Island had made do without a single private Pullman car. In 1902, their first year, the new owners ordered five for themselves. Moore's was delivered to him in May, christened *Rockmarge,* the name he would give the sumptuous mansion he was getting ready to build on the ledge of land he had not yet bought, commanding the ocean at Pride's Crossing, with an acknowledging tip of his topper, in the parlance of the Street, to "Rock Island margins."

Horses even more than houses were Moore's passion, however, and by spring of 1904 he was having his training track near his private siding at Pride's station relaid forty feet wide and a third of a mile long. In June Mrs. Moore arrived at their rented estate with the servants. Then her husband, then his special five-car train with thirty-eight thoroughbreds, twenty-seven stablemen, and various carriages and turnouts. In November Connolly Brothers, the Beverly contractors, had two hundred men spreading ten thousand yards of loam around the grounds of "Rockmarge."

That, for the North Shore to goggle at, was a sample of Moorishness.

The Moores moved into "Rockmarge" in 1905. *Impressive.* Acres of rolling lawn. A curved drive fit for a racetrack. A Grand Central Station of a mansion with a portico running the entire length of it, eight towering columns wide, topped with tiers of plain and the fanciest balustrades.

While one friend was thus engaged, Mr. Frick was asked by another but not a mutual one, Mr. Morgan, to help him with the world's largest corporation, which had gotten off to a shaky start. Frick demurred: he had an interest in Union Steel, and it would be unethical for him to assist a competitor. So J. P. simply bought Union, leaving The Man conscience-free to give Big Steel a hand through its crisis. Before the frost was out of the ground in 1905 Mr. Frick was ready to demonstrate *his* scale to his future summer neighbors, though not, he protested mildly, to the tune of the rumored half a million they were saying he was planning to spend on his new estate. But he did have, not two hundred, but three hundred men doing grading and stonework.

On from New York in a borrowed Pullman in June to inspect the progress, the Fricks stayed with the Andrew Mellons, who were renting the Alexander Cochrane estate nearby. In 1906 they were back, in their gardener's cottage. The mansion, "Eagle Rock," was approaching completion when the *North Shore Breeze* was permitted a preview and allowed to double in print the publicized cost to "the vicinity of $1,000,000, to say nothing of the interior furnishings of the mansion, where there may be represented before it is finished, well toward another million in valuable paintings, etc."

Considerable fill was brought in to create the grand expanse on the 25-acre estate from the entrances on Hale Street, along which marched in either direction the magnificent $100,000 iron fence with its handsome stone pillars. Broad avenues led up to the immense Georgian palace, which looked strikingly like the White House in Washington; at 200 feet, however, "Eagle Rock" was thirty feet longer. Forty-eight thousand yards of fill and loam, in fact (not counting other thousands spread around neighbor Moore's yard), rolled in from West Peabody by special train onto a special spur laid for the purpose at Pride's; that amounted to two and three trains a day for two months, 1,650 carloads in all. Fifty or so maple trees alone were set out, perhaps not all on a scale with the elm that was moved to "Rockmarge" from Hamilton; that was seventy feet high, twenty-six inches in diameter, with an earth ball sixteen feet across, and it took ten horses two hours to get it there.

The Frick automobile house, another Georgian brick and stone pile with portico, balustrades and Palladian windows, was bigger than the mansions of most of his richest neighbors. Similarly the "Lodge," another great house of stone and shingle surmounted by waves of gables. Across Hale Street was the stable, a hundred and fifty feet long and designed, like the "Lodge," in New England country estate style; a large clock and sundial adorned the front; inside, fourteen horses lolled in pampered ease, little used by their motorcar-mad master. Various other outbuildings, tennis court, vegetable garden and all the other amenities and necessities of an American Versailles were strewn around within commuting distance of the central pile.

The guest from the *Breeze* was impressed. The house up on the hill so very high above and back from the sea, but hardly visible from Hale Street, "is reached through a magnificent forecourt encircled with limestone columns, and the entrance has six immense colonial columns of limestone trimmings and fancy brick work. All of the main living rooms of the house will be finished in hand carved mahogany, expensive marbles and teak wood."

Ah, the Frick basement! A hotel-size kitchen, dumbwaiters, servants' elevator to the fourth floor done in Tiffany tile, pantries right and left, refrigerator room, butchery, servants' dining room, wine vault and attached unpacking room, bellows room (yes) for the organ above, great oak-paneled billiard room with marble fireplace. Ah, and the fresh or salt, warm or cold "swimming tank room decidedly Grecian in style, with artificial limestone, fluted columns, marble dado, moulded pilasters and architraves and two sets of dressing and toilet rooms."

Ah, from such a basement the rest of "Eagle Rock," and the imagination, arise! Glassed-in loggias, den, library, drawing and sitting rooms — mahogany and marble, teak floors everywhere — more pantries right and left, housekeeper's apartment, fireproof steel-lined silver vault, dining rooms (mahogany pilasters, columns, cornices and modillions), breakfast rooms, reception rooms for ladies.

Ah, and then the great hall opening onto the terraces outside through bronze doors fit for Judgment Day, and adjoining that, the staircase hall incorporating the $42,000 main pipe organ (echo organ on the third floor) playable from any of three separate consoles. And on the floor above, the bedchambers of the Fricks and their son, Childs, just graduated from Princeton, and their daughter of seventeen, Helen Clay, and governesses and guests, and servants (ten of them). And in the attic uncounted more servants' rooms, and twin ten-ton water tanks.

And everywhere, deliciously hand-carved mahogany and teak and oak and ash, and Caen stone, and breccia, and marble, marble, marble everywhere, inside and out.

There is some gentle irony in the reflection that Frick's "Eagle Rock," Moore's "Rockmarge" and Swift's "Swiftmoore," among other such Parthenons of capitalism on the North Shore, were designed by the Boston architect Arthur Little, who had graced this coast with so many mellifluous outpourings of shingle a quarter of a century earlier and was perfectly content himself to pass away the hours of summer in his stuccoed union of two old barns, "Spartivento," at Beverly Farms.

Early in September, 1906, the Henry Clay Fricks officially warmed the greatest mansion on the North Shore and no doubt north of Newport, with an *al fresco* luncheon. There was a recital on the organ and a concert by Boston Symphony players, and in the evening a cotillion. All the important people were invited, and it is ungenerous to suppose that most of them were not there, if only out of the most intense curiosity, or to put much credence in the story that on this or some other occasion the Fricks gave a great party the day a local lobsterman put on his annual cookout, and most everybody turned up at the cookout. The Moores perhaps, but the Fricks . . . not likely.

"We propose," Mr. Frick had stated during the Homestead strike, "to manage our own business as we think proper and right." And so he had. "Eagle Rock" was one tangible result of the philosophy he expanded on a few months later in one of his rare interviews, that "no legislation can be adopted or attempted in sincerity which would prove a permanent obstacle to the normal operation of sound economic law, nor should vast productions from the soil and their marketing be restrained by legislation. He [Frick] does not believe in demagogic political agitation, but in high business conscience."

While Frick was serenely sinking a fraction of his fortune in the North Shore's most thoroughly equipped summer camp and in his growing art collection, the Sphinx was milking his Rock Island Line for quite a lot more than it was worth and pouring the cream into a stable considered among the best in the world. Moore's particular forte was the four-in-hand, a very fancy coach pulled by four matched horses driven in tandem by the owner himself with such command and élan (and such disregard for the attendant expenses), in his top hat and natty greatcoat high up in the seat, that his celebrity in international equestrian circles far outshone his fame as an entrepreneur, perhaps by secondary intention.

Late every spring a special train of up to eight cars was nudged into the Moore siding at Pride's with a few dozen horses, a few dozen more stablemen, and various equipages and motor cars. In 1908 the leader of the Gang staged the first of his annual private horse shows at his Rockmarge Driving Park. Three hundred carefully invited guests had seen nothing like it on the Shore as their host whirled by at the reins of "Pride o' Prides" and "King of Kings," reportedly the top hackney pair in the country. Tea followed on the terrace.

About this time the "Judge" went world-wide. In 1910, as he would until the high seas got hazardous for horses, he shipped forty-nine of his best to the International Show in England, where he won the twenty-five-mile coaching marathon from Windsor Castle to the Olympic Arena in London. His stable manager, George Chipchase, bet, with his boss's permission, ten thousand dollars (his boss's?) that their coach would cover the course at fourteen miles an hour or better; whatever the outcome, Chipchase four years later leased the Beverly Farms cottage of James C. Barr for the duration of the war.

The Moore tallyho was without rival the smartest on the Shore, and its regular dashes between "Rockmarge" and the Myopia Hunt in Hamilton with a pounding of hooves, scurry of dust and clarion call were something to behold. The clarion call was still ringing in the memory of Ellen B. R. Boyd, a friend of Helen Frick, fifty years later: "At the very back of this handsome and unusual carriage rode the bugler. He was dressed in striking uniform to match those of the coachman and the footman. It was this young man's duty to blow his bugle as the tally-ho neared each corner or curve in the road, so that people would know they must be on the lookout. One day Judge Moore said: 'That little rascal of a bugler blows a better tune for those girls at

Thompson's Corner than anywhere else on our travels.' " The tune: "The Girl I Left Behind Me."

As for Mr. Frick, the fastest four-in-hand on earth, even at fourteen miles an hour, was a snail's pace. The arrival at Pride's of his custom Mercedes tonneau from France in the midsummer of 1904 thunder-struck the *Breeze* — seventy-four horsepower . . . one of the most powerful cars in America . . . ten passengers . . . "great speed powers and makes very little noise . . . he will cut quite a dash on the shore this year."

A dash for sure. "His real hobby," wrote Frick's amused biographer, "was speed, terrific speed, which came as a reaction from years of patient drudgery and as a revival of the impatience of an inherently eager disposition. Motoring he found delightfully exhilarating unless hampered by road regulations, to which ultimately, after securing the most expertly daring chauffeur to be found in France, he paid little heed."

To which his West Gloucester summer neighbor, John Hays Ham-mond, Sr., breathed a fervent *amen*. Frick drove around one day with E. H. Harriman, the railroad financier, to take the mining engineer for a ride in his new French car. "We started on the twenty miles of narrow, winding, unpaved Cape Ann roads. The chauffeur took the curves on two wheels and whenever we came to a village seemed to prefer the sidewalks to the streets. Hens squawked, horses reared, New England ladies scuttled into doorways. So loud was the rattle and bang of our vehicle that we were spared most of the vituperation which fol-lowed in our wake. Once we slowed down long enough to catch some salty comments which for a moment made me think I was in Billings-gate rather than in the main street of Gloucester.

"We slithered to a stop at my front door.

"Harriman and I had no breath left with which to swear, but Frick was not at all discomposed. He said, 'Harriman, how do you like the wonderful scenery of Cape Ann?'

"Harriman's trains never could travel fast enough to suit him, but now he gasped: 'To tell the truth, Frick, your French chauffeur went so fast I didn't see much of it. Another time I think I'd better ask Hammond to take me in his car. I'd really like to see the scenery!'

" 'Sorry I won't be able to go with you,' responded Frick, who, even on the golf course, had a mania for speed. 'When I go riding, I have to go fast enough to dodge bullets.' This remark referred to his experience at the time of the Homestead strike, when he was shot by Alexander Berkman."

More than the high-powered Mercedes, more even than the blue-ribbon four-in-hand, the private railroad car — usually though not invariably built by the Pullman Company — was by 1910 the steam yacht of the landbound, the mobile mansion, the plush-crusted pie in the American sky, and the more elaborately endowed (even unto gold plumbing) the better.

A much-used dodge among rail tycoons who were not overly particular about such matters was to have the company pay for the so-called "business car," which they then simply assigned to themselves. By this means Henry Clark Rouse of Cleveland began arriving on the North Shore in 1899 in Car 36 of the Missouri, Kansas and Texas Railway, one of the numerous lines over which he presided. Commodore (of Long Island's Seawanhaka Yacht Club) Rouse and his menage were sped by carriage between the Gloucester depot and his shingled castle within the Eastern Point fort, "The Ramparts," until his untimely death in 1906.

The Moore Gang, as already noted, ordered their "private varnish" wholesale through the Rock Island Road in 1902, and that is how their leader came by *Rockmarge* — the car, that is. Another rail man, Henry Clay Pierce, had his *Zamora* put on the books of the Mexican Central, of whose New York board he was chairman (he was president of the Tennessee Central), and luxuriated on its brocade and velvet lap among his several residences in St. Louis, New York, Wisconsin and Pride's Crossing, occasionally even dipping into Mexico.

There were those, however, to whom such subterfuges were anathema. John Hays Hammond rolled in grandeur with the seasons among his homes in Georgia, New Jersey and Gloucester and back in his very own *Kya Yami,* which is Zulu for "One of My Homes." A few years later Richard T. Crane had *Nituna* built to his order for arriving at Castle Hill and elsewhere with his personal plumbing under him, while Albert C. Burrage of Boston acquired *Esperanzo* after the Crash and renamed it (her?) *Alicia* for his wife, probably for more extensive travel (befitting a copper king) than the forty-minute run to Pride's.

Of course Frick had them all beat. Long after he retired from Big Steel, he charted a weekly triangular course summers among Pride's Crossing and New York and Pittsburgh on business, in various leased cars. In May of 1910, for instance, he arrived on the North Shore in the *Plymouth Rock,* which had taken first prize at the St. Louis Exposition as "the last word in luxury for travellers," then a few days later was back in the *Commonwealth* and three other special cars, one with the family baggage, one with the family automobiles, and one with his art collection, which he had decided to take with him to "Eagle Rock" for the season.

All this was mere prelude to The Man's ultimate, the *Westmoreland,* named for his native county in Pennsylvania. Pullman delivered what has been represented as the first all-steel private car in time for Christmas, 1910, when its owner was well on the way to being the largest individual railroad stockholder in the world.

When the Fricks glided into Pride's Crossing the following June, the correspondent for the *Breeze* was allowed an awestruck peek aboard at kitchenette and dining room, the bedrooms of Mr. Frick and Childs upholstered in red satin tapestry, Mrs. Frick's in pink, Helen's in pale green — each with a connected bath — and the living room in brown. The silver, china and stationery bore the emblem "Westmoreland." Lucius Beebe, who always rode first class, called it one of the best known private railroad cars of all time. After her husband's death Mrs. Frick lovingly enshrined *Westmoreland* in its own house on a Pride's siding and decreed in her will that after the retirement of a railroading friend to whom she subsequently gave it, it be destroyed; he died in 1967, and it was.

As early as 1908 Frick had been bringing at least a portion of his growing art collection to the North Shore for the summer. Isabella Gardner and two friends inspected his rival masterpieces at Pride's that August and then were driven around to Eastern Point in one of the Frick autos to visit the Philadelphia portrait artist Cecilia Beaux and her neighbor Henry Davis Sleeper.

About this time Edmund C. Tarbell, the most popular portrait painter in Boston, was commissioned by Frick to do a large and, as it turned out, striking canvas of father and daughter, full of both force and affection. The artist did three, the last of Frick alone, catching a glint of the steel in The Man, perhaps too much, for the subject was not pleased and tried to get the artist to destroy it. Tarbell was only five foot five but as stubborn as his subject; he refused, and retained it in his private collection.

Frick did seem to be gravitating more and more to the Beverly shore as his principal residence. The *Breeze* was pleased to hear in the fall of 1911 that he planned to spend most of the winter at Pride's Crossing and was "especially devoted to the North Shore and would be quite willing to call it his permanent home. The ladies of the family have many Pittsburgh and New York affiliations, so they will make frequent visits to those cities. The Frick private car is a happy medium to gratify their pleasure in those respects."

In December the *Breeze* expectantly passed on a rumor that Frick was planning to add a wing to "Eagle Rock" for his collection, which was worth millions, that would "outdo anything in New England in the way of an art gallery," including Mrs. Gardner's Fenway Court.

Then, as suddenly, the scene shifted. In May of 1912 the North Shore heard the news that its richest inhabitant had bought the entire Lenox Library block on New York's Fifth Avenue between 70th and 71st streets for $2,400,000, and that he would raze the library and build in its place for another $1,500,000 a white marble fireproof mansion with a great art gallery. Not without precedent, this classically proportioned palace across from Central Park had cost its owner $5,400,000 by the time he moved in with his family in 1914 — and his collection of art another $30,000,000 to $40,000,000 in pre–World War dollars.

Amassed and tirelessly weeded since 1895 by an industrialist of self-educated taste who had left school at the age of fourteen, the Frick Collection is one of the most glorious ever gathered by a private individual. In 1936, seventeen years after his death, his gallery was opened as a public museum, as he had directed in his will. "I can only hope that the public will get one-half the pleasure that has been afforded me in enjoyment of these masterpieces in proper surroundings," he had remarked to a friend. "I want this collection to be my monument." As indeed it is.

"Judge" Moore's monument, the Rock Island Railroad, slipped into receivership under his tender therapies. The stock plummeted from

$200 in 1902, when the Gang hijacked the trains, to $20 in 1914 in spite of steadily rising earnings.

Looking to erect a substitute monument to himself, and as a measure of the regard in which he held his neighbors, he offered in 1915 to build a granite depot at Pride's Crossing if the Boston and Maine (which he did not control) would change the name of the station, *ergo* the community, to "Rockmarge." As a measure of reciprocation, his neighbors' protests prevailed. Needless to add, there was no new depot.

In 1917 Moore and his henchmen were finally ousted after a scathing condemnation by the Interstate Commerce Commission accusing them of deliberate misrepresentation and looting. His epitaph was ante-humously engraved by Samuel Untermeyer, counsel for a stockholders' protective committee, who stated flatly that compared with the Moore Gang "the manipulators of the old Fish-Gould days were artless children." The corpse was still barely warm in 1980 when a Chicago judge ordered the remains of the railroad liquidated, with the epitaph that it was "the last chapter in the regrettably sad history of the Rock Island."

Moore the manipulator ignored a bad press to the end, which came in 1923. Frick the builder was aggressively sensitive: when the *Pittsburgh Leader* ran an annoying cartoon of him he ordered a minion to buy the paper, on second thought was relieved to hear later that a local Republican boss, similarly tweaked, had beaten him to it. When he died two weeks short of seventy in 1919, a few months after Carnegie, one "Pard" had as characteristically and grandly left his mark (a great park in Pittsburgh, too) as the other.

Henry Clay Frick and William Henry Moore both left the golf links at Myopia, where Money was never in the rough, better than they found them. Yet the only Myopian anecdote of the "Judge" for the record, a family one, concerns his discovery there of a cocktail called the martini. Remembrances of The Man are myriad, perhaps because Moore had no such biographer as George Harvey, who unintentionally penned *his* bearded subject's epitaph while describing his enthusiasm for golf at Myopia, "where he enjoyed special privileges, and where all stood aside when the good-natured warning was passed forward, 'Look out, Mr. Frick's coming!' "

He came and he went, as did they all, the kings and the captains, the wheelers and the dealers, in that wide-open game of real-life Monopoly before war and taxes cut the players down to more or less manageable size. "Eagle Rock" was razed by Mr. Frick's heirs, who replaced it with a compound still guarded by his $100,000 fence. "Rockmarge," too, was torn down by the descendants of its inscrutable builder, and the land sold for subdivision to . . . the ever-present Lorings.

9

Hail to the Chief

HE WAS SO LUKEWARM ABOUT THE JOB TO WHICH HE HAD JUST BEEN elected in November of 1908 that the ballots had barely been counted before William Howard Taft was turning over in his judicial mind how to escape from the White House and the heat of Washington the next summer.

It wouldn't do for the President of the United States to take his ease on foreign soil, even soil as friendly and fraternal as Canada's, where Theodore Roosevelt's anointed heir had been relaxing with his family for sixteen years above the broad St. Lawrence, with the forest at their backs, on the shore of Murray Bay halfway between Quebec City and the wild Saguenay. "A mere strawberry box of a place, but it suits me." So thought the vastly affable *petit juge,* as the native habitants called the former jurist.

So some cool retreat for a summer White House had to be found within the nation whose reins Mr. Taft would not very confidently take over from the dynamic driver for whom he had been Secretary of War and factotum, and whom he could never somehow quite cure himself of addressing, and regarding, as "Mr. President."

Thus it was that a couple of months before his inauguration in March of 1909 the President-elect and his strong-minded lady, Helen, were on the lookout for a summer headquarters that would suffice for his term in office (which he secretly hoped would not be repeated) somewhere on the New England coast, the family agreed, possibly along that breezy parapet of Republicanism, the North Shore, and near a golf links, at Taft's insistence.

An attractive possibility. Boston's Gold Coast offered personal as well as political haven for a son of Yale seeking admission to such a shore facility of Harvard, of which "the President," A. Lawrence Lowell's secretary once informed a caller, "is in Washington seeing Mr. Taft."

Nahant, for instance, was the den of Senator Henry Cabot Lodge, Teddy Roosevelt's closest chum, who had declined, with portentous disdain, Mr. Taft's invitation to be his Secretary of State. In Manchester summered the William Boardmans, old hosts to the Tafts when they were in the Boston area, and Senator Albert Beveridge of Indiana, who would, unfortunately, turn bitterly against the President within his own party. Manchester and Magnolia already dripped and swarmed with ambassadors and their ladies and their retinues, at least twenty of the thirty-nine accredited to Washington — a social blessing to be regarded by a vacationing President, if not his First Lady, as not unmixed.

And then inland at Hamilton, where he contentedly supervised the refinement of his "Rock Maple Farm" into one of the Shore's rural show places, resided George von Lengerke Meyer, of blood a Boston blue and TR's ambassador to Italy and Russia, later his Postmaster General, inherited by Taft and reconditioned as Secretary of the Navy — a triumph of political survival that inspired Mrs. Meyer, putting on a children's party that summer, to order her butlers out of their customary evening dress and into white ducks. Cabot Lodge urged the appointment on Taft lest Meyer, out of office and chafing, take a notion to challenge his neighbor Congressman Augustus Peabody ("Gussie") Gardner, the Senator's son-in-law. Standing for reelection in 1906, Gussie had indicated his political philosophy: "On the whole, I should rather see a few people making a little too much money than to see everyone making too little money, which was the case the last time the Democracy had a chance to tinker with the tariff."

And speaking of sons-in-law, over at Pride's Crossing every season was Congressman Nicholas Longworth of Ohio, the only man in America with the courage to marry Teddy Roosevelt's astonishing daughter Alice. Their romance on the Shore in 1904 had set every tongue wagging. "Alice Blue Gown" was the devilish darling of the social set, with the sharpest tongue of all, but at that stage in her long life, as the *Breeze* could see, preferred swimming, tennis, golf, motoring and yachting, "being of that strenuous type of which her father is the leading exponent."

Comfortable Republican country, the North Shore . . . if one didn't turn one's broad back.

In Gloucester, under the wings of the Colonial Arms on the harbor shore of Eastern Point, had sprung up a colony of damsels and their bachelor friends. "Dabsville" they acronymically called themselves, for Joanna *D*avidge, Virginia-born mistress of a New York finishing school; Abram Piatt *A*ndrew, young Harvard monetary expert; Philadelphia portraitist Cecilia *B*eaux of fabled hauteur; Caroline *S*inkler, southern belle of fabled enchantment; and Andrew's close friend Henry Davis *S*leeper, the really pioneering interior decorator and creator of "Beauport." Frequently Dabsville was joined in its capers by Mrs. Jack Gardner, Gussie's anything-but-antediluvian aunt, the capricious collector who for several summers rented the Ellis Gray Loring cottage above Mingo Beach in Beverly.

"Doc" (because professor) Andrew was the brightest brain on Senator Aldrich's team that conceived the Federal Reserve System (though the Democrats ultimately implemented it) and had so taken the fancy of the Tafts that the President was about to make him Director of the Mint.

By far the strongest magnets drawing the Tafts to the North Shore, though, were their old and close friends, John Hays Hammond and his wife, Natalie. Hammond, fifty-four, only a year older than Taft, was an adventurous Californian who applied his engineering studies at Yale so successfully out West that Cecil Rhodes hired him to run his gold mine operations in South Africa, where he made his first fortune, ran afoul of Oom Paul Kruger, was jailed, sentenced to death and ransomed for $125,000, no small thanks to the battle put up for him by his indomitable wife.

Back in the States with a whole skin, Hammond was engaged by the Guggenheims as *their* Midas at a million dollars a year. He more or less retired in 1907 to enjoy himself and his family (Natalie was the daughter of a Confederate general and conducted herself in the family tradition, and their three sons and daughter were inevitably precocious). Spending his summers at "Lookout Hill" above Gloucester

Harbor, Jack Hammond dabbled in public affairs, almost ran as Taft's vice president but couldn't get his candidacy off the ground, and turned down both the navy secretaryship, before Taft gave it to Meyer, and the ambassadorship to China.

Where, then, would the President light? The rumors flew that spring of 1909. Emissaries had inquired about Eastern Point. Was the Point's grandest, "The Ramparts," for rent? Under no circumstances, declared its rotund and redoubtable mistress, Mrs. Emma Raymond, who had inherited the fort within a fort from the late Commodore Rouse, for whom she had kept house. What about Harry Sleeper's rambling, eclectic "Beauport," separated from Piatt Andrew's "Red Roof" by Miss Sinkler's laughingly nicknamed "Wrong Roof"? "It would be difficult to imagine," chuckled a sympathetic press, "the massive frame of the President passing through one of the small doors of ancient make."

The choice narrowed to the Gold Coast — Manchester and Beverly. The late Mortimer B. Mason estate in Manchester was rumored. Nellie Taft favored the Edward Robinson cottage in Manchester, but it was too small. The First Lady settled on the green, shingled, four-teen-room cottage of the late John B. Stetson of Boston on Woodbury Point, between Beverly Cove and Hospital Point, not so far from the summer boardinghouse where President Benjamin Harrison visited his daughter around 1893, three years after he had appointed Taft his solicitor general.

Owner of the Stetson property was Robert Dawson Evans, who had come to Boston a poor boy from New Brunswick, Canada, and bounced from the bottom of the then-infant rubber industry to the top, retiring as president of U.S. Rubber in 1898, when he turned his wits to California gold mining with his friend Jack Hammond. Possibly it was Hammond who put the Tafts on to the Stetson house, which at the time was serving as an adjunct across the lawn to "Dawson Hall," the Versailles raised by Evans for himself and his consort, whose name actually *was* Maria Antoinette.

The Taft summer got off to about as inauspicious a start as the Taft administration. The identity of the summer White House was no sooner out when hundreds (the *Boston Post* claimed 5,000) of souvenir hunters invaded Woodbury Point and ripped off relics of the very house itself, leaving the grounds looking like a picnic grove on Saturday night. The *Breeze* chided: "Too much of this torchlight procession business, honorary memberships in clubs, judge of boat races, speaking to school children will prove very distasteful to the President if the suggestions ever reach his ears. Cut it out, Beverly, if you have any desire to make things so pleasant for the President and his family that they will want to return another season."

Less than two months after the inauguration Nellie Taft suffered a stroke, on May 17, that effectively put her out of action as a hostess for a year and added greatly to her husband's anxiety as he grappled with his new job. As if that were not enough to contend with, practically as the presidential train was pulling onto the special spur the Boston and Maine had laid at its depot in the Montserrat section of Beverly, landlord Evans was thrown from his horse and seriously injured. The Tafts and their youngest, Charlie, arrived on the Fourth of July in the same private Pullman *Olympia* used by the Fricks, with domestic staff, luggage and Rosebud, the family cow, in the other cars. The President returned to Washington the next day, however, to keep an eye on the tariff bill in Congress. On July 6 Robert Dawson Evans died.

The First Family was completed with the arrival of the elder son, Robert, finishing Yale, and Helen, seventeen, home from Bryn Mawr. The nineteen-year-old future Senator from Ohio set about golf and tennis with serious purpose. Helen drove herself in the family's electric runabout every day for tennis at the Essex County Club in Manchester. Charlie took to the water in the sailing dory *Bandit,* the gift of young Dick Hammond.

It seems unimaginable that there once was a day and age when a President of the United States could accept the offer of the Beverly Board of Trade of its handful of rooms in the Mason Building on Cabot Street, three-quarters of a mile from the summer White House, for the conduct of the executive business of the nation. Although the Chief did most of his work at the cottage, the *North Shore Reminder* had some fun with the prospects:

"Pretty good little rooms they are, too — for a country board of trade. One enters them by means of a marble stairway wide enough to allow two presidents to climb abreast, even though the second were of Mr. Taft's generous avoirdupois. . . . To be sure, in order to get to his room he will have to climb those marble stairs, for there is no elevator, and will have to run the gauntlet of pop corn men, candy vendors and suspender peddlers, who infest the sidewalk. Once ensconced, however, he will be all right. He can tip back in his swivel chair and enjoy the soothing strains of music, as furnished by the itinerant hurdy-gurdy man. The President has already been warned not to pay attention to any agonizing screams he may hear, for these will merely emanate from one of the dentists' offices on the same floor. It has been facetiously suggested that if the councils of state lead to uncertainty of action, recourse may be had to the wonderful powers of reading the future possessed by Mme. Zaza, occultist and palmist, whose fortune telling studio is in a nearby shop."

The tariff issue, on which he might have benefited from a session or two with Mme. Zaza, kept the President in Washington into August. Although he was not an extreme protectionist, the wall he wanted was still too high for the Roosevelt Republicans, who were already beginning to line up against TR's plainly more conservative heir under the banner of insurgency and the leadership of Progressives like La Follette and Beveridge. Nevertheless, the Payne-Aldrich Bill was rammed through and signed by Taft, allowing him a few weeks of vacation. He arrived back in Beverly on August 7, three days after the city of Gloucester, on its own course as usual, carried off a long-planned pageant in his honor, notwithstanding the honored guest was *in absentia*. The President was accompanied by his private secretary, Fred W. Carpenter, and a carload of office furniture and supplies that were hauled by the wagonload to the Board of Trade, where Carpenter set up the nation's business. The secretary thereafter commuted to his bachelor's rooms at the Salem Club in the carriage provided him by Uncle Sam.

The routine of the summer White House was now taken up in all earnestness. Not daunted by his vaunted avoirdupois, the President was a keen golfer and tried both the Essex County and Myopia club links. He preferred Myopia's more challenging eighteen, and its more rarefied roster. Four or five mornings a week he would be driven to Hamilton with one of his children and Captain Archibald Butt, his military aide, tee off around nine-thirty or ten and finish within two and a half hours. One day he broke a hundred with a ninety-eight that he boasted jubilantly about over lunch with Jack Hammond at "Lookout Hill." Frequent foursomes included Butt, Hammond, William Boardman, General Adelbert Ames, the impeached Reconstruction governor of Mississippi and son-in-law of the late General Ben Butler, who summered at Bay View in Gloucester, or the Count de Chambrun of the French embassy. "It is easier in some circumstances," observed the English writer Henry Leach, "to become president of the United States than to become a member of the Myopia Hunt Club. It is therefore all the more to the credit of Mr. Taft that he is both."

The President was surprisingly agile for one of his girth, and not a bad athlete. He had done well enough in sports at Yale, where he was a large, well-proportioned and well-liked young man, but thereafter his weight soared out of all control, especially during periods of stress. He joked a little plaintively about it, for he loved the pleasures of the table, which he only fitfully put from him, as in 1905 when he carved himself down from 326 to 250 pounds, though before long he was back over 300. Fat was the target of the President's exercise. For a while he tried horseback riding, inspiring Elihu Root to inquire politely after the condition of the horse. He was a good tennis player but followed Roosevelt's advice never to be photographed at it . . . not democratic enough, warned TR, and golf even worse. Still, his doctor had recommended golf, and the patient liked the game, and that was that. He *was* President.

One who had witnessed the President on the Murray Bay links, James A. Cruikshank, thought him then (in 1907 when Taft was Secretary of War) one of the best in public life. "He plays golf as if it were an official bit of business which ought to be transacted with as little waste of time as possible. . . . He makes a powerful drive, gets the direction before the ball fairly lands, and takes off at a pace which wearies out the little caddie. He makes another drive, holes the ball in fine score, scratches down the record on a crumpled bit of paper from the depths of a trousers pocket, and hustles on." Quick-footed as a boxer or dancer, he would leap across a ditch with the ease of a man twenty years younger.

At his favorite Myopia, a writer in *Everybody's Magazine* noted, President Taft could drive better, usually, than 175 yards. His putting, however, was *Rooseveltian* — that is, he putts like the former judge he is — it's "take that from the shoulder the way I think you ought to get it; and if you don't go in the hole, why, blast you, you can jolly well stay out and be bunkered to you."

Another time, a writer for *The American Golfer* followed him around Myopia with Hammond: "He stands very straight, keeps his head still and swings through the ball, sweeping it away. Possibly it is more of a baseball stroke than a golf swing, but it answers the purpose nobly." And on another morning the *North Shore Reminder* sought another opinion: " 'He is a good feller,' said one freckle-nosed urchin as he unslung his sticks and wiped his grimy face after a round with the President, and after the 'good feller' had patted him on the shoulder and more substantially made known his appreciation of the boy's faithful service." The pro at Myopia merely informed Hammond that neither he nor Taft would ever make a good golfer because "the brains of both of you are always working on so many things that you can't concentrate on the game."

Every morning before heading for the links Bill Taft manfully submitted to the weight-reducing regimen of Dr. Charles E. Barker, his "physical director," and grunted through a round of gymnastic exercises. Dr. Barker relentlessly added ocean bathing, and a ninety-foot pier was built out from Woodbury Point to a landing in the deep water so the Tafts could avoid traversing the rocky beach. It was a happy day when Nellie had recovered enough to swim from here while her husband watched encouragingly, but it must not have been his cup of tea because late in August he rented a bathhouse at Singing Beach in Manchester — the local Riviera for the diplomatic crowd — on his physical director's urging. It was reported at that time that all these active measures had reduced the presidential girth by seven inches and weight by ten of the twenty-five pounds they were modestly aiming for.

The inland President was not much of a yachtsman. Understandably, he liked the feel of a solid deck under his feet — an ocean liner, or at least those perquisites of the Commander-in-Chief, the presidential steam yachts. The sleek and stunningly white *Mayflower* he inherited from his friend Theodore. She was the Scots-built yacht of an American millionaire (1896) bought by the Navy at the outbreak of the Spanish War; Roosevelt expropriated her when he took office in

The First Family on the steps of the summer White House: President Taft,
Mrs. Taft, Charlie, Helen and Bob. Beverly Historical Society

The first summer White House, Mrs. Evans's Stetson cottage, Burgess Point,
Beverly. Essex Institute

Who's Who

ALONG THE NORTH
SHORE
MASS., U.S.A.

PRESIDENT TAFT AND HIS PARTY TAKING A RIDE ALONG THE NORTH
SHORE IN HIS FAMOUS "WHITE STEAMER."

THIS PICTURE WAS TAKEN BY OUR PHOTOGRAPHER AT BEVERLY AT THE TURN IN THE ROAD JUST LEADING
TO THE ENTRANCE OF THE STETSON ESTATE, WHERE THE PRESIDENT'S HOUSE IS LOCATED. THE OCCU-
PANTS ARE HELEN TAFT, CAPT. BUTT, AND THE PRESIDENT'S LIVERYMAN AND THE CHAUFFEUR ROBINSON.

The motoring Tafts made the cover of the 1910 Who's Who
Along the North Shore, *in color. Essex Institute*

Mr. Taft scores as Secretary of War on the Murray Bay links and addresses the ball as President of Myopia. Essex Institute and Myopia, 1875–1975

The Tafts leave the Unitarian Church in Beverly after services. Beverly Historical Society

Harvard economics professor A. Piatt Andrew and students, in ascending order but ungraded, Leverett Bradley, Franklin Delano Roosevelt and Thomas Beal, Jr., celebrating completion of Doc's "Red Roof" at Eastern Point, May 2, 1903. Andrew Gray

Jack Hammond, Sr., and Bill Taft. From The Autobiography of John Hays Hammond

Mrs. John Hays Hammond. From The Autobiography of John Hays Hammond

Captain Archibald W. Butt. Essex Institute

1901. She was 273 feet long, and it took 200 men to keep her in white-glove trim, including a sixteen-piece band. The luxurious presidential suite was aft of the mainmast, and it was difficult for any man to remain diffident about his status in such surroundings, especially when viewed from the profound depths of the custom-built presidential bathtub, the wonder of the crew. But the steel *Mayflower* drew nineteen feet of water. She was an "ocean liner" in all but name, for she couldn't get into the Potomac or visit other charming spots close alongshore, and had to anchor a half a mile off Woodbury Point.

So for a few hours on the water, handy to shore facilities, Taft soon after his inauguration commandeered the smaller *Sylph,* another yacht taken over by the Navy. That first presidential summer on the North Shore, *Mayflower* prowled about, sometimes in Boston or Gloucester or off Beverly. *Sylph* lay at anchor in Beverly Harbor. And a third government vessel, Secretary of the Navy Meyer's personal dispatch boat *Dolphin,* hung around in Gloucester Harbor, where she startled the city with reverberating twenty-one-gun salutes whenever *Mayflower* or *Sylph* steamed past Eastern Point flying the President's ensign. From her position on deck Nellie found these salvos anything but salutory. "They shake one's nerves and hurt one's ears, but they are most inspiring." And when *Mayflower* steamed through the fleet on review, and they all cut loose at once, "I think I know what a naval battle sounds like."

The youngest Taft — "Cheerful Charlie" to the press — was the salt of the family, out on the water every hour he could sneak in little *Bandit* to the point where his father (or mother), worried about his inexperience, laid down the law in mid-August that henceforth he was to have an expert sailor with him — an edict Charlie vowed he would retaliate for on the golf course, where Pater was teaching him the game. And so a master mariner was dragooned, an engineer from the *Sylph,* and immediately, on the afternoon of August 19, they capsized *Bandit* in Salem Bay and hung onto her bottom until a boat put out from *Sylph* and pulled them out of the drink.

No, not keels but wheels were the presidential passion — swift rolling wheels under a fine presidential Pullman emblazoned with his Great Seal, and wheels under his grand and imposing — as imposing as himself, almost — White steam automobile. After his morning golf

Mr. Taft would return to the summer White House for lunch, executive business in the afternoon, then almost without fail if the weather permitted, off with Nellie and frequently guests for the daily drive in the sedate open touring car, back in time for dinner. Two thousand miles of Essex County they traversed that summer. The President stuffed himself into a regulation motoring outfit with his golf cap pulled down over his forehead, and everyone in his party was equipped with goggles as protection against the clouds of dust raised on the country roads.

Automobile parties were all the rage, and one Sunday afternoon several converged on Beverly for an obvious purpose. When the Tafts glided almost silently from the Evans driveway, trailing a cumulus of cottony steam puffs, they encountered a line of motor cars half a mile long on the highway in wait for them. Whether these motorized kibitzers followed the presidential party in convoy is not recorded. Shades of TR's vice president, Charles W. Fairbanks, summering nearby in Danvers a couple of years earlier, driven "by its too fond attention" back where he came from, as the *Breeze* remembered; "it is said they went early and sat on the stone walls, to wait for Mr. Fairbanks to get up in the morning."

For all that, politics was politics, and the obliging President one afternoon received forty-five callers at the Stetson cottage between three and five-thirty, something of a record. There is no record of a call on that or any other occasion from a certain George S. Patton, Jr., a very brassy young houseguest at Pride's Crossing of the textile tycoon Frederick Ayer, whose daughter Beatrice he was courting. Just graduated from West Point, Patton wrote his father on April 25: "I think I will have to stay at Pride's for various reasons. Mr. Taft has the house at Beverly Point where the Ayer's were three years ago. It is about two hundred yards from Prides. I might meet the President and eventually get to Washington. . . . How sanguine youth is."

By displaying himself on the roads of Essex County every afternoon, Taft could keep his formal public appearances to the minimum, and under the most pleasant of circumstances. One such was the luncheon reception given by the Hammonds at "Lookout Hill" August 28 for the Gloucester committee that had staged the day in his honor without him. Hammond at the time was getting publicity spreading money around Gloucester right and left; if all this was a trial balloon for a run against Gussie Gardner, advised the *Gloucester Times,* forget it — Gardner was securely lodged in Congress.

Shaking hands all around, the President impressed the *Times* man as "large, jovial, breezy, his face wreathed in a continuous smile, which sent the flesh up around his eyes, so that, while twinkling merrily all the time, they had the appearance of being half closed."

In ten days Commander Robert E. Peary planted Old Glory at the North Pole, only to hear that Dr. Frederick A. Cook was claiming to have beaten him to it. "Have honor place north pole at your disposal," Peary flashed his Commander-in-Chief on September 8. The Chief flashed back from Beverly: "Thanks for your interesting and generous offer. I do not know exactly what I should do with it. . . ."

Next day, in the interests of international amiability the President was ferried out to the *Mayflower* where she lay, dressed to her trucks, at anchor off Beverly, and presented the Taft Cup to the American winner of the Sonder races off Marblehead. This was a class of small sailing yachts originating in Germany. Vice Admiral Barandon and Count Betho von Wedel, chargé of the German legation, stood on the quarterdeck bemedaled and straight as pokers. Glasses were raised, first to the absent Kaiser. "I drink to the health of his imperial majesty, the emperor of Germany," President Taft concluded his toast. "Long may he live to contribute to the peace of the world." Replying in clipped accents to the former American Secretary of War, Admiral Barandon ended his: "The good feeling which has been between the Germans and your countrymen has grown from day to day and I think it will continue to grow."

Such ironies, however, were hardly to be perceived as such except in hindsight, and it was his private rather more than his public appearances that were worrying Mr. Taft's advisers, specifically down the road a piece from the simple summer White House amid the opulence at Pride's of "Eagle Rock" with Henry Clay Frick, one of those "malefactors of great wealth" so publicly excoriated by his predecessor in office.

It seems that Secretary of State Philander C. Knox was the probable go-between. Knox was a distinguished Pennsylvania lawyer, William McKinley's Attorney General, who stayed on with Roosevelt after the assassination as a trust-buster, and after filling a vacancy in the Senate, moved into Taft's cabinet in 1909. But Knox had known Frick, and intimately, much longer — for thirty-five years — had been counsel for the Carnegie Company and represented other interests of the Pard. So it was natural that when the Secretary of State came on to Beverly late in August to confer with Taft on matters of the "Dollar Diplomacy" of which he was the author, he stayed with the Fricks so nearby. The evening of August 31 the President dined with Knox and Frick at "Eagle Rock," and the papers got hold of it.

A horrible blunder, in the emphatic opinion of Taft's biographer, Henry F. Pringle. "The occasion was hailed as further proof that Taft was no faithful follower of Roosevelt but a friend and intimate of the wealthy malefactors. The man was tired. He was suffering from a touch of lumbago, besides. He was aware that it was unwise to have his name linked with Frick. But it was easier, so much easier, to consent than to refuse." And already the fat was in the fire, for he was taking a tongue-lashing from the antitariff crowd for signing the Payne-Aldrich Bill. The worst in the Frick affair, however, was yet to come.

After entertaining their globe-trotting Imperial Highnesses, Prince and Princess Kuni of Japan, President Taft signed with Mrs. Evans to lease the Stetson cottage again next summer, bade the hounds of dissension in his administration return to their kennels (such was his vain hope) and on September 14, 1909, entrained from Beverly on the first of his annual autumn tours of a nation he wasn't really terribly enthusiastic about governing.

Farewell to the Chief

THE FIRST FAMILY'S SECOND SUMMER ON THE NORTH SHORE GOT OFF TO almost as bad a start as the first. President Taft was still feeling the shock waves from his firing in January of 1910 of one of Theodore Roosevelt's fairest-haired, Gifford Pinchot, after the keeper of the nation's forests was caught trying to undermine his boss, Secretary of the Interior Richard A. Ballinger, who had been accused by the conservationists of playing cozy with the Guggenheim-Morgan syndicate that was endeavoring to loosen the federal grip on rich Alaskan coal mining country.

Teddy the Great Hunter was due home from his year in Africa in June. Bill Taft regarded the reunion with his old friend without enthusiasm. On May 26 he wrote "the President" a dolorous letter recounting his troubles during his first year in office attempting to carry forward the Roosevelt reform program, defending the Payne-Aldrich protective tariff act and expressing confidence in the prospects for railroad regulation, but his tone was apologetic and defensive. He was dogged by his feelings of inadequacy alongside the Man with the Big Stick; he regarded TR's predictably flamboyant return to the political scene with foreboding, like the fat boy with his fist in the cookie jar, and was anxious to placate him if possible. Roosevelt steamed back to a tumultuous New York welcome as scheduled on June 18.

The former President was to come on for the Harvard Commencement in Cambridge with Henry Cabot Lodge, then call on Taft at the summer White House in Beverly on June 30. The present President planned to arrive at Beverly from Washington the day before. On June 28, son Bob Taft was at the wheel of one of the family motor cars with house guests from Yale, driving through Pride's Crossing, when all of a sudden around a bend he encountered a gang of men oiling the dirt road. Bob slammed down on the brake. The workers scattered for the ditch, and made it — all but one, Michael Grigordio, who was struck and knocked down. He was rushed to the Beverly Hospital with a fractured skull.

Notified of this bad news in Washington, the President ordered the best medical attention available, came on the next day, June 29, as planned, by train and was driven almost immediately to the hospital, where he found Grigordio evidently out of danger. The Beverly police did not fault Bob for the accident.

The following day, June 30, Roosevelt, Lodge and Charles Evans Hughes, the governor of New York whom Taft had named to the Supreme Court in April, drove up from Nahant for lunch at the summer White House. Captain Archie Butt, his aide, was Taft's "second." The principals didn't relish being alone together, and though TR proposed that he be "Theodore" and his successor "Mr. President," the talk was awkward and punctuated with Rooseveltian "bullies" and Taftian apologies that he just couldn't get over thinking of himself as "Bill" and Theodore as "Mr. President." This after sixteen months in office. Plainly the former warm friendship of the two Republican leaders was on ice. So Taft's biographer had it.

Nellie was on hand and had it differently. "Remarkably pleasant and entertaining," she recalled, finding "the old spirit of sympathetic comradeship still paramount and myself evidently proved to be unwarrantably suspicious." TR was full of amusing anecdotes of his attendance as Bill's representative at King Edward's funeral in London and convinced Helen Taft that "he still held my husband in the highest esteem and reposed in him the utmost confidence, and that the rumours of his antagonism were wholly unfounded. I was not destined to enjoy this faith and assurance for very long."

Roosevelt was soon touring the country, expounding and expanding on his "radical" position that property rights were not necessarily supreme in all cases and indicating his discontent with his understudy's emerging conservatism. The usually affable Taft was tired and tense, and though back at this enjoyable vacation spot, found sometimes as much frustration as pleasure in golf at Myopia, bursting into profanity over muffed shots and once throwing his club twenty-five feet in a rage.

On the eleventh of July Taft played at Myopia with Jack Hammond, Judge Robert Grant and Henry Clay Frick — a day worked in with a twenty-minute cruise in *Sylph* to Gloucester from Beverly to the tune of the forty-two guns of *Mayflower* and *Dolphin*. Lunch at "Lookout Hill" and a call on Piatt Andrew across the harbor at Eastern Point by Nellie Taft with her sister and her hostess, Natalie Hammond, which was returned that evening for dinner at the Stetson cottage by the highly favored "Doc."

The Frick connection was again noted in the press, and Archie Butt persuaded Nellie Taft that it was damned injudicious of her husband to be so intimately and publicly associated with the right wing. She agreed but was unable to dissuade the President, according to Henry Pringle, who "said that he liked Frick; he would not listen to arguments on the subject. He even played poker, one night, at the Frick palace. This, however, was accomplished with stealth. The President, his military aide and Secretary Norton stole past the secret service guards and went, by themselves, to the home of the steel magnate."

The vision of the massive Chief Executive giving the slip to his bodyguards of a summer evening on the Beverly shore is one to conjure up. For all Mrs. Taft's protests, the *Breeze* noted in late September the presence of Mrs. Frick at her luncheon table.

And not only the Fricks. In mid-July, biographer Pringle found out, J. Pierpont Morgan was spirited (!) into shore in a motorboat from his yacht "with the secrecy of some criminal conspiracy" and met stealthily with the President for an hour. Not a whisper of that rendezvous leaked to the press, nor of another with ultraconservative Senator Nelson W. Aldrich, errand man of the trusts whom Taft distrusted but had to work with, power on the Hill that he was. "But secrecy is rarely permanent regarding a president's activities," wrote Pringle; "news of Frick and Morgan soon reached Roosevelt and his insurgent followers."

Compounding the potential for embarrassment, it happened that Aldrich's son-in-law, John D. Rockefeller, Jr., was vacationing at

Pride's even as the President impatiently awaited the Supreme Court's okay of his uncharacteristic resolve to break the Rockefeller grip on the oil industry. Strange neighbors, that summer on the North Shore. Aldrich and John D., Jr., slipped over to Eastern Point for a visit with Doc and Dabsville, and one late August morning the old man himself, John D., Sr., was spotted in his limousine parked on Main Street in Gloucester while his chauffeur ducked into a store for a package.

Doing some ducking and sneaking himself, William Howard Taft cruised down east in *Mayflower* for ten days. They were invited to Campobello Island, off New Brunswick. The President demurred, not wishing to break the presidential tradition of territorial quarantine, but his family accepted and was entertained at the summer home of young Eleanor Roosevelt, whose husband was just breaking into New York Democratic politics. At Bar Harbor Mr. Taft sprained an ankle golfing, which probably brought on more blue language . . . on a par with the presidential purple occasioned by his efforts to conquer an especially difficult hole, known thereafter to posterity, so Phil Lewis tells it, as "The Taft Hole" — all thirty-two-odd strokes of it. On their return the Tafts entertained President Pedro Montt of Chile, who suffered a heart attack en route from New York to Beverly and died a week later on his arrival in Europe. And the President hastened to visit Supreme Court Justice William H. Moody, summering in Magnolia and ill from overwork on a bench ruled by old men. Moody admitted that his health was forcing him into resignation, and Taft found himself once again in the ironic spot of appointing others to a position to which he had always aspired more than to the presidency itself.

Following in the footsteps of Roosevelt — would he ever get out of them? — he crossed Massachusetts Bay to Provincetown on *Mayflower* August 5 and dedicated the Pilgrim Monument, whose cornerstone TR had laid two years earlier. The Atlantic fleet was on maneuvers, and five battleships anchored in Sandy Bay, disgorging onto the narrow streets of dry little Rockport 3,000 thirsty lads who were swept up by the "electrics" and on to wet Gloucester, which knew how to treat men of the sea. It was Secretary Meyer's Navy, after all, and Cape Ann was his home port, so to speak. The colorful visit and friendly invasion were repeated the remaining two summers of the Taft administration, reinforced with submarines and torpedo-boat destroyers.

Always, there were the Hammonds. Golf almost daily with Jack, glowing or glowering as the mood suited him, a clambake arranged by Natalie at Loblolly Cove in Rockport, the garden party of the ladies' auxiliary of the Gloucester Day Committee (one of her pet projects) in Stage Fort Park near "Lookout Hill," attended by Taft and his dear old aunt Delia Torrey, who lived in the minuscule Massachusetts town of Millbury, and Baron Roman Rosen, the Russian ambassador, and his family, and Archbishop (soon to be Cardinal) O'Connell of Boston. Helen Taft served punch at Mrs. Hammond's booth, but Cheerful Charlie, who was supposed to be a page, missed out — probably with relief (having already done his duty once as a "fakir" at the lawn fair of the Women's Auxiliary of the Addison Gilbert Hospital in Gloucester) when the motorboat he and Dick Hammond were coming in from Beverly happily conked out.

A bit more exciting than ladies' garden parties, and certainly more frustrating for the President's younger son, was the chance to go with his father and mother and the Hammonds to Squantum on the South Shore to the aviation meet organized by the Harvard Aero Club the first week in September, the largest held to date in the United States.

The Wright brothers had a team entered; the daredevil Glenn Curtiss was there; and three of the flying machines had emerged from the Marblehead factory of the yacht designer W. Starling Burgess, who only a few months earlier had fallen under the spell of the air and formed his own airplane company. An odd coincidence that Starling's father, Edward, the brilliant designer of the America's Cup defenders, had learned to sail from the family compound on Woodbury Point, where the Tafts were summering; hence the sometime cognomen Burgess Point, which has given way in recent times to Evans Point, but never, it must be admitted, to Taft Point. The President on this airy day congratulated Boston's mayor, John F. Fitzgerald, on "Honey Fitz's" daring flight with the star of the show, Claude Graham-White. Mrs. Taft declined the English ace's invitation to soar like a bird, and his parents forbade the eager Charlie to do any such crazy thing.

So pervasive was the network of John Hays Hammond's interests and connections that his every public and, more to the point, private move had political implications. A case in point was his former position as *fidus Achates* of the Guggenheims that led to innuendoes that he intervened with the administration on their behalf in the Ballinger-Pinchot fight. This he heatedly denied, stating that his generally pro-conservation stand was well known. One interest that he failed to mention in his *Autobiography* was his assumption this summer of 1910 of the helm of the newly organized General Cotton Securities Company, whose express object, to corner the entire American cotton market for the altruistic purpose of price stabilization, was distinctly in contrast to the expressed antitrust thrust of the administration.

Hammond did deny publicly that he had any interest in a new machine gun that was going to revolutionize warfare or that he had talked with anyone in the government about it, although admittedly his son Harris was a heavy investor in the invention. There is no reason to suppose that Jack Hammond was any more the compromiser than his good friend Bill Taft was the compromised. "I ought not to be the recipient of favors," he reflected many years later, "from an administration in which the President was known to be my personal friend."

Hammond knew every President from Grant to Franklin Roosevelt except Arthur, several well, Taft intimately, although it's doubtful he had the influence with Taft that another good friend and North Shore summer neighbor of his, Colonel House, was to have with Wilson. Presidents, emperors, dictators and tycoons, emissaries, cabinet members, Senators, Congressmen, governors — Hammond knew them all, and made a point of it — and Justices of the Supreme Court.

The President stayed on in Beverly later than usual in 1910, perhaps tarrying longer than was prudent politically. Late in September he and Nellie dined with Justice and Mrs. Oliver Wendell Holmes in their summer cottage at Beverly Farms. The Judge Lorings, in that peculiarly chauvinistic jargon of the society columns, were there, and Joanna Davidge of Eastern Point's Dabsville. Their host was still a mere fledgling of sixty-nine. Taft's elevation over the great jurist's head as Chief Justice — he saw it as just that, an elevation from the presidency — was eleven years in the future, at the hand of Warren G. Harding, who would renominate him two years hence.

Hammond was not present on this occasion but enjoyed recalling another when he and a mutual friend of Holmes, Moreton Frewen of London, motored over to the Justice's cottage on their way to Myopia for lunch and persuaded him to break away from an opinion he was hard at work on, but only with the promise to Mrs. Holmes that they would have him back by three . . . and a good job of it, too, for her husband loathed automobiles, would never own one, and could rarely be induced to ride in one. So engrossed were the three in conversation that from Hamilton they drove to the Eastern Yacht Club in Marblehead, forgetting entirely their pledge to Mrs. Holmes. More refreshments, and then at about six they boarded the Hammond yacht and arrived at "Lookout Hill" in time for a late dinner interrupted by a furious wife who had been phoning all over the North Shore trying to locate her wayward spouse. They bolted dinner and got Justice Holmes back on his doorstep, where Hammond abandoned him to his deserved fate and retreated shamefacedly.

The attempted assassination of Mayor Gaynor of Hoboken, New Jersey, on August 9 prompted the Secret Service to tighten security around the Tafts and the summer White House. Two men patrolled the Stetson cottage and the grounds day and night, and even society dowagers calling on Mrs. Taft had to wait down the driveway while an agent phoned the house to confirm the engagement. Another was constantly by the President's side when he was abroad now — golfing at Myopia or on the daily drives, riding the runningboard, while a second car manned by agents followed close behind with a large plate "U.S.S.S." hung below the Massachusetts plate, warning other drivers that the President was up ahead and they should keep their distance.

Nellie Taft bore this constant surveillance as both amusing (sometimes) and trying. "The secret service men," she wrote of the summer White House, "like the poor, we had with us always, but it never seemed to me that they 'lived' anywhere. They were merely around all the time. They were never uniformed, of course, and looked like casual visitors. They used to startle callers by emerging suddenly from behind bushes or other secluded spots — not I am sure because of a weakness for detective methods, but because they concealed comfortable chairs in these places — and asking them what they wanted."

These measures certainly contributed to what was regarded widely as the eccentric and unthinkable, if not downright unpatriotic, action of Mrs. Evans in informing her most illustrious of tenants that he need not bother to return to her cottage for the third summer of his administration. In short, she served notice of eviction on the President of the

United States . . . and this in spite of the fact that he enjoyed the setup so much and gave it such credit for restoring his wife to health that he had hoped to keep coming until his term was up!

Mrs. Evans's ostensible reason for this staggering decision was all the more staggering: she wanted to tear the house down and plant an Italian garden in its place.

Something closer to the real truth appeared in the *Gloucester Times* on October 11, 1910, a week after the news of the eviction first broke, under the headline

Mrs. Evans Disliked Publicity

"The refusal of Mrs. Robert D. Evans, owner of the cottage which President Taft has occupied for two summers, to renew his lease, was not a surprise to many people in Beverly. Mrs. Evans is a woman of strong personality, and the honor of having the President of the United States as a tenant carried no particular weight with her compared to her own comfort and summer enjoyment.

"It was stated some time after the death of her husband, a year ago, Mrs. Evans stated that this would be the last year that the President would occupy the cottage on Woodbury Point. The informant added that when Mr. Evans let the estate to President Taft, he did so much against Mrs. Evans's wish; she knew then that the estate would practically become a public place, and that practically all her own pleasure in a summer there would be spoiled. As a matter of fact, her own house, next to the cottage occupied by the President, has been closed for most of the summer, and she has been away.

"Mrs. Evans has been greatly affected by the death of her husband, and one of her friends says she is not like the same woman. She has worried a great deal, and has shunned anything like the presence of many people, especially strangers. One of her great pleasures was taking walks about her estate in the morning, but with President Taft in the estate these walks became practically impossible.

"There were many other annoyances also. The beautiful avenue of elms at all times has held the automobiles of the secret service men; their telephone nailed to a tree was in constant use; newspaper men on duty lay on the grass and the secret service men at the 'dead line.'

"Sightseers constantly drove their motors into the avenues, and these sightseers had no hesitation, being forbidden to go up to the presidential cottage, in coming to Mrs. Evans's house to ask questions about President Taft's family. This was all very distasteful to Mrs. Evans and to her sisters, Miss Belle Hunt and Miss Abbie Hunt.

"Little credence was given to the story that Mrs. Evans intends to pull down the cottage occupied by President Taft or to build a new house on the estate."

Furthermore, on the apparent theory that one White House was as much a public preserve as another, the Boston and Northern advertised special round-trip trolley rides to the "Nation's Summer Capital" at ten cents a head, with instructions how to walk to the Evans estate from the nearest stop at Hale and Ober streets . . . a bit of promotion that could have done nothing to improve the landlady's disposition toward her tenants and their crowd.

So the Tafts set about White Househunting again. The Hammonds wanted them at Freshwater Cove, or at Magnolia or East Gloucester. Nellie inspected more than forty cottages, but the location or the size was wrong, or the rent too high, and nothing had been decided when the President finally had to return to Washington on October 17, driving through Beverly between a mile of scrubbed schoolchildren, three thousand of them, all cheering and waving little flags.

Within a fortnight, however, they had found their place, and it was announced that the new summer White House would be "Parramatta," the beautiful and secluded estate of the late Henry W. Peabody, Salem and Boston merchant and shipowner, from whose widow they had leased it for the 1911 and 1912 seasons.

The wild setting had reminded the well-traveled Peabody, who had known the President when Taft was the first civilian governor of the Philippines in 1901, of the country around the Parramatta River in Australia's New South Wales. The sixty-acre estate was in the section of Beverly, a little inland of Woodbury Point and Mrs. Evans's cottages, known as "Montserrat" after the West Indies island that long past had been a source of salt for the local fishing industry. Peabody formed a development syndicate in 1887 and bought the tract of ninety acres that they called Montserrat Highlands, south of the railroad depot, from which he carved out "Parramatta." He drained and cleared a swamp for a Japanese garden inspired by a visit to Yokohama, made an artificial pond, laid out tennis courts and a nine-hole golf course and built an eighteen-room mansion nestled on a commanding ledge.

But Henry Peabody died before he had much chance to enjoy the reality of his dream — not quite as prematurely, though, as George M. Pullman, that ironfisted creator of the Pullman parlor car and the private varnish, who was negotiating with Peabody for the balance of the Highlands, planning to make an estate there to rival Frick's, when he died in 1897. What howls would have gone up from the Republican insurgents if the President had moved in next door to the malefactor who precipitated the bloodiest strike in American history — regarding which the then Judge Taft wrote vehemently (and privately) that more strikers should be killed to teach labor a proper respect for private property!

As for Maria Antoinette Evans, she was better than her word. Next spring she cut the Stetson cottage in half, rolled it down to Beverly Cove onto a lighter and ferried it across Salem Bay to a lot she had bought on Peach's Point in Marblehead, where she had it put together again.

All this unhousing of Presidents landed Mrs. Evans and the anastomosed summer White House alongside the Crowninshield compound ruled petulantly by "Keno" and peremptorily by "The Queen" — Francis Boardman Crowninshield, the short and not so prepossessing last of his unusual line, and his fabulously fat, preposterously prepossessing, regally rich and egregiously eccentric consort, the former (and ever) Louise Evelina duPont, literally *the* grande dame of the North Shore from their marriage in 1900 until her death fifty-eight years later.

Keno had his 109-foot steel schooner yacht, updated from his ancestor's, his beloved *Cleopatra's Barge II* (*"our* yacht, my dear," as another spouse of overshadowing wealth corrected her pardonably presumptuous Brookline banker husband more than once).

The Queen had her jewels, her packs of Pekingese, her raucous macaw, her limousines, her charities and her antiquing (she dropped $175,000 one casual afternoon in a Maine shop; the owner's life was never again the same) as vast as herself, her retinues at whatever seasonal duPont seat she chose to descend upon with her weighty jollity, her hats (one of which, with a torn veil, she purchased at a fair, for thirty cents, according to Charles S. Tapley, an occasional odd man at dinner), and her two million a year. The chapeau was in a class with the second- or third-hand coat Tapley swears she bought at the Morgan Memorial store in Salem for five dollars; upon being informed of the charitable object of the Goodwill Industries, she fished into her ample bag and wrote out a check for five thousand dollars on the spot.

Myriad are the stories, most of which she surely relished, concerning Louise — the great occasion when she presented the Peabody Museum of Salem with a handsome replica of the *Barge*'s cabin, acknowledging from the audience the president's fulsome praise of her as an institution, with "I presume you're referring to my size" — her unabashed bathing off Peach's Point in broad buff — and the summer this grand and humorous lady of a thousand good works had a chemical covertly added to her Marblehead swimming pool to teach peeing children a lesson, when "at once," as Crowninshield in-law and biographer David Ferguson passes the story along, "purple streams issued forth from a couple of Boston's best old dowagers in tank suits."

But we digress. Back across the bay in Beverly, overspreading the foundations of the departed summer White House, Mrs. Evans planted an Italian garden after all, laid out before a classical colonnaded tea-house of stone, with arbors, terraces, pools, fountains, statuary, walk-ways and formal plantings — a garden regarded on her passing in 1917 as quite probably the most elegant of its kind in the United States, and preserved, after a fashion, as a public park today.

An Italian Tuileries, but she could afford it, this *Maria Antoinette* with all the temerity of her namesake, as she could afford to kick out a President. "A striking illustration of American liberty and individual independence," snorted the *North Shore Breeze* in more of a compliment than it intended, while Helen Taft omitted all mention of her landlady — and the matter — from her memoirs.

When her husband's estate was probated in 1910, at $10,538,103, it was the largest ever filed in Essex County, and Mrs. Evans paid the largest personal property tax in Beverly and doubtless the county — $77,352 on possessions publicly assessed in excess of $5,000,000. One of the twelve richest women in America, it was said.

That June Maria Antoinette Evans gave Boston University $200,000

President Theodore Roosevelt on the lawn of the library at Nahant, August 24, 1902. Nahant Public Libraty

Senator Henry Cabot Lodge on his home turf during Nahant's fiftieth anniversary celebration, 1903. Nahant Public Library

The summer White House embarks on an unPresidented cruise to Marblehead
Beverly Historical Society

"Parramatta" Montserrat, Beverly, Mass.
Summer Home of
President Taft.

"Parramatta," the successor summer White House up the road in Montserrat.
Blanche Butler Lane

Mr. and Mrs. Taft, Charlie and John Hays Hammond off for a spin in the White Steamer. From The Autobiography of John Hays Hammond

President Taft lays the cornerstone of the Beverly YMCA on August 31, 1911. Beverly Historical Society

Senator Nelson W. Aldrich of Rhode Island, in wing collar, his son-in-law, John D. Rockefeller, Jr., left, and family drop in at Piatt Andrew's "Red Roof" on Eastern Point, summer of 1911. Harry Sleeper is second from left. Andrew Gray

The presidential yacht Mayflower *at anchor in Gloucester Harbor July 9, 1910, in company with the coasting schooner* Catherine. *Eben Parsons photo*

The schooner Cleopatra's Barge II. *Peabody Museum of Salem*

Louise duPont Crowninshield. Peabody Museum of Salem

Francis B. (Keno) Crowninshield. Peabody Museum of Salem

to endow a department of clinical research and preventive medicine in her husband's name. And she lived to see the immense Robert Dawson Evans picture gallery of the Boston Museum of Fine Arts, which she built for a million dollars, dedicated as another memorial, to a dedicated trustee and collector — and she endowed it for another million, and more, in her will.

A more cordial landlady than her neighbor, Mrs. Peabody painted "Parramatta" a patriotic white in readiness for the 1911 season. The President was more beleaguered than ever. As his woes mounted, he retreated into the innately conservative and apolitical depths of his nature. The Roosevelt heritage with whose keeping he had been charged was withering in his unwilling hands. His domestic policies fell prey to the ever-angrier insurgents in his own party, while his heartfelt pleas for international peacekeeping machinery fell on deaf ears in the Senate even as the House fell to the Democrats in the 1910 elections. To the east, the ascetic visage of Woodrow Wilson loomed up over the horizon; on the west, the florid face of Theodore blazed forth in apoplectic sunset.

Taft sent his family ahead to the new summer White House in Beverly but was able to escape the heat of Congress and Washington for only a few short weekends. July arrived and departed, and so did the Atlantic fleet. On August 11 the President took the train for Beverly for three days.

The next day, Saturday, at six in the evening, the presidential car was rolling nonchalantly along Boston Street in Salem. The Tafts relaxed in the back seat; Archie Butt was up front with the chauffeur. Just as they turned into Essex Street, William A. Jepson, a Boston coal dealer out for a spin with his wife, rounded the other way. "The two met on the turn," the *Gloucester Times* reported. "While the chauffeur of the President's car jammed on the brakes Mr. Jepson locked the wheels of his own machine. The two skidded for a short distance, and struck, locking together. The compact was not a hard one, and while it jarred the occupants of both cars, did not injure any one in either. Major Butt leaped out at once. He went around to Mr. Jepson as soon as he saw that President Taft, after the first scare of the collision had turned to reassure Mrs. Taft, who was manifestly uninjured, and took the matter calmly."

When the unfortunate coal dealer "endeavored to back he found that his machine had been crippled," the report continued. "The impact had broken the springs, and disturbed the gearing so that the car could not be driven."

So the nation's First Car had to give way and back off, which was getting to be a familiar story with the President. Major Butt told Jepson to have his machine towed away for repairs and send the bill to his boss, hove himself back aboard, and ordered the chagrined chauffeur to drive on for "Parramatta." The President ordered a new car off the showroom floor, a seven-passenger, sixty-six-horsepower 1912 model Pierce Arrow touring car, his third, in dark blue with a brown stripe. His seal was affixed to the door, and it was ready and waiting for him when Congress mercifully adjourned and allowed the executive branch to set up summer shop in "Parramatta" and the now-famous rooms of the Beverly Board of Trade on August 24.

Also ready and waiting back at "Lookout Hill" were the Hammonds, whom the President had dispatched as his personal envoys to the coronation of King George V and Queen Mary of England in June. They had accounted themselves well (his friends smilingly hailed Jack as "Your Excellency" and the Queen addressed him as "Mr. Hays Hammond") from the moment when the regal Natalie was asked by a reporter before their departure for Britain if it was true that her jewels would be the most valuable at the coronation. "I am tired of hearing about them," responded Mrs. H., with a toss of her head. "However, you won't have any need to be ashamed of them" — and then pointed imperially at her children: "I might say, like Cornelia, *these* are my jewels." And like the classical Cornelia, Natalie was the classic mother — almost to a fault.

The foreshortened summer routine of golf and motoring — and hobnobbing — was resumed. Helen made the papers with her tennis style in the doubles at the Oceanside: "Miss Taft is not an extraordinary player. . . . She serves with her left hand and immediately changes the racket to her right hand. Her opponents fail to get on to this peculiarity." Not extraordinary?

Helen's parents made the papers in a buried social note mentioning their presence at the "Rockmarge" reception following "Judge" Moore's annual horse show, as Helen and her mother had the previous season. Not quite as ambidextrous as his daughter, Bill Taft seems not to have been as chummy with the Sphinx of the Rock Island, who was already in very bad odor with his stock manipulations, as he was with their mutual friend Frick. But there were those, once the word got abroad, who would surely suspect that his substantial presence at "Rockmarge" belied to some degree his public distress the previous June over the failure of Congress to arm the Interstate Commerce Commission with the power to regulate railroad financing.

Taft took the occasion of the Essex County Republican Club's outing at Congressman Gardner's Sagamore Farm in Hamilton August 26 to lambaste the unholy congressional alliance of progressive Republicans and Democrats who had forced him to veto their recent tariff cuts. The speech was regarded as the opening salvo in his campaign for reelection — a prospect for which, paradoxically, he had by now so little stomach that he wrote his brother Charles ten days later: "I am not very happy in this renomination and reelection business. I have to set my teeth and go through with it. . . . But I shall be willing to retire and let another take the burden." On the twenty-first of September he left Beverly for his annual autumnal swing around the country.

A month passed, and his Attorney General, George W. Wickersham, fired the salvo that opened the final act of the Taft administration's campaign of self-immolation. In certain curious respects this unhappy drama was played to the ululations of a Greek chorus offstage on the North Shore.

On October 26 Wickersham filed an antitrust suit against the United States Steel Corporation. This was all in the Rooseveltian tradition, except that back in 1907, when it looked as if a financial panic would result if the overextended brokerage of Moore and Schley collapsed, H. C. Frick and Elbert H. Gary proposed to TR to save it by having U.S. Steel buy the five million dollars in Tennessee Coal and Iron stock the brokerage held for forty-five million; and Roosevelt agreed not to regard the purchase as grounds for antitrust action by the government.

But now, here was Taft's man four years later on a trust-busting binge, claiming in a suit that Frick and Gary had deceived Roosevelt in order to gain control of Tennessee at what proved in time to be a bargain price. Taft was so insensitive politically that he apparently was unaware of the invidious implication. But Roosevelt was furious and never forgave him.

Frick, on the other hand, rather reluctantly contributed $50,000 to Taft's campaign in 1912. To a last-minute solicitation from a campaign official for more, however, he replied that Taft couldn't win, that he (Frick) had always been against buying the Tennessee at any price as a matter of business, that he had moved to help save the country from a panic, and that the Taft administration "utterly failed to treat many of its warmest friends fairly." Pringle, biographer of both Presidents, considered the incident the worst of the strategic blunders that led to their complete breach and Taft's downfall.

The President's troubles were certainly piling up. On April 14, 1912, the liner *Titanic* struck the infamous iceberg and went down, and with it Major Archibald Butt, his faithful aide, returning from a European vacation. A few days later Attorney General Wickersham entered an antitrust suit against International Harvester, one of the giants bypassed by Roosevelt. Taft was reluctant to accuse his predecessor of having favored the corporation, so Gussie Gardner, son-in-law of Roosevelt's closest friend, charged TR with having made a deal with the Morgan interests behind International Harvester and challenged him to a debate. Roosevelt called Gardner a liar, upon which Taft yielded to the orchestrated "demands" of his political supporters and made the documents in the case public. Unperturbed by much of anything — least of all Presidents — Morgan leased one of the Ocean-side's cottages at Magnolia for the season — a ringside seat.

Roosevelt was now beginning to savage Taft, big-game style. The President responded like a wounded hippo. The battle lines were drawn. In June the two fought for the nomination at the Republican convention in Chicago. Taft steamrolled through on the party machinery. Roosevelt shouted "Thief!" and bolted, and the delirious Democrats nominated Woodrow Wilson in Baltimore.

Hence the arrival of the Tafts at Montserrat on the Fourth of July for their fourth summer in Beverly was for them the more bittersweet, in the hauntingly Far Eastern setting of "Parramatta," than ever. They were hardly settled when the next day the papers broke the news of Piatt Andrew's explosive designation as Assistant Secretary of the Treasury. The Idol of Dabsville had reached utter exasperation in his relations with Secretary Franklin MacVeagh, whose "idiosyncrasies and incapacity for decision," he charged (with an assumption of spokesmanship not unanimously ratified) were driving the other subalterns equally up the Treasury wall.

MacVeagh was a midwestern grocery wholesaler; he countercharged Andrew with inefficiency. Caught between the least popular member of an unpopular cabinet and the brilliant bad boy who was the brains behind the front man, the President (who abhorred dissent, as he would demonstrate on the Supreme Court) stuck with his establishment, as he had with Secretary Ballinger against Pinchot, and officially fired Andrew.

Another presidential friendship bent if not broken by the blasted politics Taft so detested. Indeed, he had so favored the Harvard economist (one of whose students had been That Other Roosevelt) that after raising him from the Mint to succeed Charlie Norton as assistant secretary in June 1910 he had tried and failed to convince Doc to succeed Norton as his private secretary a year later; this was after Jack Hammond got Taft, on what Hammond claimed was the only occasion he ever injected himself into White House affairs, to fire Norton at the behest of certain cabinet members jealous of Charlie's influence with the boss.

In fact, as more came out, Piatt Andrew had attended the Republican convention against MacVeagh's possibly jealous orders, to lobby for the Aldrich central banking plan which had been so much his brainchild, and to advance his own political fortunes.

Immediately, down in Nahant Senator Lodge came to Doc's defense, as did the Roosevelt wing in general. The *Boston Transcript* summed it up with an admiring profile of the handsome martyr, obviously so much more of an asset to the administration than the secretary himself. The consensus: another family squabble miserably handled by Taft . . . grist for the grinding teeth of TR, in full cry up and down the country now, in full wrath against his hand-picked successor, marshaling the insurgency.

For the rest of July the President spent a weekend or two in Beverly before delivering a lukewarm acceptance speech in Washington on the first of August. On the fifth, the Bull Moose Party convened in Chicago, keynoted by Taft's bugaboo in next-door Manchester, Senator Beveridge. Theodore Roosevelt was nominated, splitting the Republicans, and the battle was joined, to the absolute delectation of Woodrow Wilson and the Democrats. Taft remained in Washington all of August while Congress was sitting, virtually refusing to campaign, sending his party surrogates off to the hustings on his behalf — or Wilson's, for he cared not how Roosevelt, whom he now considered quite mad, was stopped.

Several prominent summer visitors to the North Shore besides Archibald Butt were among the 1,517 who had perished with the *Titanic* that spring, including Harry Elkins Widener, the brilliant young Philadelphia bibliophile whose family had leased the Eben Jordan estate in Manchester. His mother, Mrs. George D. Widener, watched from a lifeboat as the liner sank; three years later she gave Harvard its Widener Library in his memory.

Sadly mindful of the lost souls, Natalie Hammond organized a national fund campaign to erect a *Titanic* memorial in Washington. It was to be launched on the lawn of "Lookout Hill" with a gala at which the Tafts would be the luminaries. But Congress kept the President in Washington, and the show went on without him on August 27.

Amateur songs, dances, sentimental readings and self-conscious pantomimes by the young eligibles of the Shore trod one upon another on an outdoor stage, following which the dutifully attending were rewarded with a buffet. All the Tafts but the Chief were there, joined by Mrs. Grover Cleveland and her children, and fifteen hundred of the elite. Madam Hammond reigned supreme, and the occasion was hailed as the largest and most elaborate social do ever on Cape Ann and probably the entire North Shore . . . an occasion with heavy overtones, on a titanic scale, to mark the imminent sinking of a foundering political ship.

Through the soft North Shore September and for most of its golden October President Taft lurked in his summer retreat, golfing at his exclusive clubs, off on his afternoon drives in one of his five motor cars with Nellie, but without the familiar figure of loyal Archie up front.

Everything was the same and nothing was the same. The President's Navy visited Rockport as usual, and the presidential yachts swung on their anchors in Beverly and Gloucester, waiting, just waiting. But out around the country all was hue and cry, abuse and counterabuse, as old friend Theodore barnstormed the land, badmouthing old friend Bill. Cabot Lodge agonized and stuck with Taft against his closest pal and almost lost reelection to the Senate for his pains. Gussie Gardner remained loyal, and so did Doc Andrew in spite of his wounds. Nick Longworth, conservative to the bone, felt constrained finally to come out for Taft against his own father-in-law and lost his seat in Congress.

The Taft-Lodge alliance was never better than an uneasy one, and they broke over the issue of the League of Nations, which Lodge fought in the Senate and Taft supported as the only hope for postwar peace. (How the tables were turned thirty-three years later, when Henry Cabot Lodge's grandson and namesake, a fervent internationalist, swept General Dwight D. Eisenhower through to the Republican nomination over Taft's son, the isolationist Senator Bob from Ohio, in 1952 — and suffered the loss of his own seat in the Senate to John F. Kennedy as Taft and the bourbon Republicans of Massachusetts knifed him in reprisal!)

A loyal old friend and supporter visiting "Parramatta" assured Nellie that her husband would be reelected. "Well," she said, "you may be right, but just the same I intend to pack everything up when I leave Beverly, and I shall take the linen and silver home."

It was a less-than-grand fall for the Grand Old Party, and on the fifth of November, 1912, Woodrow Wilson swamped Theodore Roosevelt, who swamped the incumbent, much to the least of the losers' relief. "What a dismal petering out for Taft," Caroline Sinkler, the Lavender Lady of Dabsville and Eastern Point, wrote her dear neighbor Doc Andrew. "But I do rejoice in thinking of that jealous and spiteful and small-brained MacVeagh returning without honor to his grocery or whatever they called it."

President William Howard Taft relinquished "the burden" to the lesser of the devils, he was certain of that, in March of 1913 and retired with a sigh to Yale to teach law — and that summer and every one thereafter to his "strawberry box" above the sweep of the St. Lawrence. His good humor returned, and his game. He wrote Henry Clay Frick from Murray Bay in that dark year of 1914: "I hope Myopia Links still give you the pleasure you used to derive from them when I was at Beverly. These links at Murray Bay are by no means so difficult as you may judge from the fact that I have been around once in 82 and once in 83."

All was forgiven, after all. Frick read this note at a Myopia luncheon with the comment: "Eighty-two and eighty-three! Pretty good, I should say. And I used to wonder why I couldn't beat him. I ought to. I am eight years older than he is. I wonder if he would have mentioned the scores if they had been 102 and 103. I guess he would. There's nothing small about Taft. I must get a game with Mr. Rockefeller. He is ten years older than I am and I may have a chance." Years later he did, and lost.

Nineteen-fourteen. That was the year His Imperial Majesty disappointingly failed to fulfill the hopeful toast raised to him off the Beverly shore by the President of the United States one smiling summer day on the quarterdeck of the good ship *Mayflower*.

The next June the "Parramatta Inn" opened to the public on the rise of ground between the Montserrat station with its weed-grown presidential siding and the superb Italian garden of Maria Antoinette Evans. Nothing much had changed since the place was the nerve center of the nation. Each arriving guest, of course, was reverentially shown the oversize armchair said to have been custom-made for President Taft.

A Certain Uncertain Air of Certainty

WILLIAM HOWARD TAFT'S DEPARTURE FROM BEVERLY IN RELIEVED PRESI-
dential defeat in the autumn of 1912 left four of the last twenty years of
Republican jollity and jingoism stranded on the Cove beach. The fog by
then was rolling in from Europe.

Though as much the embodiment of the good life, Taft was no Edwardian match for Edward VII, who had the good luck to depart the
stage before his era was up, nor a Rooseveltian one for his former friend
Theodore, who didn't. The King of England was obese, self-indulgent
and complacent, and came to the job too late for it. The President was
obese, fretful and intelligent, and came to the job with no taste for it.
Both were peaceful men, but powerless against the domestic delusion
and Teutonic paranoia that neither they nor hardly anyone else understood.

A week before Mr. Taft and the Republicans formally handed the
safety of the world over to Mr. Wilson and the Democrats, the Six-
teenth Amendment to the Constitution was adopted; this raised the
first tax on private and corporate income in the history of the federal
government; it was proposed by the foxes of capitalism as a bone to the
hounds of redistribution.

The income tax was one end of the beginning of the end, not only of
the Edwardian Era, as inaccurately applied to the United States, but
belatedly of the nineteenth century. The other end occurred three
months afterward with the completely unremarkable arrival for the
summer of 1913 at Norton's Point in Manchester of His Excellency

Constantine Dumba, the ambassador from Austria-Hungary, one of many. Within a year the heir to his artificially conjoined nation's throne had been assassinated at Sarajevo, and the Emperor of Germany, awaiting the merest of pretenses, took up arms against the Emperor of Russia.

If the crowns of Europe had rested as easy as their envoys on the Gold Coast of the North Shore, it all might have been prevented over a few rounds of gin and bitters on one of the porches of the Oceanside, such was the placatory magic of the New England coastal resort hotel first invoked by Teddy Roosevelt to cool tempers between Japan and Russia at Portsmouth's Wentworth-by-the-Sea in 1905. Throughout those two rosy Republican decades, like Boston's wool dealers flocked downtown in mutual self-interest, there were more summering foreign ambassadors to the running foot of verandah on the Shore than any comparable stretch anywhere, more motor cars on the road, and more millionaires per issue, as the *Breeze* boasted of and to its readers.

With rare republican exceptions in this Age of Republicanism, the emissaries were on the Shore selling Royalty and Empire and promoting the continental drift. They found a ready clientele. Among the first was the Siamese legation, which discovered Bass Rocks and Eastern Point in Gloucester in the 1890s and took summer residence in cottages and hotels for decades after. A member of the British East Indian diplomatic staff represented Siam until its independence; his young attachés were smoothly Anglicized, Oxford-educated Siamese, the most remembered of whom was Nai Choate, an excellent tennis player and dinner partner much in demand among the socially aspiring, who wondered where he could have acquired such a thoroughly Ipswichian surname.

The general trend, however, was baronial. Toward the end of the interlude of illusion, when most were still on fairly cordial speaking terms, Baron Hermann Speck von Sternberg, the Kaiser's envoy, and Youssouf Zia Pasha of Turkey occupied Beverly Farms, Baron Mayor des Planches of Italy held down Manchester, Baron Moucheur of Belgium had staked out Hamilton, besides others of like pinstripe representing the national interests of France, England, Brazil and all shades of other colors on the map trying to relax hither and yon between Beverly and Magnolia.

One of the more popular of the barons was Roman Romanovich

Rosen, the Czar's man in America, who summered on the Shore from 1905, when he was largely engaged on important business in Portsmouth with TR and the Japanese, until 1911, usually at Coolidge Point in Manchester. Arriving in 1907 by motor car, Baron Rosen happily informed the press that "we made the trip without even killing a chicken." Next summer his chargé, one Kroupensky, threw an ultra-smart dinner party at the North Shore Grill in Magnolia for the young chaps of the Russian, French, German, British and Italian embassies and the young ladies of the *Social Register*. Youth, of course, got along splendidly.

The natives tended to regard the peerage-in-residence with amused or not-so-amused tolerance. There was some snorting on the street corners when the interlocutory corps was assigned "D" plates and exempted from the local speed limits in 1909. There was the Sunday morning when the Argentine ambassador drew up before Floyd's News Store in Manchester in a victoria drawn by a smart span of horses. His son came running in and so pestered the proprietor, who happened to be otherwise occupied, for the ambassadorial newspaper that old man Floyd finally wheeled on him in exasperation, with: "I don't give a God damn if the Ambassador is waiting; put your ass on that stool and wait until I get ready to give it to you!" And there was the day the Manchester police nabbed and grilled two members of the Brazilian embassy as suspects in a housebreak. Ultimately convinced (perhaps reluctantly) that they had the wrong parties, they released the diplomats, who swore the State Department would hear about it.

The hiatal tone of this score of years preceding the War to End War — all loose ends and bewildered beginnings and everybody ever so certain about everything in between — was established at the right time, on the Fourth of July, 1893, in the right place, Nahant, as if contrived by Sigmund Romberg, and described in the right medium, the *Boston Transcript,* the next day by the right recorder, Mr. Mason Hammond, who was there.

Several warships from the visiting Russian navy had anchored offshore, and the Nahant Club was entertaining a boatload of officers. The place was jammed. "The Russian band was playing with all its might and main. The Russian officers were scattered everywhere about the grounds, talking to the ladies, watching the tennis, playing pool and struggling with the English language, when suddenly a loud clanging of bells brought everything to a stop.

"At once there was a cry of 'Fire!' and in one mad helter-skelter stampede officers, band, ladies, guests and children rushed across the lawn down to the Nahant Road. In this free-for-all, go-as-you-please run, Lieutenant Something-or-Other of the Russian fleet won 'hands down,' and the spectacle was presented of a tall man in scarlet breeches, a long brown coat, a white fur cap, silver belt and silver dagger, leading a motley crew of Russians and Americans down across the lawn of the Nahant Club."

'Twas but a roof fire up the road, and a feeble one at that, but as can be imagined, the international brigade, filled with the spirits of amity, made short work of it, and broke most of poor Herv Johnson's windows in the fray.

Nahant, for some reason, was in a fair way of becoming Cold Roast Russia before the hammer fell and the sickle swished. Senator Lodge and Governor Curtis Guild, year-round and summer residents respectively, were as political flypaper to all dignitaries buzzing about the honey pot of the Gold Coast, especially Russians who would be touching base anyway with Ambassador Rosen at Manchester. Checking out his protocol, Governor Guild gave a posh party for William, the sailor prince of Sweden, who was progressing by yacht toward Oyster Bay to hobnob with TR in August 1907; the following July the Guv held court in his summer State House for a certain Count Dobrinskay, touring the States with a certain Dr. William D. Carlisle, whose unlikely capacity was that of court dentist at St. Petersburg . . . not Florida, but Russia. All in due course, Governor Guild was made ambassador to the Czar by his summer neighbor, President Taft, in 1911.

All the same, Nahant held coldly to its roast, distinctly so from the rest of the Shore. The town continued a summer club, the more ingrown with each passing generation, served by ingrown generations of native Nahanters and, at the center of it all, the Nahant Club, remembered at the turn of the century by James Duncan Phillips (who summered in Topsfield) for the quality of its tennis and quantity of its gossip, and for such exclusiveness that fortunate was the guest, even of a member, who got by the door. But not as fortunate as the *objectionable* outsiders from Lynn and other vulgarities of the mainland who had the cheek Saturday afternoons to stroll along the unfortunately public cliff walk that edged the estates of the insiders above their personal ocean.

" 'Why do you know [as Phillips relished the story], some objectionable people came up on our lawn to have their supper,' complained a Boston dame who had rented one of the cottages for the summer, 'and when I sent William (her humble husband) out to tell them to go away, they were very insolent and it upset William so that he had to lie down. These people never seem to come on your lawn.'

"The old Nahanter smiled indulgently. 'No,' she said, 'you see we always sprinkle our lawns very thoroughly on Saturdays and Holidays.' "

Between the Lodge estate on East Point, graveyard of the Meccan hotel, near which the men and boys skinny-dipped on Sundays, and the next headland, crowned by the replica of the Parthenon and owned by George and Mary Crowninshield Mifflin, was snuggled the colony's almost as perfectly private bathing beach, descended to by forty rickety steps. "Forty Steps" was the daily miserable destination of a Mifflin granddaughter, Eugenia Brooks Frothingham, who shivered in her retrospective book *Youth and I* at the very recollection of such a purgatory, bereft of "the coquetry of green and white awnings such as one finds at resorts, nor yet a man in a boat to wave a threatening arm to anyone who gets out beyond the waistline. Nahant would have considered such things contemptible. Our bath houses were of weatherbeaten clapboards and from these we descended painfully over a stony beach to bathe in pure and icy water, or swim dangerously above undertows."

(Margaret Nichols Shurcliff at about this time was plunging into the just as icy waters in front of the Greely Curtis summer mansion, "Sharksmouth," at Manchester, where she visited as a girl under hardly less Spartan conditions. Family and guests alike must fortify themselves before the morning dip with draughts of a concoction called raspberry vinegar, followed by a spirited round of "Swimble in the Swough," a familial twist on tennis played in an erratic fashion against the dormers of the stable roof.)

Half a century before Eugenia Frothingham's girlhood summer at

Nahant the journalist George William Curtis was struck by the resort's repose, its "freedom from the fury of fashion," and sensed it as a retreat "where you may breathe the fresh air awhile, and collect your thoughts, and see the ocean and the stars, and remember with regret the days when happiness was in something else than a dance, the days when you dared to dream."

But had anything changed? "The compact social world was just as adroit, just as assured, and even more secure than a European group of the same size," Mrs. Frothingham reflected on the summer of 1904. "Sure of our loyalties, a forced departure for any social indiscretion — provided it was at all discreetly contrived — was unthinkable. In our midst were about three married couples who liked to hear themselves called the 'Gutter Club' and justify the name by their actions. They were all distinguished by birth, intelligence and education, so their chosen sobriquet was only partly descriptive. We thought them amusing. . . . The whole of that summer is a pretty picture, but I was not especially happy. I knew myself to be outside of a circle within which were the idioms of a social temperament which was strange to me. It had a thinness, a gayness, a sort of necessity for continuous enjoyment that I could only carry with effort to ultimate defeat."

This from a Mifflin, a Crowninshield, a Frothingham!

Needing to go nowhere, being already there, Nahant remained Nahant as the centuries changed. On the other hand, the Gold Coast from Beverly Cove through Manchester, principally, grew ever more golden in the agglomerating manner of wool merchants and ambassadors, though continuing strung through with threads of silver, Old Boston sterling.

Frick's and Moore's, as prime examples, weren't the only nuggets at Pride's Crossing, many of whose residents, though not all (certainly not the Lorings), seemed sworn to outcross one another therewith. Boston men, too. The tantrum-prone, polo-playing banker and Frick backer Fred Prince, for example, who kept forty-five horses and seventeen miles of bridlepaths for them on the 1,500 acres of "Princemere" — not to mention sixty or so more in his stables at Pau in France.

Or Oliver Ames and his palace with its formal gardens the envy of a prince, or William Amory Gardner's stone shack of twenty-three rooms and eleven baths above Mingo Beach, or Quincy Shaw's, parlayed from a mining fortune, or Francis Bartlett's from his father's forays into the mines and rails of the Great American Century.

High on a Manchester hill commanding 260 acres, Philip Dexter employed 150 men in 1910 blasting his cottage 140 feet long from the solid ledge, leveling for tennis courts, dredging for a pond . . . one of the biggest in town but still not as grand as the grandest out on Coolidge Point, where T. Jefferson Coolidge, Jr., one-upped his old man, the tycoon, in 1904 with a monument to dynastic riches 230 feet in length that people promptly dubbed "The Marble Palace," rather to his annoyance and eventually to *his* son's, who ripped it down and replaced it in the late 1950s with one as consuming but less conspicuous.

In West Manchester, Eben D. Jordan's prodigious pile was as much as Coolidge's a temple to family wealth, accumulated, in his case, by means of the retail penury to which Cleveland Amory credited not a few Boston fortunes.

Jordan was not a Brahmin, never could be; his father came down from Maine at fourteen with $1.25 in his pocket, founded Jordan, Marsh and Company, the massive department store, and bought a piece of the ground floor of the *Boston Globe*. The son's obituary in 1916 carefully noted that he "worked his way from the humble position of packer to head of the great concern, asking no favors and winning his way upon his merit." Nothing inconspicuous about the younger Jordan's consumption in the bright dawn of the Age of Retail Consumerism; he was a large patron of music (the Boston Opera House, which he built, and Jordan Hall, which he added to the New England Conservatory in honor of himself), fine horses (he was regarded in his and their prime as the leading show man in America) and summer houses on an operatic scale ("The Forges" near Plymouth on the South Shore, where he kept his important stables, and with canny impartiality toward his clientele, "The Rocks" at West Manchester on the North Shore).

Length serving as good a yardstick as any, "The Rocks" at 185 feet stretched halfway between Coolidge and Dexter. Completed about 1905 when the owner was forty-seven — Neo-Elizabethan Department Store inside and out, crushingly deposited upon the landscape, overpoweringly ornate in brooding oak panel, mahogany and cypress, marble and fancy plaster work, with the essential billiard rooms, stablemen's cottage and the rest. When wearied of the environs of Boston, the Jordans leased various estates in Scotland, for which they entertained a partiality, culminating in Drummond Castle at Perthshire, one of the show places of Britain. All rather well done on buttons, lingerie and Morris chairs.

Withal, as *Town and Country* sized him up after a guided tour of his just-completed Manchester cottage in 1905, "Mr. Jordan is a representative American in his fondness for home life on the country estate." It was reassuring to know that the son of the Maine lad hadn't forgotten his humble and unfavored start in the packing room.

Eben Jordan's summer neighbor on Smith's Point across Manchester Harbor was George Robert White, whose career outsold, if anything, the retailer's father's. White humbled along as a chore boy for the Boston druggists Weeks and Potter until they admitted him as a partner in 1888. In no time he had organized the Potter Drug and Chemical Corporation, biggest of its kind in the country; he invested heavily and wisely in real estate and by his prime was the heaviest (and wisest) taxpayer in Boston.

Bachelor White bought one of the original summer places overlooking Manchester's Long Beach in 1898, tore it down and built on the heights a spacious shingled summer cottage, which he called "Lilliothea." By 1912, like Jordan, he hankered for a change. But instead of relocating, he set to work enclosing "Lilliothea" within a brick and stone shell, leaving a three-inch airspace between the walls, old and new. That winter, as this fancy overcoat of petrified gingerbread arose around the simple shingle, the eccentric soapmaker (Cuticura was his brand) ordered the contractor to enclose the entire project within a second, temporary epidermis, heated so that his more than 300 workers could continue uninterrupted by the weather.

Thus insulated in what his neighbors called his "Cuticura Soap Palace," George Robert White lived the remaining summers until his death in 1922, with his sister and brother-in-law, Mr. and Mrs. Frederick T. Bradbury. In his will this self-made old soap king established the philanthropy he is remembered by, the George Robert White Fund for the benefit of the people of Boston, but left nothing to his adopted Manchester, to the disgruntlement of some of the natives such as Frank Floyd, proprietor of the news store and gossip center.

After White's departure, it is said (leaving everyone the cleaner), a prodigious safe was discovered in the basement of the Soap Palace. The locksmith was summoned, lawyers and relatives were gathered, and it was cracked. The ponderous door groaned open, all peered inside . . . at a dozen bars of Cuticura.

"With all the society columns of the summer papers filled with stories of what society is doing in its pursuit of personal pleasure, it is refreshing to note that not all its devotees are purely selfish in their activity," editorialized the *North Shore Reminder* in 1907. This was eight years after the publication of Thorstein Veblen's uncomfortably (to those who chanced to read it) trenchant *Theory of the Leisure Class.* "Palatial summer homes are opened to the public for functions, which though fashionably attended, are to result in funds for the happiness of less favored fellow beings. Society women, though wearied by their innumerable social duties, unselfishly give up an off day much needed for rest, and go up to town to superintend an outing of their pet charity. Others with a commendable desire to share the blessings which the gods have bestowed on them, invite properly escorted parties of children from city tenement districts to come for a day of delight in the beautiful grounds of their summer estates. . . . The inter-dependence of humanity's widely differing strata is coming into prominence as the problems of human existence are being taken up by the great minds of the day. . . ."

The pursuit of leisure had so far been institutionalized — in no season more so than summer, when it laid claim to all outdoors — that society women were finding that wealth and its uses and misuses imposed a drudgery as taxing as the domestic slavery from which the suffragettes were marching toward liberation. Social duties bred more social duties and the escalation of pretense. An American petty aristocracy was in the making, contrived and effete — not in Nahant, perhaps, where the blood lines had long been drawn — but along the Gold Coast without a doubt. Witness the *Breeze,* May of 1908:

Coachman

English, wants situation, thoroughly experienced in the care and
training of horses, total abstainer, highest of references, with some
experience in autos, 16 years in last situation, well acquainted with
North Shore.

And the same summer, society women, wearied by their duties,
pleading in the public print for tutors, French teachers, French lady's
maid, French dressmakers, laundress, chambermaid, seamstress, parlormaid, governess, gardener . . .

For the North Shore matron who was longer on pretension than on
staff, the "Bureau of Social Requirements" in Boston advertised that
its staff was prepared to handle the purchase, sale and leasing of summer property, to close and open city and country residences, interior-
decorate, shop, market, pack trunks by the hour or day, provide visiting stenographers and amanuenses by the hour, mend and repair,
shampoo and manicure at the patron's residence, and, wrapping it all
up, fill mourning orders promptly.

The ultimate in hired elegance that made every matron an Adelaide
Frick for a day was provided by William J. Creed, who in 1908 established in Beverly the catering business without whose total takeover no
function even today can be considered quite de rigueur.

Before striking off on his own, this Englishman raised in the Wode-
house tradition of domestic service buttled for the family of Robert G.
Hooper in West Manchester; before that, in the 1890s he was Henry
Clay Pierce's steward in St. Louis and Pride's Crossing. Twenty years
after entering catering so successfully that he alternated his annual
vacations between England and the South, Creed enjoyed picturing
himself, The Man's Man Supreme, arranging his master's trek to the
Pierce lodge in the Brule River country of Wisconsin, accompanied by
a veritable tribe of Indian guides and four canoes loaded to the gun-
wales with provisions. A man's man who could cater such an expedition into the wilderness in 1898 could meet any social challenge the
lionesses of the North Shore would come up with, and did.

The fact is that the help question, if a summer resident of sensitivity
thought about it overly, could bring on a migraine. Perhaps taking a

preliminary reading on his readership, young J. Alexander Lodge sent out an editorial feeler when his *North Shore Breeze* was but a month old in June of 1904. The leading summer hotels of the Shore had announced that they would no longer employ blacks: "While we do not object to the negro and have no race prejudice, we believe this is a step in the right direction. The attitude of the negro servant in our summer hotels along the shore has become so overbearing that it has become a nuisance and we might almost say insulting." So much for that.

A problem of another complexion was presented by the servant population explosion. By 1906 recreational rooms euphemistically called "clubhouses" had been found for male and female servants in Magnolia who hitherto, the *Breeze* sympathized, had no off-duty amusements except to "sit, or walk, or go to bed." In 1909 the Men's Club House was built in Magnolia out of a fund subscribed by summer cottagers and hotel guests, with rooms mainly for "the rapidly rising class of chauffeurs" at least fifteen of whom (and here's the rub) had to be boarded by their employers at the Oceanside at sixteen dollars a week. Such was the craze for one-upmanship that servants were being imported faster than quarters could be provided for them, indeed were simply left to fend for themselves. A trained nurse had to hire an apartment for a year in order to occupy it two months in the summer, and the second gardener on a West Manchester estate was forced by his boss's frugality to hike seven and a half miles every day just to eat.

By 1911 editor Lodge had undergone a change of heart and was taking the landowners of Manchester, and Beverly Farms particularly, to task for demanding such exorbitant prices for open property that thrifty and industrious domestics could not possibly afford to build homes for themselves; hardly one small cottage a year had been put up in the Farms in the last ten. "The bane of the North Shore has been its unwise and unAmerican class distinctions," chastised the *Breeze* in February. "The peril works damage to the best interests of all and the dreadful housing condition does more to irritate honorable men and women worthy of better opportunities for decent living to discontent and unhappiness than any other one thing. That there is not a single first class public house where a stranger can find a place to lay his head for a night, at Beverly Farms, or where a party could obtain a simple meal, served with ordinary decency, is an unfortunate

As befits dignitaries, Senator Lodge, Lieutenant Governor Curtis Guild, U.S. Surgeon General Robert A. Blood in epaulets, and town father J. Colby Wilson in derby ride a shining black double victoria in Nahant's fiftieth anniversary parade, summer of 1903. Nahant Public Library

Quite as happily, this bevy of patriotic beauties flatters a four-horse dray and drivers on the same occasion. Nahant Public Library

The Nahant summer colony gathers above its private beach, Forty Steps, in 1913 to observe a youthful tub race. Hammond Collection, Nahant Historical Society

Hard rocks and a beach of pebbles at Forty Steps suit Cold Roast Boston to a T. Summer of 1913. Hammond collection, Nahant Historical Society

Miss Eleonora Sears, first women's squash champion — among a galaxy of other titles. From Myopia, 1875-1975.

Three belles in bows. The Bremer sisters, Manchester, 1913. Essex Institute

Children of Eastern Point summers put on their own pantomine, "The Royal Family," beside one of Commodore Rouse's antique Spanish mortars atop the earthworks of "The Ramparts," August 1909. Lila Leonard Swift

A child of Gloucester fogs and fancies, Thomas Stearns Eliot, on the piazza of the Eliot cottage, Eastern Point, 1897. Henry Ware Eliot collection, Sawyer Free Library

On his terrace at "Red Roof" overlooking Gloucester Harbor on October 6, 1910, Piatt Andrew sits beside Isabella Stewart Gardner, with the Japanese artist-scholar Okakura-Kakuzo, the pensive Lavender Lady, Caroline Sinkler, and Henry Davis Sleeper. Andrew Gray

Mrs. Jack and John Singer Sargent, her portraitist and protégé, on the terrace at "Red Roof." Andrew Gray

His Dabsville neighbor, "the female Sargent," Cecilia Beaux, takes Doc Andrew, right, and friend in tow on the "Red Roof" rocks in the whites the host fancied for himself and male guests. *Andrew Gray*

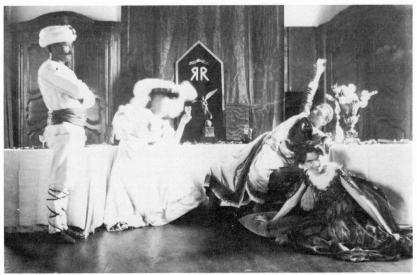

Dabsvillian bacchanalia. Professor Andrew raises his glass, perhaps to himself, in Cecilia Beaux's studio adjoining her "Green Alley" on Eastern Point. Others are unidentified. The occasion is probably the farewell party his friends, including Isabella Gardner, gave him in August 1908 before he sailed for Europe as an expert with Senator Aldrich's National Monetary Commission. *Andrew Gray*

truth. . . . It is peculiarly lamentable when one considers the other side of the North Shore life with its splendid mansions, costly display and luxurious ease."

Within four years, to be sure, the Great Leveler was solving the servants' housing shortage forever.

One should not retire from the field of domestic service on the North Shore without paying respects to a couple of collateral amenities, Robbers Row and the *Flying Fisherman*.

Robbers Row, so designated by those who could and those who could not afford to patronize them, consisted of the score or so of exclusive stores that sprang up almost overnight on the Magnolia land of Miss Frances H. Stearns, an astute Boston businesswoman, who in about 1906 built a charming colonnade shading a blockfront on Lexington Avenue that she leased to a variety of Boston, New York and Paris specialty shops. These she added to, and anchored with the leading night spot north of Boston, the North Shore Grill Club, before she died in 1911. Their names were enough to send a cold chill down the backs of the men with the checkbooks, even on the hottest day of summer: Grande Maison de Blanc, Dreicer, Bonwit Teller, DePinna, A. Schmidt and Sons, Cammeyer, Harlow and Howland, and Mme. Mogabgab, to select a gingerly few, and they offered the fashionable everything from trousseaus, linen and jewelry to imported *objets,* furs and antiques.

The exclusive integrity of Robbers Row was maintained even unto the Second War, when it dwindled bravely, pathetically. But in its snobby glory in the months before America entered the First War, the Colonnade, Lexington Row, the Colonial and the Arcade, shading their haute-couture storefronts, throngs of sophisticates and curbside lines of shining limousines, chauffeurs liveried and waiting, were thus hyperbolized in the *Breeze:*

"For years Magnolia has been acknowledged the premier style center of America and second only to Paris. . . . It has been the fate of many splendid resorts that hordes of lesser personalities have followed in the wake of the more select groups whose names and persons first graced the resorts and made them famous. In turn other multitudes of vacationists have swarmed to these centers to bask in the light shed by the socially prominent. The result has always been the same; society has sought new haunts. . . . Having prevented the incursions of crowds, which would make this section 'popular,' by the establishment of large estates and the exclusion of the cheap hotels, the North Shore — particularly Magnolia and vicinity — has become the headquarters of American society in summer."

As for the *Flying Fisherman,* it was neither a schooner yacht nor an oilskinned aviator but a special commuter train on the Boston and Maine's Gloucester Branch that made one round trip a day for the benefit of wealthy summer subscribers only. The first "Dude Train" (so called by the jealous who couldn't qualify) ran into Boston from Magnolia and Gold Coast way stations in the morning and back in the afternoon in 1892; at about the same time the New York, New Haven and Hartford scheduled a similar train on its Old Colony Branch between Boston and the Buzzards Bay resorts.

Subscribers to the *Fisherman* at first paid a hundred dollars a season plus fare, an arrangement so lucrative for the B & M that in 1907 the railroad placed five big chair cars with cane seats, green leather upholstery and vestibules in service, custom-built by Pullman. By 1914 the Dude Train had four cars and about a hundred subscribers who guaranteed the B & M $13,000 for the season, and some spoilsport on the Massachusetts Public Service Commission was questioning the legality of what were "officially called 'club trains,' implying that they are for the exclusive use of some men of social distinction who live on the North Shore or down in the Cape district during the summer." He was right, of course, but nothing, as might be expected, came of it.

Times changed, and the Dude Train, having survived the Great War, died with the peace, to the dismay of one devotee, whose chauffeur for years had been dropping him off at the Magnolia depot in the morning, then driving hell-bent over the road to Boston and picking him up at North Station and on to the office — as Robert Rapp tells it — so that he shouldn't miss his game of cards en route. Presumably this mad race was reversed in the afternoon.

In the potentially hazardous game of racing railroad trains, only Mr. and Mrs. John Lowell Gardner, Jr., had both the means and the merriment to apply the maxim about joining 'em if you can't beat 'em.

The Gardners of Boston were old summerers of Beverly, and one day at the height of the 1891 season, being sports, they reserved seats on the maiden run of a new tallyho from Pride's Crossing to the Myopia Hunt Club in Hamilton. They missed the train at Boston, however. An hour later, as the gala coach-and-four was about to pull out, down the track thundered a locomotive of the B & M, belching smoke and steam, whistle screaming, bell in an urgent clanging. This apparition screeched to a grinding stop at the Pride's station, and out of the cab jumped Jack to help his Isabella down from her seat beside the fireman. All in the nick of time. Arriving at North Station and a missed train, the Gardners had hired a spare engine on the spot, which was something you could do in those days if you had the right connections to rectify the wrong ones.

In seven years Jack Gardner was dead, leaving Mrs. Jack with the jack to create his and their memorial, Fenway Court, for their growing art collection . . . and to perfect another institution, herself, as Boston's gayest and grandest of dames (and most glacial, if need be) — and the North Shore's whenever she chose to set every haute monde tongue there awagging with her mesmerical presence.

As much the Talk of The Shore in her own right during these deceptively docile decades along the primrose path to perdition was Eleonora Sears, another redoubtable female quite as self-liberated as Isabella Gardner. The younger of the two by nearly fifty years, Eleo (always Eleo in the press and everywhere) was the improper daughter of proper Frederick R. Sears, Jr., of Boston and Beverly Farms and the granddaughter on her mother's side of T. Jefferson Coolidge of Manchester.

As a girl Eleo was a tomboy. Where Isabella was an unabashed devourer of younger men and grand larcenist of other women's husbands (she never remarried after the death of her own), Eleo achieved national fame as a female "jock" in a day when that sort of thing just wasn't done, not in the best of circles, anyway; *she* was a devourer of men on their own turf, grand larcenist of sports trophies, and never married at all.

It *was* rumored in 1906 that the remarkably handsome and lithe Miss Sears was engaged to John Saltonstall. Already she was in the spotlight for her athletic prowess, already rather an enigma. Saltonstall was one of a gallery of fascinated eligibles, as was a Vanderbilt, they said, but nothing ever came of anything, and the lady's press after a while shifted more or less permanently from the gossip columns to the sports pages, and ultimately to the political, where she became a patroness, of sorts, of the Far Right.

A prodigious distance swimmer, Eleo was reported to be preparing for an alongshore match race the summer of 1907 with Baroness Elizabeth Rosen, daughter of the Russian ambassador. By 1908 she was the eastern tennis champion in the women's singles, doubles and mixed doubles.

Betwixt dashes between Beverly, Magnolia, Boston, Newport, New York, California and Europe at tennis, golf, riding, swimming, squash, skating, backgammon and driving fast cars, Miss Sears announced in 1910 that she would defy the previous season's male outcry against her latest projected invasion. "Those who have seen her give an exhibition of whirlwind polo," the *Reminder* applauded with glee, "feel that she is quite capable of taking care of herself and will give some of the crack polo players of the opposite sex a good run for the honors." With her berry-brown skin and twinkling blue eyes, she is "a busy and tireless example of the up-to-date society girl. At the same time, in evening clothes, she is as charming and womanly as the most feminine of her sex and carries herself with ease and grace."

But then she turned around and shocked Propriety by striding along Beacon Street in riding britches — or turned up on a dare on the stage of the Majestic as a matinee extra. And there she was, at a Boston society dance in December 1915, sitting out a number with the great Castles, Irene and Vernon, "wearing that snappy, cool little smile that has baffled a lot of the youth of the day, and presently everybody gasped to see her usurping the position of Mrs. Castle, gliding about on the cleared floor — the epitome of litheness and grace. . . . In a few short minutes," gasped the *Breeze,* Eleo had "added dancing as an expert accomplishment to the already incredibly long repertoire of pastimes in which she more than excels."

With the years Eleonora Sears assumed a certain mannishness in style and habit, presiding with haughty horsiness over her extensive stables at Beverly Farms, ever the more eccentric exhibitionist plodding along on well-publicized hikes from Boston to Providence followed by her limousine in low gear, chauffeur at the ready with fueling drafts of hot chocolate, firing off guns over the startled heads of beach-combers with the gall to pollute her beach with their presence, forming committees against the income tax, demanding the impeachment of President Truman and so on. Bitchy, ruthless and unreasonably rich, yet richly endowed in the bursting bloom of her youth, peremptory, one of the first of the modern playgirls, this super Amazon smashed the sports barriers against her sex right and left, and in those innocent years before the Great War — before she had left most of her grace behind — imparted to the North Shore an air of her own special snappy coolness.

Having not inherited, but only married her place (her money came by both routes), Isabella Stewart (a New Yorker) Gardner had per-force to win Boston, which she did by storm, leaving its North Shore simply to be wooed, which she did by charm. One of those deceptively plainfaced coquettes, Mrs. Jack was in fact fancy-bodied, subtle, se-ductive, soulful, direct, adept as a conversationalist, supremely manip-ulative, outrageous in her behavior, gifted with a sixth sense for printer's ink, and yet, by turns, as midsummerish as Mab. A self-sculpted Pygmalion she was, who would deserve all the distinction she earned if only for her influence on the world of arts and letters (better, artists and writers!) and all the notoriety she craved for her impact on Boston's prewar world of drawing-room dustiness and studied stuffi-ness that she startled, shocked and always ended up by delighting as no one else before or since with the highly dubious exception, perhaps, of the late occasionally Honorable James Michael Curley.

By 1907 Isabella abandoned summering in the shingled Gardner cot-tage, "Alhambra" at Beverly, and her car too, according to her biog-rapher, Louise Hall Tharp, and set upon an unashamedly regal progress of visiting around her North Shore friends and bumming rides from them, for she was feeling frugal; Fenway Court, her pala-tial chef d'oeuvre, had opened to a stunned Boston in 1903, and it is doubtful that even she knew how much it had cost her.

Around 1910, however, bank accounts were back in perspective and Mrs. Jack commenced building "Twelve Lanterns," a cameo replica of a Spanish villa, above the shore on the ocean side of Marblehead

Neck. The place had all the haunting otherworldliness of Fenway Court, and its creator similarly supervised every detail, touched every corner with her intuitive taste.

But if Mrs. Gardner planned to make this aerie her new North Shore base, she never did. In 1911 she presented it outright to one of her stable of handsome protégés, now no longer quite so young, the talented but lazy pianist George Proctor, on the occasion of his marriage to a former pupil, Margaret Burtt. George had been under Mrs. Jack's wing since 1892, when he was eighteen and she fifty-two . . . but a voluptuous fifty-two judging by the advice of an admirer that the portraitist Anders Zorn "ought to do your Beverly shore and you, bathing in the gloaming with a corn-colored moon rising behind your pearly back." Within a year, however, the Proctor union was on the rocks, Margaret complaining that frequently they didn't eat unless Mrs. G. sent over food, and "Twelve Lanterns" was sold.

Another protégé — no, a *friend* — was the magnetically handsome, aquiline-featured Harvard economist Piatt Andrew of the dark and searching eyes, who was to rise and fall so rapidly in President Taft's Treasury Department and personal favor. Soon after it opened, Doc was introduced to Mrs. Gardner at Fenway Court by their mutual friend Cecilia Beaux, the interesting and very definite portrait artist from Philadelphia who, like Piatt, was a recent discoverer of Eastern Point. Bachelor Andrew in 1903 was just occupying his strangely dark and Gothic cottage "Red Roof," honeycombed with secret rooms, hidden passages, bedchamber peepholes and unexpected mirrors, and hosting such favored Harvard "ec" students as Franklin D. Roosevelt. His neighbor, Joanna Davidge, the cultured and precisely precious proprietress of Miss Davidge's Classes for young ladies in New York, was moving into hers, with her Mama.

"Bo" soon bought land beyond Joanna (both were ten years older than Doc, who was thirty-three years younger than Isabella) and moved into her "Green Alley" (for the *allées* she had cut through the underbrush) with its nearby studio in 1906. That was the year Bo's irresistible friend, Caroline Sinkler, the Enchantress of Philadelphia, bought her cottage on the other side of "Red Roof." To the Carolina manor born, Carrie had worn and surrounded herself with Southern lavender since the winter day in 1896 when her betrothed, the architect John Stewardson, drowned while skating on the Schuylkill, and would forever mourn with enchanting grace.

And that was the same spring, 1906, that the soft-faced interior decorator with the hatpin wit, Henry Davis Sleeper, met Piatt Andrew, same age, same nonmarital status, and was invited down to "Red Roof" for the first time. Within three years Harry had bought the lot next over from the Lavender Lady on the other side — and moved with *his* Mama into the dramatically promising core of his great house-museum, "Beauport."

Mrs. Gardner was invited down in September of 1907 by Piatt Andrew, for her first visit to this acronymic little community-within-a-community of masters and misses on the magic Gloucester Harbor shore of Eastern Point, self-styled "Dabsville" by the stylists of self.

On returning to her Brookline estate, "Y" (as soon she would be to all in her relation to Andrew) wrote "A" (as he would be to her) a rushing, gushing note: "In a few hours, what a change! The land change does not make one into something rich & strange — alas! Your village is Fogland with the sea's white arms about you all. Don't let outsiders crawl in — only me! For *I* care. I love its rich, strange people, so far away. . . ."

Again and again "Ysabella" returned to the rich, strange people of Dabsville, and their rich, strange guests — the James brothers, novelist Henry and psychologist William (or was it the other way around?), the amiable editor Richard Watson Gilder, the imperious John Singer Sargent — with the sea's white arms about them all, as if . . . as if on the fourteenth of April, 1910, she wouldn't, couldn't, be seventy. But she was, and for four more years time stood still, or nearly so, in Dabsville, on Eastern Point, and the length and breadth of the North Shore, until that fatal June day in far-off Sarajevo.

Likewise the boy Thomas Stearns Eliot returned to the salt-scented brier rose, the rusty granite, the song sparrows, the "sea howl and the sea yelp" of Eastern Point until he was twenty-three, when in 1911 he exchanged forever those impressionable summers for the seasoning summers of England. Time — that time sailing, tramping, staring at the blue sea and the blue sky, curled up with some arcane volume on the piazza of the Eliot cottage above Niles Beach, from 1896 until this so-cerebral son of the St. Louis brick manufacturer graduated from Harvard in 1909 — clamored and clanged in the poet's memory of fog in fir trees and "the heaving groaner/Rounded homewards," so hauntingly and disturbingly evoked in *The Dry Salvages.*

Out of the Great War had emerged *The Waste Land,* and out of that waterless watershed of modern poetic expression were expunged seventy-one lines describing the outward-bound trip of a Gloucester fishing schooner and her fatal collision with an iceberg, a voyage canceled in the manuscript on the urging of Ezra Pound. And in total contrast, the lightheartedness of the bird-lover in that concise panegyric with the surprise ending, "Cape Ann."

Although many the literary laborer has found the North Shore hospitable to his muse, few have drawn inspiration from their surroundings as directly as the artists have; far fewer have succeeded in universalizing their perceptions of the place and the people. T. S. Eliot's immersion along a particular shore of the Shore was granted him during his formative years. The imprint remained as fresh in his mind's senses as the fog in the firs. Nearly fifty years after he left, this alienated soul returned one summer day to sniff it out, and was gone again, satisfied or not, as suddenly as he had reappeared.

Piatt Andrew had loved France and her people ever since his graduate studies had taken him there, had Frenchified his house and everything in it. Though a native Hoosier, he was a Princeton man and an internationalist. In September of 1914, as the Germany army advanced on the Marne, he ran in the Republican primary for Congress against, of all people, Isabella's favorite nephew, Gussie Gardner, the incumbent, and was beaten.

Stinging from defeat, burning for the great cause he knew his country must sooner or later join, Doc organized the American Field Service for the purpose of helping the French to evacuate their casualties from the front . . . and as a ploy, he hoped and prayed, for drawing America into the war. Inspector General Andrew, chief of the Field Service, sailed for France in December of 1914, leaving his loyal Harry

Sleeper behind in charge of raising money for ambulances and recruiting idealistic young college men to drive them.

Well, it all started as a North Shore project. Mr. Crane stood for three ambulances, Mr. Frick for two, and in no time that somehow seemed a singularly North Shorish thing to do, too. Mrs. Gardner's, incidentally, had a cryptic "Y" painted on the door.

12

Tous et Tout pour La France

It was during this summer that the then Italian Ambassador, Marquis Cusani, was established in the neighborhood and often came to the studio at [Eastern Point]. I did a drawing of him and it was from him, on that splendid summer afternoon when the news came, that we heard it. His view, in his clear and perfect English, would have been interesting to remember — but how little we guessed that we — *we* — were just entering the most awful moment of History.

— Cecilia Beaux, *Background with Figures*

EUROPE WAS A TIME BOMB THAT SPRING OF 1914, TICKING AWAY WHILE the world waited and trembled. Woodrow Wilson sent Colonel House across to see if cool American reason could disarm disaster. In May the President's Silent Partner met with Kaiser Wilhelm in Berlin and reported back on the twenty-ninth: "It is militarism run stark mad. Unless someone acting for you can bring about a different understanding, there is some day to be an awful cataclysm. No one in Europe can do it. There is too much hatred, too many jealousies. . . ."

"Someone" did almost succeed in getting England and Germany together, but fate was unforgiving, and a month later the fuse was touched at Sarajevo. House sailed with heavy heart, arriving at Boston on July 29, and went straight to the cottage he had rented for the season at Pride's Crossing. On the first of August, that "splendid summer afternoon," the bomb exploded with Germany's declaration of war, sooner even than he had feared. On that day House wrote Wilson, hoping he would cruise up to the North Shore on the presidential yacht *Mayflower* for relaxation and talk, but it was not to be.

Pouncing on Belgium while Austria-Hungary held off the Russians, Germany aimed for the heart of France. In far-off Beverly chauffeurs gave notice and booked passage *pour la patrie*. Not entirely fair exchange, perhaps, but Fifth Avenue's Grande Maison de Blanc's Magnolia shop announced that a shipment of children's coats and bonnets in the latest (and last, for some time) mode had fortuitously arrived from Paris. Anxieties were expressed about the safety of friends and relatives abroad, and the sanctity of foreign business connections. Even the weather frowned. Fewer found solace upon the beaches, or in their clubs. There was a temptation to retrench, to hedge somewhat nervously.

Two weeks after the armies of Europe marched, the Royal Hungarian Orchestra, onstage, was the popular dancing attraction in the North Shore Grill's new outdoor garden. Well offstage, however, the *Breeze* sounded an uncertain trumpet: "It is impossible for the new world to entirely forget the conflict in the old world, but it is a rare spirit that has the ability to find rest and peace of mind in the midst of this martial conflict. The point at issue is not that one should steel one's heart to the old world troubles, but the question is whether the exhausting emotions which our sympathies create will help the foreign situation."

Nowhere, one might have supposed, were spirits rarer or emotions more exhausting than within the concupiscible confines of Dabsville, dubbed by some sharp-tongued neighbor the "Sheshore" of Eastern Point. Yet, it was from the queer cubbyholes of "Red Roof" and the quaint closets of "Beauport" that Piatt Andrew's and Henry Sleeper's American Field Service emerged. Their creative sympathies and unsteeled hearts — Doc's initiative and Harry's sensitivity — devised the *deus ex* that by early 1915 was siphoning off the first flow of fiery young idealists from the college campuses to the battlefields of France. Inspector General Andrew set up his headquarters in the small hospital in Neuilly-sur-Seine supported by the American colony in Paris. Henry Ford had invented the moving assembly line in 1914 and the next spring was shipping across the first of the 1,200 chassis ordered by the Field Service to put under its French-built ambulance bodies. "We received no favor or assistance from their manufacturer," Andrew wrote later of Ford, "who with his peculiar ideas of philanthropy, was averse to giving any assistance to war activities, even to the relief of suffering entailed by war."

And then the flood of hellbent volunteers shuttling between the trenches and the shellholes and the *postes de secours* with their bouncing burdens of the maimed and dying, and dying themselves, and "busily writing and agitating in terms that were not neutral," as their leader assessed the effort after it was all over, "sending to their families and friends throughout the Union, to their home papers, to their college publications, and to American weeklies and magazines the great story of France and her prodigious sacrifice. . . . Herein lay by all counts the greatest contribution which the men of the Field Service could make and did make to France. . . . The epic and heroic quality of France's whole history, and especially of that chapter of which we were eye-witnesses, the quenchless spirit and unfaltering will of her people, the democracy, the comradeship, and above all, the calm, unboasting, matter-of-fact courage of her troops, kindled something akin to veneration in all of us. The Field Service motto was *'Tous et tout pour la France.'* We all felt it. We all meant it. It is forever ours."

Among the graphic, horrified snatches of eyewitness to find their way into wider print were the letters sent back to his Gloucester friends in Dabsville and his special friend Jack Hammond, Jr., by the good-looking young English émigré-actor Leslie Buswell, holder of the Croix de Guerre; they were published as *Ambulance No. 10,* edited and prefaced by Sleeper and Andrew. After his return in 1916 Buswell and Hammond were "extended guests," as the *Breeze* phrased it, at Sleeper's "Beauport."

The younger Hammond had his father's genius if not his hail-fellow sociability and had followed him through Yale's Sheffield Scientific School, where he developed such an interest in radio, then in its infancy, that the senior staked him to a $250,000 laboratory, which he built on "Radio Point" below "Lookout Hill" in 1911.

Soon Jack, Jr., was startling fishermen with an unmanned, radio-controlled motorboat that he raced around Gloucester Harbor from his lab. In March of 1914 his remote-controlled radio-gyroscope steered the experimental *Natalia* to Boston and back with a naval observer aboard. Here was the brain behind the brain behind the autopilot and the guided missile and the space shuttle in action. Then on to radio-controlled torpedoes, 128 patents for which he sold the government for $750,000 in 1916, though he was not to collect from Congress until 1932. As a side venture in 1914 Jack invented a light incendiary aerial bomb that was rejected by both the United States and Britain. But when it fell on London he was accused of having peddled it to the Germans and was not cleared, so it is said, until a former employee admitted stealing and selling the plans to the enemy.

Italy's entrance into the war against the Austro-Hungarian Empire on May 23, 1915, dealt another rude reminder to the North Shore of Old World troubles. Italians, as the *Breeze* had remarked only six weeks earlier, had replaced the Irish as the dominant laboring class in the area, making less than two dollars a day, living accordingly, some well trained, most unable to speak English. "It is true that they are selfish in their desires to learn English, but on the other hand there is a moral and economic reason why the New England towns and cities should try to do something for them."

This uplifting advice came too late. As the French chauffeurs had responded to the call, so now did the Italian reservists, and in such large numbers that in August the John Hays Hammonds were persuaded to sponsor at "Lookout Hill" an Italian Fiesta for the benefit of the families of the patriots under the patronage of the Marquis Macchi di Cellere, the ambassador who was summering at Beverly Farms. The social event of the season. Not America's war, yet the shortage of laborers was already a noticeable inconvenience. But one made the best of it.

There was not exactly a home *front,* for that would violate the President's strictures on neutrality . . . except that the ladies of the North Shore branch of the French Wounded Emergency Fund met twice a week in Mrs. Walter Denègre's coach house at West Manchester and turned out medical supplies at a rate exceeding 15,000 a month. Not bad for unpaid piecework in a dowager's summer cottage industry.

Something was happening to home and hearth. For five years the suffragists and those who could not suffer them had been having at it in the letter columns of the *Breeze* when Lillian McCann, a not dull observer of the summer scene, awoke one day in July of 1916, as Europe lay bathed in blood, with a sense of elevated consciousness:

"Do you realize that North Shore society is in an extremely interesting period of its development? This period, which is growing in interest daily, began only one season ago. Do you know how the women of the most exclusive homes of America, gathered on the North Shore for the summer, are toiling to make life pleasanter for the soldier at the front, to help the nurse in the hospitals, and to aid the family at home, left without its breadwinner? The ability to do something worth while — to stand for something, is gaining many a society woman a new zest in life. The ability to open and build up such work-rooms as are on the North Shore might spoil any woman for the life she has always been supposed to lead, by men. Before the war, the world seemed made for the comfort of the well to do and travel was as safe as staying at home. But all that seems tame and uninteresting now. Action is the word, and practically all of our women have interests vastly more important than golf, tennis or tea."

Action *was* the word, male and female, neutrality be damned. First the Field Service, and now, at long last, another return of favors to the Marquis. Twin horses of Troy. It came about this way:

W. Starling Burgess had inherited not only the depth of his late father Edward, who designed three America's Cup defenders in a row in the 1880s, but his breadth, which some called eccentricity, others genius, and all agreed was something to behold in action. Ned had died too early of typhoid in 1891, on the verge of new worlds of yacht design. Starling in due course picked up the paternal torch and was a successful fashioner of boats of beauty in Marblehead when in 1909 he was accosted by one August M. Herring, an irascible but truly pioneering airplane designer who had fallen out with Glenn Curtiss and wanted Burgess to build a biplane for him in his yacht yard.

Flying Fish emerged from this union of minds and skittered a few hundred wobbly feet low over the sands of Plum Island on April 17, 1910. Among the aviation nuts on hand were two scions of rock-ribbed North Shore families, Norman Prince and Greely S. Curtis, Jr. A Grottie and Harvard 1908, Prince was a compact, rugged, clean-cut, aggressive but nonetheless affable student of twenty-two at the Harvard Law School. His distinguishing mark was a yellowish moustache. He was a chip off Frederick Prince, the tempestuous co-founder of Myopia, and grew up on "Princemere," the family acres at Pride's Crossing. Curtis was much older, pushing forty, a son of General Greely Curtis, commander of the First Massachusetts Cavalry in the Civil War, who had come up from Boston and built "Sharksmouth," the first of the truly grand summer mansions, on the Manchester shore in 1868. With some background in aeronautics at Cornell, Curtis persuaded Starling Burgess to let him take the controls of *Flying Fish* a few days after the Plum Island trial and immediately cracked her up. Herring took a perhaps understandable dislike to Curtis, quit the company in a huff and was replaced as Burgess's partner by his nemesis.

Prince finished law school and was in Chicago practicing in 1912 when he joined a syndicate that hired Burgess to build an entry in the Gordon Bennett Cup Race that September. Norman wanted to fly her but was outvoted on the grounds of his inexperience. The plane was not finished on time, and they had to withdraw anyway.

Meanwhile, Burgess, being Burgess, just naturally had to work a boat in there somewhere and that year built his first hydroplane; the Navy began ordering his improved model in the spring of 1913. A year later the Burgess Company produced a radical new hydroplane under the patents of the English designer J. W. Dunne; the Burgess-Dunne it was called, and by the end of that first war year both the Army and Navy were taking delivery.

Piatt Andrew, campaigning for Gussie Gardner's congressional seat in June, was flown up one day, cap on backward, to land on the Merrimack River in this open-aired contraption, leaning out with his camera on the way to snap the first aerial photo ever taken of Cape Ann. Doc mailed a picture postcard to his Dabsville neighbor Carrie Sinkler, traveling in Italy, who replied: "Fancy dear AP my perplexed and excited interest over your postcard. After close scrutiny I even soaked it in water thinking something would develop on it! When suddenly I realized that the tiny mark was you aloft. . . . How I wish I had been there to see you soaring over us. How like you to have done such a dashing thing, but it must be a terrible and thrilling feeling. . . ."

Europe had been hardly a month at war when Greely Curtis's younger brother, Frazier (though thirty-eight and with limited flying experience), sailed on September 2 on the *Arabic,* hoping to enlist in the Royal Flying Corps — the first American to volunteer abroad as an aviator. Politely rejected on account of his age and his citizenship, which he would have had to renounce, Curtis returned to the States with the notion that he might be accepted if he bought a Burgess-Dunne and brought it back with him. But first he had to learn to fly it, so he enrolled in the school Burgess had established with the object of turning out pilots as fast as planes.

It happened that Norman Prince was back in Marblehead from Chicago with the same object as Curtis's, very much against the wishes of his father. Together Prince and Curtis now conceived the idea of getting up a volunteer Yank squadron to take to the air against the Boche.

The elder Prince was a reckless polo player himself, and his opposition to his son's heroics seems out of character, especially in view of their shared devotion to France, nurtured during many summers riding the family spread at Pau, "Villa Ste. Helene"; Norman knew France intimately, spoke the language volubly, loved the people. Still, flight training, let alone actual combat, in those pioneer days of flimsy flying machines with their wings of fragile fabric held together by struts and wires, and uncertain engines, was by the seat of the pants, as someone said, and a father rightly worried for a son. Indeed, in one year at a Texas training field more than forty students were killed in crashes, and no fewer than 200 more were injured.

After another battle with his father, who was dead set against it, Norman sailed for France on January 20, 1915, to organize an American *escadrille,* an air squadron to fight alongside the French. Frazier Curtis returned to England *sans avion,* where his offers were again declined, then joined his friend in Paris. The linguist of the two, Prince tackled the French bureaucracy, which only after months of his insistent argument began to sense the potential of his proposal for enlisting more direct American involvement in the Allied cause. At last both men, with Elliott C. Cowdin of New York (a year behind Prince at Harvard), as a device for hanging onto their citizenship enlisted in the French Foreign Legion along with scores of their countrymen who were willing to carry their ideals into the trenches if necessary.

The three aviators shifted to Pau, in the lower Pyrenees — Prince horse country — for flight training, joined by Bill Thaw, a seasoned pilot already flying with the French forces. Injured in several crashes and not an adept airman, Frazier Curtis washed out, returned to the States and organized the Harvard Flying Corps. In the meantime, they got the financial backing of William K. Vanderbilt.

That December (this was still 1915) Prince, Cowdin and Thaw inveigled eight-day leaves back to America in time for Christmas. With her son home for the holidays, Abigail Prince was suddenly possessed with the terrifying thought that she might never see him again, and on January 2, two days before his departure, determined to have his portrait painted. The Princes engaged Frank W. Benson, the Salem artist and etcher of waterfowl, reportedly for $10,000. Benson took the train that same night to New York, where a room at the Hotel Vanderbilt was improvised as a studio. There Benson painted the young flyer all the next day, the third of January. At dusk the portrait was done. The following day Norman sailed on the *Rochambeau* with his older brother by two years, Fred, Jr., who wanted to enlist in the French Army and utimately gain his wings too.

For three more months Norman Prince stormed the Quai d'Orsay. And the French surrendered. On April 20, 1916, *l'Escadrille Américaine* was officially organized and assigned to the most horrible of the western fronts, the slaughterhouse of Verdun. Their headquarters, in the idiotic irony of war, were in the idyllic village of Luxeuil-les-Bains, their mission to provide fighter escort for a French bombardment squadron. While the Americans waited for their planes they borrowed a trainer from a nearby field, and Prince, whose faulty depth perception should have disqualified him at the outset, flew it through the hangar wall on his first try and wrecked it.

Six new disassembled French Nieuport single-seat fighters arrived by van at Luxeuil the first week in May, and the whole squadron pitched in putting together their *Bébés,* as the French aviators affectionately called them. On May 13, eleven months before the United States entered the war, the volunteers of *l'Escadrille Américaine* flew their first mission against Germany. The rest is history.

Some of the early members of the Escadrille who joined up by way of the Field Service and Foreign Legion had already experienced the horror of the stalemate in the trenches. For others it was a romantic

Daredevil congressional candidate A. Piatt Andrew, with pilot Clifford Webster at the controls of the Burgess-Dunn "hydroaeroplane," takes to the air against incumbent Augustus P. Gardner on June 24, 1914. Andrew Gray

Defeated in his first political bid, Andrew organized the American Field Service. The inspector general poses in France with ambulance driver Leslie Buswell, left, in 1915. Andrew Gray

Lt. Godfrey Lowell Cabot, pioneer pilot at fifty-four. From New England Aviators 1914–1918

Lt. Norman Prince, founder of the Lafayette Escadrille. From New England Aviators 1914–1918

dash from the polo fields to the flying fields that soared above the misery and the carnage in the mud below. It was in tribute to them that the father of a dead machine gunner, after viewing the photographs of airmen from New England, wrote that "the Yankee race has never produced a handsomer type of young manhood . . . the facial type of the young American of today of the best race."

But it was *not* a private war. Or was it, joined in by that silent ally, the New England conscience (blood ties to old England, old romance with France), self-consciously emasculated by the doctrine of neutrality?

Precisely as Norman Prince and his Escadrille flew their baptismal missions over the tortured earth of Verdun that verdant May morning of 1916, another Brahmin of an age to be their sire, Godfrey Lowell Cabot, was organizing his own private squadron back on the North Shore as yet another spin-off from Starling Burgess's yacht yard/airplane factory at Marblehead.

One of the wealthiest and healthiest (he died at 101 in 1962) men in Boston, America's leading manufacturer of carbon black was only fifty-four when he learned to fly the Burgess-Dunne at Marblehead in the spring of 1915. In a year he bought the western end of Misery Island, directly offshore of his Beverly Farms summer estate, and erected a hangar for the first of the four B-Ds he got a few rich younger fellow patriots to buy and learn to fly and fight in against the day when he was convinced America would make Europe's war its own. At the same time he leased Gooseberry Island, a chunk of rock southwest of Baker's Island, as a target for gunnery and bombing practice.

For all his crusty Bostonism, Cabot had the soul of the innovator: in the course of announcing these plans for his Massachusetts Independent Aviation Corps he proposed that for less than $4,000,000 the Navy could equip twenty-four warships with torpedo, fighter, spotter and patrol planes, and the catapults to launch them with. After a year, American belligerency and his own commissioning as a Navy pilot ended the private Cabot air corps. Lieutenant Cabot patrolled Boston Harbor in his seaplane, *The Lark,* and invented and developed the technique of in-flight refueling between aircraft.

As for that ladies' man with the carbon-black moustache, Starling Burgess, the yacht designer who generated all this activity aloft, he quit his own company when he was commissioned in charge of the Navy's Bureau of Construction and Design in Washington in December 1917, and when his airplane plant burned on November 7, 1918 (perhaps in premature celebration of the false news of that day's "False Armistice"), it never reopened.

Over in France, the myopic Prince vision that had vaguely visualized the Myopia Hunt dogged Norman on the ground and in the air, drawing from one historian of the Escadrille the mournful comment that his "notoriously poor depth perception had caused him to wreck more Nieuports than any other man in the squadron." Frustrated by many nearsighted misses but never a kill, he for a while settled on being the first in the Escadrille to down a German observation balloon with a battery of electrically fired Fourth of July skyrockets. Finally, on August 23, 1916, he picked off the machine gunner in an Aviatik six miles behind the enemy lines and herded the Heinie pilot triumphantly back to land in captivity. On September 9 he downed a Fokker.

On the morning of October 12, still in the Verdun sector, the Escadrille convoyed a bombing raid across the Rhine. Prince shot down an attacking E-111, his third confirmed victory out of 122 engagements.

As he approached a patch of an emergency field in Corcieux at dusk, his eyes deceived him again. Coming in too low, he struck a high tension cable with his landing gear and flipped. His seat belt snapped and he was flung to the ground with such impact that both legs were badly broken. Two days later Norman Prince died of an embolism in the field hospital. Croix de Guerre. Legion of Honor. His place was taken by his waiting brother, Fred, Jr.

Two months later, on the suggestion of her ambassador in Washington, France changed the name of *l'Escadrille Américaine* to *l'Escadrille Lafayette*.

The premonitions of a mother . . .

13

Right Here and Over There

BACK ON THE NORTH SHORE FOR THE SUMMER OF 1914 AFTER HIS FRUITLESS intermediary mission to Europe, Colonel House continued proselytizing for peace among the vacationing diplomatic colony, several times in September with Ambassador Dumba of Austria-Hungary. In spring of 1915 he sailed again for Europe, on the Cunarder *Lusitania*. But when a German U-boat torpedoed her on May 7 on her return trip with the loss of 1,198 lives, many of them Americans, in the submarine effort to circumvent British naval supremacy, all chance of an American-negotiated cease-fire sank with her, and he returned to America on the *St. Paul* on June 5, determined to persuade President Wilson to prepare for inevitable war with Germany.

House was still at sea when a cabal of like-minded alarmists organized the Conference Committee on National Preparedness under the influential industrialist Henry A. Wise Wood, a summer resident of Annisquam. Wood was one of the sixteen children of that interesting New York City mayor and congressman, Fernando Wood — a wealthy inventor and manufacturer of newspaper printing machinery, an early aviation editor, accomplished yachtsman and all-round gadfly on behalf of the numerous causes that arrested his attention, including the considerable challenge of awakening America.

As keen a Democrat as his summer friend and neighbor John Hays Hammond was a Republican, Wood from the beginning of the war had nevertheless been at odds with the secretaries of the Navy and War, Josephus Daniels and Lindley M. Garrison, over their foot-dragging under the yoke of the President's dedication to his see-no-evil, hear-no-evil policy of neutrality. That summer Wood put Hammond up to pressuring *his* summer neighbor Ed House to urge on Wilson the political importance of armament if for no other reason than that the Republicans were liable to make a telling issue of the country's lack of preparedness in the coming election campaign.

Certainly the Silent Partner needed no such prod from his old schoolmate from New Haven days, but every new voice swelled the chorus. A season or so earlier the heavyset multimillionaire had him to dinner at "Lookout Hill" one evening and got great satisfaction from relating how "he told me that he was called 'the John Hays Hammond of the Wilson administration.' I said, 'I hope you will have more influence with President Wilson than I had with President Taft; I failed to use such influence that perhaps I should have exerted.' "

That summer of 1915, however, House was unable to push the President as far or as fast as the preparedness advocates urged, in spite of the horror of the *Lusitania*. He met openly and secretly several times with the British ambassador, Sir Cecil Spring-Rice, who had a cottage at Beverly Cove. The basically pacifist Secretary of State, William Jennings Bryan, had resigned in a difference of policy after the *Lusitania* crisis, and his successor, Robert Lansing, late in July traveled up to Manchester to talk with the President's kitchen cabinet minister. In August Josephus Daniels arrived at Gloucester aboard the *Dolphin,* visited the Colonel, whom he disliked, and dined at "Lookout Hill" with Jack Hammond, Sr., who thought the Secretary of the Navy was finally coming around to the necessity of beefing up the fleet. All the same, quarter-steam ahead was too slow for Henry Wise Wood, who in December walked off the Naval Consulting Board in disgust, went over to the Republicans and after the war wanted to impeach Wilson for his advocacy of the League of Nations.

The Wilson-haters on the dominantly Republican North Shore were rabid on the issue of the President's apparently doctrinaire attitude of neutrality and his unwillingness to arm the nation, a state he had of course inherited from his Republican predecessor. Godfrey Cabot fumed that Wilson didn't have the ability to run a peanut stand. Young Lieutenant George Patton, Jr., wrote his father, who was campaigning as a Democrat for the Senate in California in 1916, "I would like to go to hell so that I might be able to shovel a few extra coals on that un-speakable ass Wilson. . . . He has not the soul of a louse nor the mind of a worm. Or the back bone of a jelly fish." And when Patton, Sr., lost, his loyal son credited him with carrying California for Wilson all the same and was mad as hell when his father wouldn't push himself for Secretary of War. Georgie was a foamier mouth-frother than most.

In the spring of 1916 Colonel House made the rounds of the bellig-erent capitals for the third time, returning to Sunapee, New Hamp-shire, for the summer to escape the incessant interruptions at the North Shore, which had become, as Hammond wrote, "a veritable 'hub of the universe': every important diplomat who came from Europe was sent by President Wilson to consult with the colonel." As the year dragged on and the nightmare of the war deepened, hope for peace talks glimmered once more, only to be doused altogether by Germany's sudden decision to attempt to bring Britain to her knees with unre-stricted submarine warfare in February 1917.

Visions of U-boats prowling off the beaches of the North Shore had a thrilling effect in certain quarters. The President was two weeks away from declaring war when the *Breeze* rejoiced over prospects of a boom season — "the war has meant much to the shore resorts of New England" — practically every available cottage rented (at $2,500 to as high as $6,000 that summer). A week later: "Jocular references to sub-marine attacks on this side of the water have little terror for residents of the North Shore, as is evident by the number of early arrivals this season. . . . In the minds of city dwellers there is confidence that on the North Shore there is security from any of the sufferings incident to the war."

In short, a lark. Then on April 6 Woodrow Wilson abandoned the role of peacemaker, and the United States of America, prepared or not, jumped in. The early exodus to the "safe haven" of the Shore, the *Breeze* decided just a little nervously the same day, was inspired by widespread fear of disorder and sabotage around munitions plants and naval bases. "The chance of a German submarine picking its way among the hidden reefs and jagged rocks of the North Shore to get near enough to land to fire a shot, is about as remote as the possibilities of the German fleet itself being able to get out of its 'bottle' into the Atlantic Ocean."

Lieutenant Patton, the abrasive West Pointer who had dreamed of attracting President Taft's approving attention in the summer White House days next door on the Beverly shore — and of shoveling coals on his successor — had won beautiful Beatrice Ayer after all. His first important victory. They arrived on leave from Texas at palatial "Avalon," her family estate in Pride's Crossing, some days after the "jelly fish" declared war. Patton wrote General John J. Pershing, whose aide he had been in the Punitive Expedition against Mexico, in his own highly individualistic style: ". . . All the people here are war mad and every one I know is either becoming a reserve officer or explaining why he can't. It looks to me as if we were going to have Too many reserve officers many of whom are meer children. . . ."

George and Beatrice had joined forces and fortunes one triumphal May day in 1910 before the flowered Episcopal altar in Beverly Farms. A jeweled throng attended, many by means of a special train from Boston commanded thence by the snowy-bearded father of the bride, Frederick Ayer, eighty-eight, patriarch of the Ayers and of the giant, sprawling, smoking, whirling American Woolen Company. Georgie honeymooned Beat to Europe, prophetically for himself, on the *Deutschland*. Back from the Mexican border, this more than faintly Prussian-type cavalry officer of thirty-one must have noticed that the war madness he remarked on to his chief was depleting the roster of the family club, Myopia, where fewer than six of the usual thirty started a meet that season. The casualty rate appears to have inspired one Hamilton huntress to pronounce fiercely, "We are all too busy and have too much on our minds and hearts to think of feasting at the clubs or sitting around just for mere amusement."

In pursuit of mere if rare amusement, the yacht *Mayflower* with her presidential cargo steamed into Gloucester Harbor in defiance of the Kaiser's *Unterseeboote* and dropped anchor broad off Hammond's "Lookout Hill" on the ninth of September, 1917. A Navy launch ran the Wilsons in to the public landing, where they were met by the Houses, who had been given only a few hours' notice; almost on the spur of the moment, the exhausted President had slipped out the back door of the White House and boarded his official yacht in New York.

It was Sunday, and the Commander-in-Chief and his party drove through the streets of the fishing port almost unrecognized, on along the western harbor shore, past Hammond's estate and through Magnolia to Coolidge Point, where they paused briefly at the House cottage and the Coolidge mansion to inspect memorabilia inherited by T. J. from Thomas Jefferson. Then a two-hour drive along the North Shore, the high point of which, one may imagine, must have come in Beverly, where they stopped to inspect the marvelous Italian garden that Mrs. Robert Dawson Evans had planted at Burgess Point in place of the summer White House from which she had summarily evicted the President's rotund predecessor, as *he* had evicted him from his winter headquarters. Alas, within a month the dauntless Mrs. Evans would be dead.

That evening the Houses dined with the Wilsons aboard *Mayflower*. Did the talk drift back to that easygoing summer of 1903 when Princeton's new president lolled with his wife across the harbor at the Harbor View whilst a couple of miles away the rich Texan and *his* wife relaxed in Magnolia, these partners who would not meet face-to-face for another eight years?

On Monday morning the men golfed, again in broad Taftian footsteps, at the Essex County Club. In the afternoon, another motor tour from Salem to Ipswich. Back aboard *Mayflower* for dinner, and on Tuesday morning the President headed back for Washington and the burdens of the war he had sought for three years to keep his country out of, an effort that rewarded him narrowly with reelection in 1916.

Now that the nation was in the thick of it, or soon would be, the *Breeze,* North Shore Society's conscience in such matters, predicted that summer activities must and would assume "a more serious tone." As indeed they did. Mrs. Congressman Gardner of Hamilton signed a summit agreement with eight other Washington socialites, viz: "1. No meal to exceed three courses. 2. One meatless day a week. 3. Simplicity in dress and entertainment." A flotilla of yachtsmen organized a Coast Guard auxiliary patrol out of Marblehead, where the Navy was in the process of taking over the Eastern Yacht Club as headquarters for its subchaser fleet.

And suddenly the "benefit," hitherto no more than a nonbelligerent excuse for a sometimes belligerent party, was transformed overnight into the determinedly belligerent one for a spate of indeterminately unbelligerent gatherings. There were house and garden tours, readings, concerts, musicales, specialty dog shows and so on for hospitals, surgical dressings, the Red Cross . . . and song recitals, God condemn the mark, such as the one presented at the Gallery-on-the-Moors in East Gloucester by the Duchess de Richelieu on behalf of the French Tuberculous Soldiers' Relief Fund, tickets five dollars, on invitation of the Duke and the Duchess and an extended retinue of patronesses from the North Shore summer colonies.

Albert C. Burrage was a small-town boy from Ashburnham who made it to Harvard, studied law and piled up a fortune speculating in Chilean copper. He summered at "Seahome" in West Manchester, grew prize orchids by the tens of thousands in his Beverly Farms greenhouses, cared for sick and crippled children by the hundreds in Burrage Hospital, which he established on Bumkin Island in Hull Bay, and entertained guests by the score aboard his steel, 260-foot schooner-rigged steam yacht *Aztec,* one of the ten biggest in the America of her day.

No lip-service chauvinist, Burrage offered Uncle Sam the use of his personal hospital for sick and wounded sailors, proposing to stand the expense of it up to $4,000 a month . . . and *Aztec* as a hospital ship up to $8,000 a month — both for a minimum of four months. Obviously Boston's Copper King figured the doughboys would make short work of it, once over there.

Over at Pride's a patriot of a different stripe, William H. ("Judge") Moore, was moved to admit the public for the first time to his private horse show, for the benefit of the Red Cross.

In Ipswich the Cranes opened the gates of Castle Hill (or at least the casino at one end of their vast swimming pool) for the benefit of the Scottish Women's Hospitals for Foreign Service. There, among the eighteen or so solid marble dressing rooms and the famous gardens, Society heard Miss Kathleen Burke explain the work of the hospitals, followed by Mr. Crane's "stirring little speech in which he urged all to stand behind the fighting men, to make one more step up the road of sacrifice we are all called upon to make today, and to help out the marvelous work which the women are doing in the hospitals."

Frederick Prince had by then stood behind a son, and in another step on the road he sacrificed the greenhouse to the coal shortage and a flower garden or two to vegetables under the "Hooverizing" of Federal Food Administrator Herbert Hoover. The *Breeze* sacrificed space every week for the explicit instruction of the Irish cooks as to the exact number of jars of this or that to be put up from the vegetable/ex-flower plots, and the wisdom of the Swedish cooks such as Mrs. Augusta Gallagher, long with the Ayers: "On the family table you can Hooverize, but you cannot on the help's table. The family will do with a made-over dish, while the help will turn up their noses at such a dish. If the help were kept to some rules, then the cook would know what she has in her ice-box for the different tables. The help rule the kitchen in many places and if the cook says anything, then she is considered hard to get along with."

Forty Society girls, as the war dragged into planting time in 1918, sacrificed nine hours a week in the four acres of vegetable gardens on the Dudley Pickman estate at Beverly Cove — equal, it was proudly claimed, to the labor of eight men. In manless Britain a quarter of a million brown-smocked members of the Women's Land Army were in the fields fighting the U-boat blockade with "veggies." Falling in step, the North Shore Garden Club organized a service auxiliary of "Farmerettes" to grow produce for the Beverly Hospital. Estate owners supplied land, horses and manure; the girls brought their own seeds, tools and automobiles, with and without chauffeurs. Most wore the national garb of the Farmerettes — khaki smocks, bloomers and leggings designed by Miss Gregg of the *crème de la crème* Winsor School for Girls in Boston.

In her library at Pride's Mrs. Bayard Warren taught her friends how to machine-knit socks for the doughboys. At Beverly Farms Mrs. George Lee permitted the folding of surgical dressings in her garage. At Manchester Miss Charlotte Read borrowed a car from the local Ford dealer, took it apart in *her* garage and taught herself how to put it back together again. Then she hied herself overseas in January of 1918 and signed up with the Hackett-Lowther ambulance unit of twenty-three English and two other American lady drivers. They were attached to the French Army, rated as *poilus* . . . and won the Croix de Guerre.

Relief work and rest from the arduousness thereof, soothed the

Breeze, would be the summer's theme for 1918. And though the U-boats had sunk more than a score of merchant vessels off the coast, the sensible Shoreite need hardly take notice, "for there is good reason to believe that our resorts will not be molested. . . . They would hardly waste time or valuable ammunition killing a summer boarding house or a cottage that costs less than one of their torpedoes."

A more sensitive barometer of war hysteria was the rise and fall of Karl Muck, so esteemed as the conductor of the Boston Symphony Orchestra in 1914, so reviled for his refusal, after America's entry into the war with his fatherland, to render "The Star Spangled Banner" before every concert, and defended almost alone by the BSO's guardian, Henry Lee Higginson, and angel, Isabella Stewart Gardner — both of North Shore summers. Dr. Muck resigned under the pressure in March, 1918, and was interned. Major Higginson backed him to the last. Mrs. Jack hurried to the jail cell of the maestro with an armful of goodies, as related by Louise Tharp, to the malicious satisfaction of *Town Topics,* which snipped that "her activities in thus rendering 'comfort and aid to the enemy' have turned her most loyal friends, as well as the public, much against the lady."

Inspector General "A" the while was directing 1,200 volunteers and a thousand ambulances in thirty-one sections spread across the entire Western Front and in the Balkans, and having his usual magnetic effect on raw arrivals at the rue Raynouard HQ on the Seine, where one of them never forgot to his dying day being brought before " 'Doc,' who greeted you cordially, told you how glad he was to welcome you to the Service, warned you of the — ahem — evils of Paris, made you feel you were the one man in all America he had been hoping would come over."

So magnificently did the men of the American Field Service perform that the initially skeptical French asked Andrew to organize an adjunct of transport camions after America got into the war, and soon another 1,800 of Sleeper's recruits were trucking ammunition and supplies to the lines. The ambulance sections and camions wound up in the U.S. Army, Doc wound up a colonel, and Harry wound up in Paris running the headquarters.

In June Helen Clay Frick, apple of The Man's eye, returned to Pride's Crossing after seven months with the Red Cross in France putting her

Beatrice Ayer and George Patton on their wedding day, May 26, 1910, at "Avalon," the Ayer estate in Pride's Crossing (below), and three years later with Frederick Ayer, Sr., Beat's father. Patton album

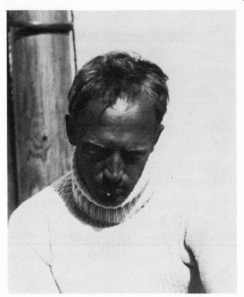

George and Beatrice Patton cruising on the Ayer yawl Tempest, *June 1913. Patton family album*

Frederick Ayer, Sr., his daughter and son-in-law, Beatrice and George Patton, and their firstborn, Beatrice, above the beach at Pride's Crossing. Patton family album

Pierrot et Pierrette. Who else but George and Beat Patton? The occasion and date are unrecorded. Patton family album

President Wilson and Colonel House relax with a promising member of the next war generation, probably at Manchester during the visit of August 1918. From The Intimate Papers of Colonel House

Charlotte L. Read of Manchester on the running board of her British ambulance, somewhere on the French front, 1918. Essex Institute

War or no war, fashion rules the Shore, and elegance holds sway. Cammeyer's ad ran in the North Shore Breeze *during the 1916 season, Schmidt's in 1917. Both were fixtures on Magnolia's "Robbers' Row." Essex Institute*

Summer Store
7 Lexington Row
Magnolia, Mass.

CAMMEYER
Branch De Luxe 381 Fifth Avenue New York
Exclusive footwear for Men Women & Children
De Luxe Catalogue on Request to Department 100

A. SCHMIDT & SON.

FINE CHINA AND GARNITURES

ENGLISH SILVER AND SHEFFIELD PLATE

MAGNOLIA, MASS.
Opposite the Colonnade

New York ... Washington
4 WEST 39TH STREET 706 CONNECTICUT AVE. N. W.

SUMMER STORES
Newport - Bar Harbor - York Harbor - Magnolia

A Bit of Unintentional "Acrobatics"

How an Observer Was Thrown from His
Plane 2000 Feet in the Air
and Came Back

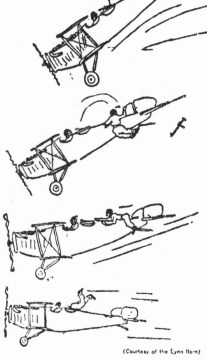

(Courtesy of the Lynn Item)

Lt. Samuel P. Mandell II. New England
Aviators 1914–1918

*Fighter pilot Sam Mandell of Hamilton
dove to get a shot at the same German
scout plane his observer, Lt. Gardner
H. Fiske of Weston, was peppering,
with the results pictured back home in
the* Lynn Item. *After the Armistice
the lucky Fiske married a North Shore
girl, Constance Morss, and summered
in Manchester. From* New England
Aviators 1914–1918

slender shoulder to the reconstruction of villages retaken after the devas-
tation of the first German offensive. Destined never to marry, this com-
passionate soul in 1909 had bought H. H. Melville's twenty-five-acre
"House with the Iron Railings" summer estate in Wenham as a country retreat for the poor girls from the mills of her millionaire neighbors. The estate was to be known variously as the Iron Rail Vacation
Home or "The Frick Rest," and eventually, when she made it the National Camp of the Girls' Clubs of America in 1954, simply as The
Iron Rail. Miss Frick spent the summer of her return from France producing *Home Fires,* an amateur motion picture filmed by Norman
McClintock that she planned to show at the Red Cross canteens in
Europe as a morale-booster for the boys.

On July 18, 1918, the French and Americans launched the counter-
attack that drove the exhausted Germans back across the river in the
second Battle of the Marne and turned the tide of the war. On August 8
the British opened the Allied offensive at Amiens that never again let
up. A week later President and Mrs. Wilson, accompanied by the White
House physician, Admiral Grayson, arrived at Manchester, this time
wisely by special train, which stood by for them at the Magnolia depot,
for a few days of rest with the Houses at Coolidge Point.

The President was pale and tired. Mrs. T. Jefferson Coolidge turned
over the "Marble Palace" to the Wilsons and their aides — servants,
automobiles and all — and moved in with her mother, Mrs. C. W.
Amory, in a small cottage on the estate. Thirty-three Marines pitched
their tents on the grounds, and heavily armed guards were all about.

The tense atmosphere and tight security were contagious, taxing the
credulity even of the usually phlegmatic Manchester police. The second
day of the visit the Wilsons and the Houses drove over to the nearby
home of the latter's son-in-law, Randolph Tucker. "A policeman on
the beat eyed us with suspicion," the colonel recorded in his diary.
"After remaining in the house a few minutes the President, Grayson,
and I walked out the back way, strolling along the grounds and taking
a walk in the neighborhood. We did not know until after we returned
that the policeman had followed us and had stopped one of the Secret
Service men to tell of his suspicions. He said he knew the owners of
the house were away, and having seen us drive up to the front door
with two machines, one of which he thought was for the 'loot,' and

then come out the back way bareheaded, he was convinced something was wrong and was about to put us under arrest. The Secret Service man had some difficulty in making him believe that it was the President of the United States he had under suspicion."

The Silent Partner had for some time been cerebrating over the implications of the war's impending end and drafting — with deep skepticism — a Covenant for a League of Nations that would incorporate the President's determination that all nations, large and small, should have an equal voice. The two discussed the dilemma in depth on the loggia of the "Marble Palace" overlooking the Atlantic, with flaming, ruined Europe out of sight somewhere beyond the shimmering horizon. Sir William Wiseman, Chief of British Intelligence in the United States, who chanced to be visiting House, was sympathetically impressed.

"I remember one afternoon in particular the President and Colonel House sat on the lawn in front of House's cottage with maps of Europe spread out before them, discussing ways and means of organizing Liberal opinion to break down the German military machine, and how the nations which had suffered from oppression might be safeguarded in the future. The Allied embassies in Washington were keenly interested and somewhat disturbed about the conferences at Magnolia. Rumours of peace overtures were flying around, and, with one excuse or another, various embassies tried to reach that part of the North Shore where they felt the destinies of Europe were being decided."

For the rest of it, there were walks, auto rides, golf at the Essex County and Myopia clubs, and plain loafing. Mrs. Wilson knitted socks for the soldiers, almost without letup. After five days, the sunburned savior of democracy departed for Washington with his party. Admiral Grayson said it had done him a world of good.

George Patton was General Pershing's boy, and when Black Jack sailed for France with the first units of the American Expeditionary Force in May 1917, he took him on his staff. George wanted to get Beatrice over too, but Pershing had already put the ban on wives overseas. In September Beat wondered if John Hays Hammond's pull with

Colonel House mightn't get her over, but nothing came of it. The "unspeakable ass" evidently was wired into neither the Ayers nor the Pattons.

Bored with staff work, itching for action, intrigued by the mechanized tin cans that the French had been using in the field with some success, George got the general to put him in charge of the tank school at Langres in December. He was promoted to major. Training, training, training in the horseless cavalry . . . plans, plans, plans.

Colonel George S. Patton, Jr., led the First Brigade of the Army Tank Corps into battle at St. Mihiel on September 12, 1918, under the commander of the IV Corps, a general by the name of Douglas MacArthur. Never before had American tanks been under fire. ". . . Passed some dead and wounded. I saw one fellow in a shell hole holding his rifle and sitting down. I thought he was hiding and went to cuss him out, he had a bullet over his right eye and was dead. As my telephone wire ran out at this point I left the adjutant there and went forward with a lieutenant and 4 runners to find the tanks, the whole country was alive with them crawling over trenches and into woods."

Patton was still looking for his first good tank fight four days later when, an ocean away in Pride's Crossing, Helen Frick's morale movie *Home Fires* flickered across the greensward of her father's "Eagle Rock" in its benefit premiere before an appreciative audience of the patriotic elite. To remind the doughboys that the nation was behind them, there were shots of school letting out in Manchester-by-the-Sea, the GAR parade in Beverly Farms, Farmerettes plying their hoes, and classes in surgical dressings, sock-knitting and canning. To remind the Yanks of what they were fighting for, Miss Frick had selected vignettes of the beloved "Bunny" Woods's outing classes for little boys and girls of the North Shore summer colony, a tennis match between Eleo Sears and Alice Thorndike, hunting and golfing at Myopia, polo at "Princemere," and whippet racing on the private track at Charles G. Rice's "Turner Hill" estate in Ipswich. More than $4,000 was raised for the Red Cross.

As if exhausted by the effort, with the Germans on the run, editor Lodge suspended publication of the *North Shore Breeze* on the first of

October for the duration (plus a few months, as it turned out). He blamed high costs and went to work on Henry Ford's assembly line in Detroit.

It would be the last American air raid of the war, this morning of November 5, 1918. Argonne-Meuse sector, 20th Aero Squadron of the First Day Bombardment Group. Objective: railroad and warehouses at Mouzon. The Armistice was six days in the offing. Piloting one of the Liberties was Lieutenant Samuel P. Mandell, St. Mark's and Harvard, polo, in every feature "the facial type of the young American of today of the best race," son of George S. Mandell (publisher of the *Boston Evening Transcript* and Master of Fox Hounds emeritus, Myopia Hunt) and Emily Proctor Mandell, and summer resident of Hamilton, on the North Shore of Massachusetts Bay. The previous day, on his seventeenth bombing raid, Lieutenant Mandell shot down his first Fokker.

They prayed for rain, but no dice. Returning from Mouzon after dropping its bombs, the 20th was attacked three times by Fokkers. On the third pass, German tracers knocked out an aileron, and Mandell's engine. Out of control at 12,000 feet, his Liberty "sank in great spiral vrilles from which its occupants managed to right it about every 1000 feet. The last recovery was less than 100 feet from the ground. It fell within a few yards of the canal at Martincourt. Lieut. R. W. Fulton, of N.Y., his observer, was practically unhurt; Mandell's leg was badly broken. The exact details of his other injuries are doubtful. The Germans marched Fulton away, and left the wounded pilot propped against his plane.

"The rest of the story is gleaned from the inhabitants of the town. About 4 o'clock in the afternoon, a German captain of infantry came to the bank, took a rifle from one of the guards, and deliberately fired a number of shots into the helpless American."

Lieutenant Mandell was twenty-one.

Total of dead, wounded, missing and prisoners (rounded off): 37,494,000 . . . plus one.

Anna Coleman Watts was a sculptress married to Dr. Maynard Ladd of Boston. They summered on the North Shore in Manchester. Toward the end of the Great War they went to France for relief work with the Red Cross. Making the rounds of the wards with her husband, appalled at the wreckage of humanity, she got the idea of making artificial faces for the disfigured soldiers. Her method was to make first a plaster cast from what remained of the patient's features, upon which she sculpted his likeness in plastic as nearly as she could project it from old photographs and her own imagination. After coppering this mask in a galvanic bath, Mrs. Ladd trimmed it to fit exactly the portion of the face that had been shot away, enameling it in flesh color, painting in an eye where one was missing.

Anna Watts made face masks for five American and seventy French soldiers. Two *poilus* in particular had refused to go on the street in daylight because of the horrified stares they attracted; the American sculptress masked them and went out with them for a stroll, and hundreds passed them by without a glance.

Back home again, the gentle lady let it be known that she would make a new face for any American soldier who had left his over there.

14

Wine, Women and Weariness

If for us there is some poignance in having finished an era of unselfish labor, even less stimulating it must be for younger men to suspect, as some of these doubtless do, that they have reached their zenith. . . . The spirit that led them to France by inclination, before the time of obligation, is the same that in considering the future makes them hesitate to dedicate themselves permanently to a purpose with little human interest.

— Henry D. Sleeper, in *History of the American Field Service in France,* 1920

FOR THE ADVANCEMENT OF SUCH PURPOSE AS REMAINED AFTER THE DEFEATS of the Kaiser and Woodrow Wilson, destiny decreed a reversion to Republicanism in the person of Warren G. Harding.

The new President's promised "return to normalcy" could not arrive soon enough for the nation and most particularly for the summer colony spread along the North Shore of Boston, which, having enjoyed a fuller measure of leisure than the rest of America before the war, quite naturally felt the more keenly the sacrifices incident thereto.

The first of the future's distressing waves had been of immigrants, eastern and southern Europeans for the most part, million after million from the turn of the century until the flood of 1914 was shut off, mercifully for ethnic purity, by the war — but only a year after the inundation of the land of the free and the enterprising from within by the most ominous alien of all, the income tax.

In the years before the hated levy many of the more pretentious spreads on the Shore were built out of surplus income by the plentiful, cheap and therefore welcome labor of Italian immigrants. The new tax began, almost apologetically, to skim off the thickest of the cream. Then came all the inconvenience of the war.

Patriotic estate owners bit their lips, cut back on maintenance and work force. New construction all but dried up until, as Nahant's historian Fred Wilson bemoaned (his father was the leading summer home contractor on the Shore), their establishments "may lack that last spic-and-span touch of perfection which was possible when money bought more." Many of the Italian laborers returned home to fight. Many more remained, at first as welcome as the Irish were in Boston when there was hard work to be done, but now, after the Armistice, regarded with as much hostility by such takers of the summer pulse as the *Breeze* (editor Lodge was back from the Ford assembly line), which considered them unfair competition for our returned boys "strong and true," living as these foreigners did under conditions "in marked contrast to the general prosperity of the Shore . . . a shifty, unreliable element . . . a distinct menace when they are interested only in prosecuting their own pleasures and interests according to old world ideals."

In response to such postdiluvial alarms Congress adopted the first quotas in 1921, limiting immigration in any one year to three percent of each nationality according to the 1910 census, up to 357,000. On the eve of the adoption of a far more restrictive new quota, aimed at eastern and southern Europeans, that didn't actually go into effect for five years because of widespread opposition, the *Breeze* chose the Fourth of July, 1924, to suggest that "any community has a right to resent being ruined by such an admission of aliens that our institutions and customs are endangered."

Long since, as early as 1920, Lodge had perceived an even more insidious peril from within, citing an unnamed student "who arises to call the attention of the white race to the appalling increase in the number of men in the colored race. So he sees the cloud in the sky of the coming storm, but it will be another generation which will have to stem it, if it comes." The editor's views continued singularly unchallenged in his letters column.

Surplus-siphoning, belt-tightening and the postwar depression occasioned by all the national and international gear-shifting — and the rediscovery of the wheel under the influence of gasoline, and the self-loss of the war generation under that of bootleg booze — augured the moribundity of most if not quite all of the patriarchal estates of summer and of the way of life they had sheltered on the Shore since the Civil War — and of their dismemberment and division, or, as with the inevitable matriarchies, their demise and distribution.

By the winter of 1921–1922 there was a definite trend toward year-round occupancy of summer homes, in Beverly Farms especially, as pronounced as the preference for the smaller estate observed with the revival of construction activity twelve months later after a ten-year drought.

Henry Clay Frick went out with his era, on December 2, 1919. There would be no more "Eagle Rocks" on the North Shore. Still, if the fortune was great enough and properly trusted, as the most Bostonish were, it was almost impervious to death, war and even taxes, and quite a few held their feudal grip on the land unscathed. The polo field at "Princemere" reverted to the pounding hoof and swinging mallet in 1919 — a hundred auto parties on the sidelines there one Saturday — thirty horses in the stables, thirty hounds in the kennels; that September the Princes reverted to Pau for the hunting, taking twelve and twenty with them on the boat now that the seas were clear. Soon "Princemere" had grown to a thousand acres sprawled across Beverly, Manchester, Wenham and Essex.

Mere Princes aside, the dowager queens of the Shore had a postwar problem on their hands within to match their spouses' without: cooks whose talents for hitting the spot had been welcomed in munitions factories were indignant at offers of fourteen a week with room and board, as were maids at ten. The word was out, the women's vote was in, the new quotas were choking off the supply of young innocents from abroad, and a red-blooded American girl, if she was willing, was finding that she could command twice as much in a steaming North Shore summer kitchen as her business college counterpart in a steaming city office.

The war had liberated more than bleeding France, but the bonds of female sexuality, sometimes self-imposed, frequently self-enjoyed, varied broadly according to class and custom. Fully forty years after the world of Victoria inspected and rejected *A Doll's House,* Lillian McCann offered it as her opinion in the *Breeze,* with a shade less than the accustomed deference of her sex, that it had not been entirely a man's war, for "back of the surface joy of the season that is to come [1919] will be the thought that we all helped to set the old world right. . . . Knowing that we tried to 'keep our home fires burning,' American society [women] will enjoy the coming summer as never before." And again: "Pre-war days of society, it has been said, will never come again. Everyone [women] was awakened and 'carried on' in some manner during the war. And everyone is at it in some form or another since. Society will always want to be doing something now."

One thing that Society wanted to do, now that the silliest law ever passed by Congress over a President's veto and adopted by the states was on the books, was to drink itself silly in the flouting of it. Between them, the Eighteenth and Nineteenth amendments to the Constitution worked to liberate both libido and spirit. And when Detroit put wheels under her (by 1924 at a mere $265 for a Model T Ford runabout), the goofy, garish day of the red-blooded American flapper — the first abortively liberated female — clattered in all its transient dizziness along the shore road at three in the morning, with all the boozy bedlam of a tin lizzie laden with loaded lads and lassies.

Still the mecca for the smart set, the North Shore Grill in Magnolia was bought in 1918 by Joseph P. Del Monte, Boston hotel man who acquired immortality with the Lost Generation that wove a path to his door. Del Monte promised his young patrons the best avowedly liquorless meals and the best dancing to the rhythms of the best jazz on the Shore, and he was as good as his word on all counts. In 1924 Del's four-piece band was featuring a youthful violinist named Ruby Newman, whose "full, round and accurate tone" was approved by the press. Next year Ruby had his own orchestra, playing for *thés dansants* in the late summer afternoons, evenings from eight til midnite, and New England's best-known society band leader was ascending his own scale.

Blanche Butler Lane, the little darling who nearly torched off East Gloucester's Hawthorne Inn leading her gang in Hare and Hounds with live matches, was a big girl in 1919, and still at it. "One night on our way home from Del's we decided we would collect all the red lanterns which sat on the little dummy cops (sort of pedestals) at the various intersections. This we did. Result, an article in the *Breeze* about the *vandals* who *stole* the lanterns!"

Liberation appalled and occasionally amused convention with the appalling gaucheries and occasional mere affectation of social adolescence. "Petting parties, without even the cover of a sunshade, girls smoking cigarettes and baseball were popular pastimes," the *Lynn Item* observed of Nahant's Short Beach one July Sunday in 1922. "The sight of two young women parading the beach attired in men's trousers and swimming jerseys, nonchalantly puffing cigarettes, entertained hundreds in the early afternoon."

Ah, the confrontations between the old hair shirts and the new shirtless, the itchy black woollen bathing suits (shot through with moth holes after one season) and the rubber caps, unisexed and sexless . . . and the beach flapper in her wetless getup of voiles, cheesecloth, nets, cretonnes, stockings, ballet slippers, scarf, feather boa and coyly carried sunshade! A "perfect figure" of a girl strolled along a North Shore beach, marveled Marion Dodge one July day in 1924. "She wore a brilliant red woollen bathing suit, no cap, but her hair, curly and bobbed, was as red as her suit. A pair of red, white and blue stockings were on her legs and around her neck a white fur. In one hand, she had a cherry ice cream cone and in the other she held a huge red parasol over her ruddy Fourth of July self."

The new sexual freedom inside the curtained flivver, the feast rollable from the woods to the beach and back, was neither to be marveled or laughed at, however, by those who knew a woman's place, and knew they knew. The goings-on and takings-off the length of Long Beach by midsummer of 1923 so alarmed the clubwomen of Lynn that they laid plans for an antipetting drive against the hated flappers and their naughty escorts. The churches got up a purity league, and the heat was on the local cops. The minister of Advent Church, Mr. Frederic Brooks, hurled a thunderbolt from the *Item*'s paper pulpit: "This splendid gift from God's hand has been used by Satan as a spawning place for the propagation of his species. Not only are the lecherous libertines and the painted vamps there seeking prey, a menace to our virtuous youth; but the sons and daughters of some of our so-called respectable homes are there in attire and posture that give convincing evidence of moral dereliction. I have not dared, personally, to allow my wife and daughters to frequent the beach because of what I have witnessed when riding by."

And to think that seventy-five years earlier the poet Longfellow had strolled so sedately along this selfsame strand, watching the innocent cows wend their way across and wondering how "their red hides and the reflection of the wet sand light up the gray picture of the sky and surge!"

The roaring side of the Twenties, and the awesome accomplishment of the same Congress that killed the League of Nations in creating, and creating order among, criminals in America, confound the chronicling as the waves of the sea. Every tenet of sane behavior having been broken in such ghastly fashion for five hellish years previously, a few billion more minor slips, 'twixt the ship and the cup, and the cup and the lip, during the fifteen of the Ignoble Experiment added up perhaps to no more than momentum of a sort. The Asinine Amendment was at long last repealed; but the underground of malefaction it institutionalized can apparently never be, nor the grip of cynicism on the public conscience.

Being a resort of both summer sailors and winter fishermen stretched along a coast of covert coves, bits of beach and involuted inlets perfectly suited for the midnight rendeznous, the North Shore imported and exported, it seems likely, even more illicit beverage than it consumed. Such of the saga as surfaced in the press or by word of mouth is more bizarre than jocular. A few examples will suffice.

Bill McCoy, a towering Florida boatbuilder and master mariner with a leaning for adventure, turned up in Gloucester early in 1921 looking for a fast fishing schooner, which he found in the *Henry L. Marshall*. Captain McCoy refitted the *Marshall* for a liquid cargo (the kind that frequently enough ballasted a hold visually full of codfish) and started running the best stuff he could lay his hands on up from Nassau to New York, where he stood just outside the territorial limit and unloaded into speedboats fast enough to outrun anything the Coast Guard then had in service. Thus he founded "Rum Row," the floating wholesale hooch business that kept the Atlantic seaboard and the Feds occupied until Repeal.

A few months after acquiring the *Marshall,* "The Real McCoy" —
applied equally though not originally to the man and his goods —
wooed and won the love of his life, the beautiful Gloucester schooner
Arethusa. She cost him $21,000 in swag — half her appraised value —
cash on the line to her receiver, General George W. Goethals, retired,
the builder of the Panama Canal. McCoy registered her with the British
as *Tomoka* and moved squarely into the big time . . . for a short time.
In 1923 she and he were captured. Big Bill served *his* time in Atlanta,
briefly — relieved to be gotten out of the business just as the gangsters
were getting in. He never did realize his dream of sailing *Tomoka* to
the South Seas and died in 1948, the most legendary and innovative of
all the personages of Prohibition in its heyday. They made him an
honorary Gloucesterman, you might say, and while ashore between
trips he dearly enjoyed to sneak in a round or two at the Bass Rocks
golf course with his fellow businessmen, and a customer or two.

The spotlight of public embarrassment focuses:

This here is a real plush summer mansion in Manchester — which
the hoity-toities call Manchester-by-the-Sea, see, so the visitin' swells
won't mix it up with Manchester-by-the-Mills — on Boardman Avenue,
which belongs to Mister Lester Leland, Esquire, of Beacon Street in the
Back Bay of Boston, a very important man indeed in rubber who
happens to be doin' the European circuit right now, which explains
why there ain't none of the family around.

So it's the fourteenth of March, which is the day before the Ides of
March, whatever the hell that is, in the year of nineteen hunnert and
twenty-one. This here Mister Leland's servants are holdin' down the
joint under the ever watchful orbs of the housekeeper, and there's a
whole gang of workmen, see, tramplin' the shrubbery, poundin' holes
in the roof, racin' around paperin' the woodwork, spillin' paint on the
Orientals et cetera.

Up the private driveway slides this big black sedan, and bringin' up
the rear a panel truck. They screech to a very polite stop, see, skitterin'
gravel all over the grass, and three very businesslike-lookin' gents climb
out of the sedan, march up to the front door hup, hup, hup, and the
front man gives the button a jab with a manicured forefinger.

Comes the butler.

BONWIT TELLER & CO.

The Specialty Shop of Originations

FIFTH AVENUE AT 38ᵀᴴ STREET, NEW YORK

DISTINCTIVE BEACH FASHIONS~

FOR·ALL SMART BATHERS AT ALL SMART BEACHES

Smart bathers in 1925 shimmied into the North Shore Breeze, *or elbowed into Peter McCauley's collection by way of Revere Beach*

A pair of Gloucester Midgets, the harbor's first postwar racing class of sleek little sloops, dashes along inside Eastern Point in 1923. Edward Williams photo

The glorious Columbia, *perhaps the fastest Gloucester schooner ever launched, smashes along off Eastern Point during an international fisherman's race with Canada in the early Twenties. The mainmastheadman waves his cap at photographer Adolph Kupsinel.*

Anyone for croquet? Under the matriarchal eye of Mrs. Emma Raymond, the mistress of "The Ramparts," who is suitably in black, a few of her numerous family wield their mallets behind the embrasures of the former Eastern Point fort, 1925. Madeleine Williams

Anyone for a trot? Sir Esme Howard, left, British Ambassador to the United States, leased the E. G. Black estate in Manchester for the 1924 season. Essex Institute

Sir? sez he.

The boss guy, very neat in his pinstriped serge, identifies himself as Mister William J. McCarthy, Supervisor of Prohibition Enforcement in New England, and these are my men, see, and he quick-flashes a badge and a John Doe warrant, and lemme talk to the housekeeper.

Up she comes on the double.

What's this? she wants to know.

They flash their stuff at her, and she backs away, and then like they know just where they're goin' the three of them waltz right across the carpets, past the lines of flunkies and workmen watchin' with their mouths hangin' open and down the cellar stairs, the lady in charge trottin' along behind, see.

Right to the door of the wine cellar. Where's the key, lady? Oh, dearie me, I don't have it. Mister Leland must have taken it to Europe with him.

Well, that's all right, sez the Chief, and he sends one of the boys hot-footin' it out to the sedan. He's back in a jiffy with a bag of very interestin' tools like you never saw in the hardware store, and in another jiff the door's open, and there it all is.

Aha, exclaims the Chief, rubbin' his hands, these are the beauties now. They sure look natural, those labels, now don't they, boys? Let's hustle along.

And he trots up to the front door, gives the truck the high sign, see, which they bring right up to the steps and two characters jump out of the front and four more hop out of the back.

This way men, orders the Chief, and they two-step in betwixt the rows of spectators, peelin' off their jackets and down the stairs to the wine cellar. Lively now and pile all this stuff in the truck, but don't break nothin', see.

And boy, don't the cases and the bottles start movin', and the finest kind of stuff, like the bucket brigade at the fire, and when the housekeeper offers to put up a squawk the Chief throws her a hard look and growls she better not interfere with the process of the law.

So the servants and the painters and all are standin' around takin' all this in, see, watchin' the hooch bein' passed up to the truck, and a couple of the carpenters commence to mumble and make noises like maybe this don't look to them like it's entirely on the up and up, know what I mean.

Well, it's right then that some of the Chief's deputies, while they're workin' along there handin' the booze along, get to talkin' kinda loud about the time on the raid they had to use their revolvers, and the mutterin' on the sidelines stops like somebody shot out the light.

In another coupla minutes the wine cellar is bare as Mother Hubbard's cupboard, and on with their jackets, and pack up their tools, and out past the servants and the guys.

Pardon the inconvenience, sez the Chief, and he tips his lid politely and bows to the housekeeper, and then into the sedan and off out the driveway, the panel truck behind, slightly down on the springs.

But the housekeeper smells a rat, maybe nine of them, see, and she calls the Manchester cops and informs them that a very fine-appearin' man who said he was Mister McCarthy, the Prohibition Chief, showed up with his deputies, a rather hard-lookin' crew, and carried off a hunnert and forty bottles of the best rye whiskey and fifty-seven cases of very, very good gin, which Mister Leland had stocked in his wine cellar all legal and proper before the Volstead Act was ratified.

When the cops telephone Mister McCarthy in his office in Boston, he is extremely angry and in fact fit to be tied because this gentle little heist pulled off in his good name at Manchester-by-the-Sea, see, at the bootleg price of fifteen bucks a jug, is worth a cool twelve thousand three hunnert and sixty smackeroos.

Two years pass, and our attention is directed to Nahant, where on a biting cold February day in 1923 investigators arrest Edward (Big Ed) Furey of New York at gunpoint. Known in the West as 270 pounds of confidence man, he is wanted on various counts in various places. In due course Big Ed, who drove a Cadillac and possessed several guns, was indicted and found guilty of numerous raids on North Shore clubs and homes in the guise of a federal Prohibition officer, seizing caches of liquor or extorting substantial hush money for his silence. Low tide suddenly struck Nahant in the neighborhood of Bass Point after Mister Furey's arrest.

Revere Beach, too, was said to be a busy nocturnal port of entry, "a profitable but dangerous business for all concerned," in the words of historian Clarke. "The danger came from hijackers." The ingenious Revere firemen converted a confiscated still into a serviceable pumper.

The art of the hijack reached its most amiable, possibly, with the disclosure by a prominent Eastern Point resident at a cocktail party, to a prominent Annisquam widow thirty years or so after the fact, that one night he had lifted $10,000 worth of booze her husband had run ashore and stashed in a Squam barn for safekeeping.

A common practice on the back side of Cape Ann was to torch a summer cottage at Folly Cove, and while everyone rushed to the scene, land a load across the point in the quiet of Pigeon Cove — or, for variety, vice versa. On the other hand, more than one summer resident of the North Shore arrived in June to open up and find an anonymous bread-and-butter note and a wad of thank-you bills on the kitchen table.

And then there was "Blighty."

Among those unaffected by the rather severe postwar recession were Arthur Leonard, stocky builder of the Union Stockyards in Chicago (financed by the explosive Myopian, Freddie Prince), and John Wing Prentiss, suave senior partner in the investment banking house of Hornblower and Weeks, who, indeed, is said to have profited prodigiously by it, buying up deflated Liberty War Bonds on margin and waiting it out. Son of Irish immigrants, Leonard fought to the top from railroad office boy, found and fell for Eastern Point and in 1921 moved his family into "Druimteac" (*drum-hack*), Gaelic for "House Back of the Ledge," a solid summer mansion of remarkable elegance for all that it was quarried from the ledge itself within reach (to the ultimate dismay of his heirs) of the winter surf that smashed the Point's dramatic Back Shore.

Always "Colonel" (a staff lieutenant colonel in the Great War), Prentiss began the climb from Harvard as a three-dollar-a-week Boston Stock Exchange messenger. Twenty-five annual rungs later, in the mid-Twenties, he had the sublime satisfaction of offering Henry Ford, not once but three times in a row, one cool billion dollars cash for his company on behalf of sundry interests he represented — and of course the sublime disappointment of being as coolly turned down three times in a row. By then Colonel Prentiss owned the twenty wild acres of shore between Leonard's and Brace Cove and had spent on his own self-quarried manse twice as big a quarter of a million dollars that he publicly admitted to. He and his Marie christened their pile "Blighty," or in the language of the blighters, "one's home place." They moved in down the shore from "Druimteac" the year after the Leonards, in 1922, complete with tennis courts, bowling green, and an abbreviated six-hole golf course.

Arthur Leonard was the dour, self-made man, always "Mr. Leonard" to "Mr. Prince" in tacit mutual abeyance to their unequal social status, Canute to the seas that filled his great hall with sand, rocks and salt water frequent Februarys, lone pragmatist, practical worker with his hands, solitary viewer of Gloucester's glorious sunsets. Jack Prentiss and Marie were childless; he had not his summer neighbor's inner resources, it would seem, hence was more lonely, more sociable, and on occasion the more mordant, particularly when in the liquor that he had no trouble stocking throughout the dry years when "Blighty" was the colony's social oasis.

Once in "Blighty" (to borrow a page from *Eastern Point*), the Prentisses established two institutions now indelibly of the lore: the July 4 and Labor Day all-day buffet, golf and tennis tournaments which by consensus opened and closed the season at Eastern Point for the sixteen years of the Prentiss primacy.

All the Point was invited. The luncheons were sumptuous. As for the tennis and the golf (and bowling on the green for those so inclined), everything was provided, including liquid fuel. The courts and the links were maintained as if with whisk broom and manicure scissors, and if one had arrived unequipped, racquets, clubs and plenty of balls were available in the hall closet.

Andrew Volstead might as well have saved himself the trouble, for the Prentissdom of "Blighty" recognized no twelve-mile limits. After the buffet and during the afternoon's play the popping of corks mingled with the crackle of distant firecrackers, and every spirit lifted on the flooding tide of champagne. There was always a bottle of champagne presented for a hole in one. All summer the courts and the links were crowded, and on weekends from noon until suppertime the "Nineteenth (seventh?) Hole" was open, a terrace room at the end of

"Blighty" with Teachers Highland Cream, soda, ginger, ice and glasses on the table. Every afternoon during the week Marie Prentiss presided at tea, warm and gracious, everyone invited.

Fanning (just Fanning) was the Prentiss chauffeur, mechanic, man of all work, arbiter of the fourteen servants, keeper of the Prentiss mutts, Hooch (an English bull) and Booze (an Airedale), and steward. In the latter capacity this estimable factotum (every factotum is estimable or he wouldn't be one) kept a spacious and seaworthy power dory moored off the estate in Brace Cove; by means of this modest craft he filled the liquid needs of the household on periodic nighttime cruises to some well-laden schooner out on Rum Row, financed with two or three of his master's numerous crisp thousand-dollar bills.

Not that Fanning had to crank her up that often. The boathouse of the local volunteer rescue station of the Massachusetts Humane Society above the Brace Cove beach was an undisturbed and convenient drop point from the sea, as one young fellow discovered one day while delivering fresh fish to the summer homes thereabouts, when two men suddenly emerged, stuck a gun in his belly and suggested he move on, which he did.

In time, Fanning did too, after the colonel's death. Legal liquor accomplished what the contraband never could, and after he drove Marie's brand new Rolls Royce, her very pride and joy, into nearby Niles Pond one night, "Blighty" saw Fanning (just Fanning) no more.

"We got our alcohol in a drugstore on the Main Street of Gloucester" (Blanche Butler Lane speaking, the grown-up little girl who perched on the piano and waved the flag at the Hawthorne Fourth-of-July parties) — "*not* good old Barker's! Down the street a bit further. We brought the gallon jug home and 'aged' it by rolling it across the kitchen floor several times. Gad, what days *those* were! A wonder *any* of us are still alive!"

A wonder indeed.

15

The Prince and the Ham Sandwich

A horse! a horse! my kingdom for a horse!
— *Richard III*

MIDWAY IN THIS DARING AND DECADENT DECADE OF THE TINSELED TWENTIES
the North Shore was visited by a prince, and once again by a President,
each as modestly endowed as he appeared to be, each endowing the occasion with all the modesty it so patently denied. Of the President, more
later.

Although long on names, Edward Albert Christian George Andrew
Patrick David was short on the stuff it took to cut the "figger" that his
grandfather Edward the Seventh did.

Still, in sacrificing his throne on the altar of an uncommonly common love, he carried it off about as well as most of his predecessors . . .
whether in battle, in bed, or under the business end of the executioner's
broadax. Shirtsleeves to shirtsleeves in three generations and all that.
The two princes of Wales were both rebels against the established
order of primogeniture; the denouement for both was somehow sadly
anticlimactic. But princes are not born to be pitied.

There is at least one reason to suppose that Edward Albert, Prince of
Wales — Eddie, among other epithets, to the American press — as a
horseman held a more graceful if not a more solid seat than Albert
Edward, Prince of Wales. Not that it mattered, but America, which
endowed the young Prince with a pleasant reflection of the glamour
that his countryman Leslie Howard was born to, and copied his every

cravat, had a perfectly matchless opportunity to judge for itself, and more or less publicly, in the autumn of 1924, when the gadabout heir to the honorary board chairmanship without portfolio of the British Empire was thirty.

The whole of *the* North Shore, and possibly some of the rest of the country, had been in a tizzy since the word was handed down that during his second tour of the former colonies (he had visited the States and Canada, where he bought a western ranch on the spur of the moment in 1919), His Highness would pause for a day at the Myopia Hunt Club. There he would be the houseguest of the Bayard Tucker-mans at their beautiful "Savin Hill Farm," and not only that . . . he would ride to the hounds . . . absolutely the most extraordinary coup since Harpo Marx actually played a harp *sans grotesqueries* in a musicale one evening inside the broodingly Gothic stone penitentiary on Eastern Point of Evelyn Ames, the shovel heiress.

The Tuckermans, it was revealed, had met Wales (as he was also known familiarly in the press) two years earlier while they were in residence with their horses at Melton Mowbray in the Leicestershire hunting district of England. They had gone over with Tuckerman's cousin, the Myopia Master of Fox Hounds, Jimmy Appleton. Phyllis Tuckerman was a Sears, and her husband was in the insurance business in Boston.

An awful lot of people — not all of them awful by any means — agreed that the Prince, though not brilliant, was amiable company when not pressed, and enjoyed a good time as much as the next fellow, and — unlike a couple of New Yorkers who some years back had traveled to Boston for the hunt — if he did not know his Greek, knew enough not to admit it. In Boston the New Yorkers had hired a hackney carriage to convey them to Hamilton. "What's Myopia mean, anyhow?" one of them inquired of their driver. "Myopia," replied the hackie coolly, "is derived from the Greek and it signifies nearsighted-ness." "Drive on!" groaned his fares.

The question of a number of lifetimes, of course, was: Who would be invited? Or more to the point: Who wouldn't?

Edward's destination on his second tour of the New World was his once-seen ranch in Alberta. But first he swung through Washington for an unusually awkward luncheon at the White House with the

Coolidges on August 31. H.R.H. was dressed with his usual startling informality, for some reason that has escaped posterity. Evidently this faux pas, combined with the usual taciturnity of the President, unnerved him so that his usual presence evaporated, and the royal guest was so painfully ill at ease that Silent Cal surprised his wife, his cabinet and his staff with a sympathetic torrent of unusually monosyllabic volubility.

Then on to Long Island for the polo matches between America and Britain, and the round of house parties and swell times that produced the famous headline "Prince Gets in with the Milkman" that so annoyed his father when the dastardly example of American bad press manners and vulgarity was brought to the attention of King George V.

From Syosset, Edward resumed his royal progress to Canada and the ranch, planning his return to Olde England via the New England hunting country. Security precautions for his October revisit to the States were notably less offhand than the odd ruse dreamed up for his grandfather, who, while Prince of Wales, visited Boston and even paused at Ipswich in his Scots guise as "Baron Renfrew." Originally the instant Wales was to have arrived in Hamilton on October 22, but he came down with a chill in Montreal that threatened at first to cancel the entire affair.

A day late, Edward's special train puffed into the Lowell station at ten in the morning of Thursday the twenty-third, and he descended the steps behind his white-coated valet, followed by his aides, Brigadier General G. F. Trotter, known to his intimates as "G"; Major Edward D. (Fruity) Metcalf; and Captain Alan Lascelles. The general was twenty years his liege's senior but so close, nevertheless, that the later Duke of Windsor wrote of him "I learned from 'G' Trotter that life should be lived to the full." Genial Fruity Metcalf, almost lifelong bosom companion and accomplished horseman, was most particularly in charge of the none-too-expert though terribly game equestrian side of his boss's life. Lascelles was a bit of a stick, admittedly smarter by far than his charge; his principal function seems to have been wherever possible to keep the reins on a chap he disliked more the more he saw of him.

The royal entourage was greeted effusively by its opposite Myopic numbers — Tuckerman, Mr. Jimmy in a great bearskin coat, Charles S.

Bird, Jr., and Dudley Rogers. All immediately departed the Lowell station in the host's "high-powered [never low-powered in the press] motor car" and upon arrival at the imposing English-style brick mansion house set upon the prime crest of the two hundred acres of "Savin Hill Farm" off upper Asbury Street, were greeted by Mrs. Tuckerman and her awed household. Light refreshments were served, after which everyone drove over to Myopia for a tour of the clubhouse and stables.

Dashing headlong into the clubhouse before the others, the prince found himself alone for a few moments with Blanche Wheeler, the telephone operator, who told an inquiring reporter later that "he just stood there and dropped his eyes, fingered his cap around nervously and then started walking toward the pool room. I think he's nice, but he's too bashful, I'd say."

The report of the day's events reads as if it were sent in by someone who knew horseflesh and the hunt — if not an insider, then a most knowledgeable observer caught between exhilaration at chronicling such a memorable occasion and journalistic cynicism. "Wales" struck the reporter as slender and of medium height, giving "the curious impression of being boyish and at the same time utterly sophisticated." The grounds and buildings of the Tuckerman estate were crawling and creeping with local police and state troopers, mounted and afoot, Secret Service men and, so it was said, private detectives.

"The prince's sartorial equipment," according to this account in the *Salem News,* "created a deal of interest. The initial impression of his clothes was that they were striking, not to say loud; at least they would have been loud if worn by an American. He wore a black derby hat, set jauntily on one side of his head. When he half raised it at a feeble cheer from the crowd, a white silk livery could be seen. His loose knee length overcoat was made of tweed, with astounding black and white checks, and was garnished in front with four large brown buttons." Light blue shirt and "razor-creased" checked tweed trousers topped off the outfit.

Edward and his hosts returned from the Myopia clubhouse to "Savin Hill" and at about one sauntered down to the Tuckerman stables, where Thomas Walton, the head stableman, had three horses saddled and waiting. The prince mounted Desert Queen, a nine-year-old chestnut mare he had seen his hostess ride at Melton Mowbray. Salem observed that the Queen, "sensing that she was carrying a noted guest for the day, proved equal to the honors and with her sleek body aquiver from tip to tail, loped away with her royal charge. Mrs. Tuckerman followed on Old Bachelor and Mr. Tuckerman on Buckskin. The Tuckermans have a dozen fine horses. Hostlers in their cockney were bemoaning that 'Desert Queen's too quiet a horse for His Highness.' "

Accompanied by Major Metcalfe, James W. Parker, the president of Myopia, and Dudley Rogers, guest and hosts proceeded at a pleasant pace across the lovely October countryside to Appleton Farms, the oldest and greatest of New England family spreads, as guests of the Francis R. Appletons for the start of the long-awaited hunt.

And now tallyho! The course was to be across Appleton Farms, through the Blair and Adams estates into Nancy's Corner at the junction of Cutler Road and Highland Street in West Hamilton. The corner was named for Lady Nancy Astor, who for three years or so occupied a house there (no longer standing) when as just plain Nancy Langhorne of Greenwood, Virginia, she was married to her first husband, polo-playing Robert Gould Shaw II of Boston. From Nancy's Corner Chuck Haley had dragged the anise bag (lifting it twice to provide breaks for the hounds) through the Burroughs estate over Vineyard Hill into the Smith Farm, through the Sargent and Hobbs estates and on to the finish at "Savin Hill."

Fifty or so of unquestionably the best and irrefutably the most socially impeccable horsemen and women on *the* North Shore were gathered at the Appleton stables, as Leicestershire-looking as could be in brilliant hunting pink on down through the spectrum of the chase — all but Wales, whose style was his international hallmark: namely, light britches, brown coat and that same black derby.

The pack yelped and strained in a furious wagging of tails and scuffing of dust, salivating with excitement. Every hair in place, the horses pranced and pawed and shook their handsome heads and whinnied with the contagion of it — the unaccustomed human air of deference, the pungent smells of manure and sweat and leather, the soft afternoon sun, the fiery foliage, the slight autumnal snap to the atmosphere. Old England in New England. What an astounding and anachronistic, playfully class-ridden tableau! Yet how perfectly, how movingly, was it all carried off! What style! What theatre! How deliciously was belief suspended!

Unhappily, it was the visitor, the monarch of all that he might have surveyed had his ancestors prevailed, who was not entirely at his ease for all the wishful thinking of his loyal countrymen, the grooms. His was the *noblesse* least *oblige,* too obviously to the perceptive observer.

True, Edward was gracious to the pushing photographers and willing to pose, but only if some American hunter posed with him ("His fellow guests," Salem noticed, "were not bashful about participating before the camera lenses"). And as the Master's horn signaled the start, and royalty touched Desert Queen into motion, he did smile and wave to the crowd of some three hundred — "mostly," Salem smiled, "pretty girls of the flapper type."

And yet the Prince of Wales seemed nervous and ill at ease, his smiles perfunctory. For he *was* rather out of his class, and he knew it. So too, without a doubt, did the owner of the last name on the roster of the hunt, Major (back to his Regular Army rank) George S. Patton, Jr., who with Beatrice was wintering in "Sunset Hill" at Beverly Cove, where he — they — had a string of polo ponies.

Early in the chase, while the crowd was still in sight, Wales appeared to take the jumps easily enough and was seen to glance back over his shoulder repeatedly at the other hunters and to spur his mount when his lead was threatened. But it was clear to the watchers — so contended the *Salem News* correspondent, at any rate — that the royal guest held the lead by the courtesy of his hosts. He kept his seat, though he twice nearly lost it taking high walls.

The ever-gallant Gordon Prince, who succeeded Mr. Jimmy as Master, recalled that "unfortunately the Prince preferred to ride with a snaffle bit, which was not what Desert Queen was accustomed to. Of course the Prince was supposed to ride up front with the Master, and this he had no trouble doing whatsoever as Desert Queen, with that in her mouth, could 'take quite a hold.' " This Prince graciously called the other's "a flawless performance under most difficult circumstances."

Unexpectedly as generous was the "mannish" North Shore sportswoman Eleonora Sears, Phyllis Sears Tuckerman's cousin, whom one Boston paper enjoyed pitting against her rival "bachelor girl," *demure* Olivia Ames of Pride's Crossing, for the royal attention. Although at

Of the Boston newspaper cartoonists, Collier was on the cool side.
Tuckerman scrapbook

Edward is met at the Lowell railroad station by his host, Bayard Tuckerman, Jr., left, and Myopia Master of Fox Hounds James W. Appleton in bearskin coat, and soon is up on Desert Queen, derby and all. Tuckerman scrapbook

The Prince of Wales takes two North Shore walls in stride. Tuckerman scrapbook and Phyllis Tuckerman Cutler

Prince Takes Tumble—but Not Wales

According to the humorists, a prince must fall off his horse, so the Myopia hunters lived up to the custom. Photo shows the upholder of the tradition. It is Dr. Morton Prince, who is being assisted after "coming a cropper."

Mrs. Bayard Tuckerman, Jr., in riding habit welcomes her royal guest to "Savin Hill." To the prince's right is her husband, and behind him, her father, Herbert M. Sears. Phyllis Tuckerman Cutler

Cartoonist Norman limns a more gracious good-bye. Tuckerman scrapbook

the last minute she elected not to join the drag (she had a superb sense of timing), Eleo gained the day in an interview that made a point of her long acquaintance as both riding and dancing partner of the prince, and his disappointment at her absence from the hunt. "Slight accidents that would never be mentioned were he not the Prince of Wales are repeated over and over until people believe that he only gets on a horse to fall off," snorted Miss Sears. "He is a daring rider and rides as if born to the saddle."

The Salem reporter thought otherwise. "Edward of England took punishment, though, on the last two miles of the drag hunt in the late afternoon that even the chivalry of the red-coated Myopia hunters in drawing rein to let him come first into the public view could not conceal from the thousands who lined the back roads and filled the seven hills of the Tuckerman estate. . . . The hunt had to wait for him at the check back of Vineyard Hill, two thirds of the way from the start. The Prince was all blown when he came in, almost last of the nearly fifty riders he had led over the Appleton Plains for the early, very public jumps. They made it a very long check on his account, and Hunt Master Jimmie Appleton then urged him to ride as slowly as he wanted to. But the Prince spurred on close behind the master when the hounds were let go again. And the courteous Myopia riders held back for him as they faced the colorful throng along the finish."

Two thousand spectators were all over the lawns and stables of "Savin Hill" at the finish, and they sent up a rousing cheer as the Prince of Wales panted in. Where they all came from, Salem was not so sure, but there were hundreds of pretty girls in the crowd, "all dressed in their Sunday best, with an extra dab on their cheeks. Some of them tried to give the impression that they were members of the exclusive set — and some of them succeeded."

Well, he had carried it off in the American limelight that fascinated and repelled him, and he had kept his seat. Edward climbed the terrace to the mansion with his host, changed rather wearily, one supposes, and then descended to meet "the neighbors," as the Tuckermans cozily referred to them — two hundred of them — and tea to the tunes of a small orchestra.

Afterward, a nosy reporter persuaded Helen Graham, the Tuckermans' Scots parlormaid, to open up her diary: "I took part in serving tea in honor of the Prince of Wales. I have been with Mrs. Tuckerman for a year and a half as parlor maid and during the tea His Royal Highness shook hands with me. The butler, who is also a Scot, has been with Mrs. Tuckerman for two years. He served for them in England, then they brought him over with them. He served four years in the Great War and saw much of the fighting in France. His Royal Highness was delighted to see Mr. Edgar with his decoration, and he asked him quite a few questions about where he comes from and how long he served in the Great War, etc."

And then — for the royal day was not yet done, nor could the princely bones yet rest — it was off to Topsfield for dinner at their "Gravelly Brook Farm" with the John S. Lawrences and fifty-four other extra-honored guests — and yes, oysters, lobster, chicken, and gigantic pots of Ayrshire cream for the princely stomach so recently indisposed.

And then — dancing in the Lawrence ballroom to the strains of William Boyle's Copley Plaza Orchestra — dancing first, His Highness, with Isabel, the Lawrences' nine-year-old, after which Cinderella was packed gently off to bed — and then dancing, dancing, dancing until three in the morning, when the most socially acceptable visitor the North Shore had *ever* entertained felt he *must* call it quits.

The high-powered motor car was there at the door. Good-bye! Good-bye! Jolly good time! Jump in! And Wales and his aides were driven by their elated hosts back to Lowell in time for his special train to get under way for New York and the liner *Olympic,* sailing for England later that very day.

As he was leaving the dance Edward did something that struck one of his American cousins as . . . oddly democratic? The memory stuck, and came unstuck in print eleven years later in 1936, just a fortnight after he had ascended the throne of Great Britain and Ireland as His Royal Majesty, Edward VIII. Dashing for the waiting motor car, "the Prince refused the food that was proffered, the finest and most select that could be procured, and whispered into the ear of Creed, the caterer, that he would like a ham sandwich that he might eat as he scurried along."

And, as all the world knows, they did not live especially happily ever after.

16

Swampscott's Silent Summer

PRESIDENT COOLIDGE WAS EVERYTHING AMERICA THOUGHT IT WAS BORED with but was good for it, like prune juice for a hangover, as the Prince of Wales was a bit of what it thought it envied but didn't want steadily, like double martinis before lunch. Both were throwbacks to the times, the values, the misguided views of reality that had led the nations one presided over, the other would reign over so transiently, into a tragic war and an aftermath fraught with folly.

Calvin Coolidge, the marbliest of Vermonters, was so indifferent a rider that for a while, until he was laughed off it, he resorted to a hobby horse for exercise in the White House. So it was not the chase that drew him to Swampscott for the 1925 season but the escape from it, from the most distasteful aspect of the presidency — people — just too damned many of them.

The agent for this second Republican summer White House on the North Shore was the Chief Executive's strangely devoted, self-appointed President-maker, Frank W. Stearns, son of the founder and head of the well-known Boston dry goods firm of R. H. Stearns, Tremont Street opposite the Common.

Stearns was the picture of the dry goods man. He was dry, good, short, pleasantly paunchy, gray hair and moustache, mild, unassuming, vest sprinkled with cigar ashes. One could fancy a tape measure draped around his neck at the ready. The perfect Colonel House or Jack Hammond for a Calvin Coolidge . . . except that, quite consistent with their unusual relationship, the President cautioned his mentor, who was sixteen years his senior, one day after glancing over a copy of the *Intimate Papers* of Woodrow Wilson's alter ego (the Stearnses had a suite in the White House): "Mr. Stearns [always *Mister*], an unofficial adviser to a President of the United States is not a good thing and is not provided for in our form of government."

The caveat was faithfully honored by the devoted merchant, who conceded to an admirer once that he had some fair influence with his lofty protégé, then governor of Massachusetts, "but it will last just as long as I don't try to use it, and not one minute longer."

The two Amherst alumni first met in 1912 concerning some legislation affecting their alma mater when Coolidge was in the Massachusetts senate. In 1915 Frank concluded that Calvin was the cool star for his wagon that would carry him beyond mere immortalization in the dry goods hall of fame. So he spent the balance of his ledger of the prime of life marking up Coolidge's political pricetag with extraordinary acumen, devotion, persistence, selflessness and, obviously, success, to the astonishment of a world that couldn't believe good old Frank Stearns wasn't getting anything more out of it all than vicarious satisfaction.

The Stearns family had summered in Hull on the South Shore but moved out with other wealthy cottagers in disgust after the garishness of Paragon Park was imposed above Nantasket Beach in 1905. After the Great War Frank rented "Red Gables" on Little's Point in Swampscott, entertaining Calvin and his savingly gracious Grace for several weekends in the summer of 1920 even as the governor's star was rising so rapidly over the national horizon as the result of his coolness in dealing successfully with the Boston police strike of the previous September. That winter Stearns bought the sprawling place.

Vice President and Mrs. Coolidge were planning to weekend at "Red Gables" on August 2, 1923, when President Harding died so suddenly of what was at first thought to be ptomaine poisoning but which was probably coronary thrombosis. Instead, they remained at the old family home in Plymouth, Vermont, where Cal took the oath from his father, Colonel John, in the famous lamplight scene.

The first presidential visit to Swampscott was to get away from it all after the death of their younger son, Calvin, Jr., of blood poisoning on July 7, 1924. In November this tight-lipped image of old-fashioned

Yankee values, hardly opening his mouth, so engaged the conscience of a nation scandalized by the excesses committed in the name of his predecessor (and encouraged by signs of recovery from the postwar depression) that he was swept over a lesser nonentity named John W. Davis back into office in his own right with the greatest Republican majority in history.

The inauguration stand had not yet been taken down in March 1925 when the White House let it be known that Mr. Stearns had leased "White Court," the stately estate next door to "Red Gables" on Little's Point, as the summer White House for the coming season. Standing on a six-acre knoll behind four hundred feet of ocean frontage, "White Court" commanded a view to the southward toward Nahant and Graves Light at the entrance to Boston Harbor. It had been built about 1905 by the late Frederick E. Smith of Dayton, Ohio, and was up for sale by his heirs. The executive offices for the summer would be located on the seventh floor of the Security Trust Company in Lynn.

Naturally this announcement set great social wheels in motion. North Shore real estate brokers were swamped with demands for estates where one could make a splash in the hope that the Coolidges would show up. All at once anyone of any importance in the country expressed an interest in visiting Swampscott that summer. The New Ocean House, where most of the White House crowd stayed, and the Preston were booked solid for the season, and there was a scramble among the Washington press for roosts.

A certain awkwardness among the summering diplomatic corps, lately at official swords' points, had been cleared up to everyone's relief, and the embassies were back on their favorite North Shore in full panoply. The Right Honorable Sir Esme Howard, the British ambassador, and Lady Isabella, already exposed to the social frigidities of the administration in Washington, did choose to forgo their usual sojourn on the Shore this of all seasons, it is true, but the new German envoy, Ago von Maltzan, Baron zu Wartenberg und Penzlin, manfully brought up the rear in a manor in the Magnolia woods.

If the President pleased State by choosing to summer on Embassy Row, he caused Treasury no end of aggravation by selecting an ocean view of Rum Row. Or so it was joyously claimed by certain newspaper correspondents in search of copy, who swore the fleet could be observed from the rocking chairs on the piazza of 'White Court." This vision of potential embarrassment was a hundred times compounded by the well-known fact that bootleggers for some time had outnumbered bathers on the beaches of Swampscott after sundown. In June the Coast Guard had come down with such a vengeance that the town fathers had to fire the police chief. There was a report that the Prohibition agents swooped down on Little's Point and confiscated $30,000 worth of whiskey from a cottage next door to "White Court," supposedly not "Red Gables." On June 21, a Sunday, fourteen of the Coast Guard's fast new rum-chasers steamed into Boston, with more expected along with a couple of Navy destroyers and a hydroplane.

For the rest of the summer the closest Rum Row got to Swampscott was thirty miles. The Coast Guard denied that there was any connection between the arrival off the North Shore of this task force and the impending arrival of the President, who was most certainly in favor of vigorous enforcement, though a spokesman admitted to hearing that the rum ring was going to try to land booze under his nose, just to give the whole country a horse laugh.

Two days after the show of dry force, June 23, 1925, the Coolidges arrived at Salem from Washington in three Pullmans and a baggage car. They were greeted by a local delegation, including the now Republican Congressman A. Piatt Andrew from Gloucester, who had entertained Vice President Coolidge at "Red Roof." The President was dressed with his accustomed ascetic precision and emerged from the train, according to the wide-eyed reporter from the *Lynn Item,* with "an actual smile on his face and a friendly nod for all around him."

The executive party piled into limousines for the drive to Swampscott and "White Court," where one of the Chief's first orders was to disarm the Marines encamped on neighboring Lincoln House Point of their rifles, leaving them only with their pistols; Mr. Coolidge, it was explained, disliked the military aspect. Almost at the same time, the presidential yacht *Mayflower* arrived quietly at Marblehead and anchored off the Corinthian Yacht Club, back in familiar North Shore waters.

The First Family (son John, an Amherst student, was along) had hardly tracked down the bathrooms in the summer White House when the cold water faucets decided to belch forth steaming hot water. Vice

President Charles G. Dawes happened to stumble in upon this domestic crisis and could not restrain himself from wisecracking to the news-hungry reporters that the attention given his arrival rivaled, almost, that accorded the plumber's.

On June 27 Mr. Coolidge held his first press conference of the summer. That is, it was held on his behalf. The press was summoned and permitted to submit written questions fifteen minutes in advance. At the stated hour an aide appeared and responded to those selected by the President for a reply. Oral questioning was not allowed.

Two days later Colonel John Coolidge was operated on in Vermont, and the Coolidges were driven up to be with him for the day. On the way the cavalcade of twelve cars was stopped near Charlestown, New Hampshire, by a large lady gate tender in a sunbonnet, who refused to let the President of the United States across her toll bridge until a Secret Service man came up with fifteen cents. The Coolidges were back at Little's Point the thirtieth, and on the first of July the Commander-in-Chief inspected the Marine camp on adjoining Lincoln House Point.

Thus the summer White House relapsed into its routine. The President was there for a rest, period. He occasionally walked about the grounds, now and then went for a drive, did some reading, and worked. He was not interested in sports or games, didn't fish, ride, swim, sail, golf or play cards. His single recreational weakness was the jigsaw puzzle, to which he was said to be virtually addicted.

Grace Coolidge, a pleasant and rather outgoing Vermonter, bore her husband's creed of the tight lip with resignation, declining all invitations, to the bitter disappointment of the North Shore set, which, in common with nearly every other set of society save his Plymouth neighbors, was anathema to Silent Cal. She enjoyed being driven over the shore roads at ten miles an hour so that she could take in the scenery and ocean views, and she walked briskly every morning, once almost at her cost when four state troopers on motorcycles came roaring around the bend into Little's Point, forcing the First Lady to leap into the ditch. Sunny mornings she swam in the natural rock pool down on the shore dammed with concrete. Reported the *Breeze:* "Mrs. Coolidge prefers to wink at the sun from under a broad white hat, rather than let him toast her to a ruddy brown. Passing up the lane between the hedges surrounding the Mitton and Brush estates on either side, Mrs. Coolidge only has to wander across the field, humming happily to herself after her refreshing dip, through the gap in the hedge and she is on the green lawn of White Court, her Secret Service escort with her as always."

The Brush estate, "Shingleside," was one of the architect Arthur Little's early shingled creations and had been acquired in the early 1900s by Charles N. Brush, a most sedate and distinguished-looking merchant of Boston. His grandson, William R. Brush, a boyhood chum of the author, was told that one spring — surely not the spring of 1925 — "Grandfather arrived at 'Shingleside' with his entourage only to find rather threatening rum runners present. At their suggestion, he returned to his home on Longwood Avenue, giving them time to complete their work, and found on his return some rather elegant champagne awaiting him."

Yes, that *must* have been another spring, for all agreed that *this* season on Little's Point, quiet was the word, so quiet that the high point of the day came at the end of it with the lowering of the flag at the Marine encampment. A brace of color sergeants and a bugler. With the first flash from Graves Light across the water, down came Old Glory and, as the plaintive notes of "Taps" trilled along the shore, likewise the flags of the cottagers. A moving sight and sound for the guests on the spreading porches of the New Ocean House, and always a gathering on Blaney's and Fishermen's beaches for the event.

President-watching was a calm and rarely rewarding pastime, as discovered by a crowd of Baker's Islanders whose destination one late July afternoon aboard the good launch *Melba* was the Swampscott shore. "A halt of 15 minutes was made in front of President Coolidge's summer home, giving the party ample oportunity to take in all the surroundings, observe the sentries pacing about the grounds and finally to cap the climax, receiving a friendly wave from the group on the piazza." As exciting as watching the grass grow on the "White Court" lawn, or the President having his portrait painted inside by Edmund Tarbell.

Less exciting than bootlegger-watching. What a scare one August evening when a notorious rummie cruised audaciously through Swampscott at midnight in his high-powered car! Six of the local cops were on

A smiling President Coolidge and his First Lady pose pleasantly with Rob Roy on the lawn of "White Court," the White House for the summer of 1925 on Little's Point, Swampscott. Lynn picture collection, Lynn Public Library.

"White Court" from the water. Swampscott Historical Society

Mr. Coolidge regales the press at "White Court." Lynn picture collection, Lynn Public Library

The terrace at "White Court." Swampscott Historical Society

The Marine camp on adjoining Lincoln House Point, Swampscott, on June 23, 1925. Swampscott Public Library

The President visits his executive offices set up for the summer in Lynn's Security Trust Building, August 1925. Lynn picture collection, Lynn Public Library

Silent Cal and his old political pal, Congressman Piatt Andrew of Gloucester, on one of the vacationing President's rare public appearances at a fete in Swampscott. Essex Institute

Mr. Coolidge, in a rare show of action, raises the flag above Lynn Common August 27. Lynn picture collection, Lynn Public Library

his trail in a twinkling as he idled along the streets near Little's Point for half an hour, then crossed into Marblehead, where he got the same kind of welcome. The Coast Guard and Feds were alerted up and down the coast for the rest of the night. The President slept on, and the bootleg chief moved on, chuckling no doubt over having more or less accomplished his mission for the rum ring: Objective Last Laugh.

In her own very special category of citizenry underwhelmed by the presidential presence was my Uncle Phil Lewis's great-aunt Emma Ireson Newhall, one of the seven Ireson sisters of Lynn. Ever since anyone could remember, Emma had been driven out around Little's Point on her daily outing. (If they happened to be on the sunny side of the road, which she abhorred, she ordered James to drive in the shade, on the left, oncoming traffic be damned.) One late June morning the carriage halted at the entrance to the Point. "Why are we stopping, James?" "There's a Marine at the gate with a gun, Ma'am." "A Marine? Drive on, James." And he did . . . and the astonished guard stepped aside.

Calvin Coolidge, son of the soil, had been at Swampscott eleven days before he set careful foot on *Mayflower*. On the Fourth of July, his birthday, he and Grace were driven to Marblehead for dinner in the main saloon, at anchor in the harbor. A week later they assayed their first voyage beyond the mouth of the Potomac, which until then had been the extent of the Coolidge cruising ground. The stunning white yacht, with her crew of 165, steamed presidentially the few miles down to Boston for a tour of the harbor defenses. Mr. Coolidge, in an admiral's hat, was seen on the bridge. His spouse spent the round trip knitting a pair of socks for son John, who would soon be off for a month of citizens' training at Fort Devens, west of Boston.

The photographers for some reason or none were excluded from this first venturing forth in *Mayflower* and raised a cry. To make up, they were the only press taken on the second, July 15, to Quincy, when the Landlubber-in-Chief posed as patiently in his nautical cap as he seemed out of place. Another week, and the presidential yachting party plunged valiantly across the bay twenty-five miles to Hull and back in what were described as rough seas — rough anyway for the press corps forced to follow *Mayflower*'s boiling wake in a twenty-four-foot launch that was nearly swamped by every swell, taking on water that threatened to douse the engine, pumps going, most of them hanging over the rails interviewing the fishes.

Twice more *Mayflower* poked out of Marblehead, for the Charlestown Navy Yard and the South Shore. Insouciantly that summer she would steam through the starting line of whatever race was forming outside the harbor, as she did one Saturday when Phil Lewis was crewing for Alfred Chase, scattering the fleet, almost capsizing the contestants in that wake. Mr. Coolidge was seated up in the bow in his sea-going cap, all by himself, preoccupied perhaps with the ins and outs of his tax cut program, or the coal crisis, regarding which he had lunched with Mr. John Hays Hammond, or an especially challenging jigsaw puzzle. "Fact is," Uncle Phil recalls, "we rode her bow wave, got a head start across the line, and it was the only race we won all season."

For a week in mid-August the Coolidges retreated to Vermont as if in respite from the seashore, though ostensibly to visit the President's ailing father. Hard put to it for news (how the press ground out a reported 200,000 words a week was the mystery of the summer), the reporters seized on the arrest of two Marines late in August, who were cast in *Mayflower*'s brig charged with neglect of duty while on guard. One of them, it developed, had been found asleep at his post one night. The dereliction did not produce any particular outcry.

Somehow, some silver-tongued politician persuaded the President to make his one public showing of the summer and raise the flag on what was touted as the highest wooden flagpole in New England, just erected on Lynn Common. The twenty-eighth of August. Twenty-five thousand converged for a glimpse of their nation's leader. It was a regular mainsail of a flag, and the President had a little trouble managing the halyard as it flapped furiously in the breeze that rattled his coat and ruffled the always carefully brushed Coolidge hair. But when it was done, and the banner waved proudly aloft, and the thousands of schoolchildren massed around the reviewing stand lifted their voices in patriotic respect, the Chief Executive turned to Mrs. Coolidge and was clearly heard by those near him to say:

"That's a wonderful sight."

Labor Day was around the corner, and the week after, the nation's business would revert to the capital. The President, a spokesman earnestly declared, had bent every effort to be impartial in his relations with the communities of the North Shore — residing in Swampscott, maintaining his offices in Lynn and his yacht in Marblehead, and attending divine services in Salem.

Mr. Coolidge was paid a call on September 4 by Donald H. Smith, owner of "White Court," setting off a flurry of speculation that he might be considering the well-advertised hope of Frank Stearns that the President would be tempted to purchase the estate as his permanent summer residence. It was not to be. The matter was not brought up, Smith told reporters. Early in the summer the press had reported that friends of the President had pledged $125,000 to buy "White Court" for him. He had demurred, so it was said, with his usual laconic finality: "I might not like it."

On the ninth of September 1925 the Coolidges motored to Salem and boarded the night train for Washington, even as *Mayflower* raised anchor and steamed for the last time out of Marblehead.

Whether or not Calvin Coolidge liked "White Court," his neighbors, or any of the North Shore at all, he wasn't talking. But then, why should he?

17

ainted Place

IN THE SPRING DAWN OF THE 1921 SEASON, W. LESTER STEVENS, AN ARTIST and sometime writer of Gloucester, made one of those off-the-top-of-the-head surveys and announced that there were more representations of Cape Ann in more styles in more museums and private collections than of any other place in America.

Surely he was right. Such a bottomless market naturally brought all the more artists buzzing around the honey pot at the end of such a rainbow (he calculated the summer invasion already at 600), and all the more buyers with cash to burn, some of whom, he observed, were attracted to the North Shore's famous art colony as simple lovers, some because it was the thing to do, "while a few, whose Ford incomes of 1916 have grown to Rolls-Royce proportions in 1921, come here that they may absorb and carry back to their woman's clubs in White Horse Junction, Arkansas, or some similar locality, the message of the 'Moderns.'"

Thus did Master Stevens, traditionalist among traditionalists, with one stroke of his verbal brush patronize both the patrons *and* the moderns, of whom there were precious few, for at that moment Gloucester's single brief experiment in modernism, the Gallery-on-the-Moors, was on the brink of defeat and collapse. Not that there wasn't a stray comet still in the offing for a firmament that had glowed to a Lane, a Homer, a Hunt, a Duveneck, a Twachtman, a Hassam and a Sloan. But quantity had clearly won the day, many of them, and by the end of the decade, in the rueful words of art historian James F. O'Gorman, the country's most prolific art colony was trademarked by "a kind of rubber-stamp Impressionism."

And such an outcome in the midst of such inspiration! Or perhaps because of it. Few are the artists, fewer the writers well starred enough to have come to terms with this most beguiling, most elusive, most durable of American marine settings.

The native Fitz Hugh Lane was the first, and as not infrequently is the case, probably the best — a man crippled by polio in childhood who yet captured the vitality of Gloucester and the fishing, the beguiling, elusive durability, as no other quite has. Lane was well appreciated by his knowing contemporaries before his death in 1865. Yet Lester Stevens in his 1921 chronicling of the artistic heritage of Cape Ann mentioned every name but Lane's. Twenty years later Lane's canvases (at least one of them, anyway) were being fished, if it was a lucky day, out of Gloucester's trash barrels. Forty more, and Fitz Hugh Lane, the Launcelot of luminism, was the star of the National Gallery, hailed — with and without Winslow Homer — as the greatest American marine artist of all.

Homer certainly knew Lane's work as painter and lithographer when he made his own discovery of Gloucester in 1873 at the age of thirty-seven. He stayed at the Atlantic House, still standing and restored now on the waterfront at the foot of Washington Street, and was busily, if not too significantly, engaged.

At almost the same time William Morris Hunt, of bald pate and flowing beard, back in Boston from his Barbizonian affair with Europe's ancient muse, was roaming the North Shore for subjects for his new-found insights, sometimes in his gypsy wagon of a painting van drawn by a span of horses, sometimes accompanied by a clutch of worshipful female students, seventeen of whom invaded Annisquam in his wake to immortalize the apple blossoms of 1875. Two years after that, Hunt bought an old barn in Magnolia and converted it with the help of his architect friend William Ralph Emerson into a studio and umbilicated, elevated gazebo of legendary eccentricity, which they called "The Hulk." In two more years, after creating an oil of Gloucester Harbor whose capture of light pleased him immensely, so masterfully realized that in a few strokes it ushered in the era of modern luminism, Hunt drowned at the age of fifty-five — by accident or suicide — at the Isles of Shoals off the New Hampshire coast while visiting Celia Thaxter.

The following summer, 1880 — perhaps drawn back by the tragedy of Hunt's death and the auctioning of his Gloucester work in Boston — Winslow Homer returned and boarded with the lighthouse keeper on Ten Pound Island in the middle of the harbor. Here, splendidly isolated within the mainstream, he perfected his watercolor technique with a hundred living, breathing, glowing, mysterious and supreme examples of the art. Homer the illustrator was as taken up with the interaction of man and the sea in all their moods as Lane the panoramist with the uneasy truce between ship and sea. And from Gloucester, her wharves, her fishing, her life and death, her work and play, the wider-ranging of the two was nigh overwhelmed, one imagines, with the inspiration for some of his most dramatic works.

Lane and Homer were as intimate with Gloucester as Hunt was detached, perched up there in his one-man crow's nest thirty feet above the ground. Somewhere between these extremes of impressionability was the best teacher of them all, the one who came closest in his diffident way to fathering a "school," the German-born Cincinnati painter-etcher-sculptor, Frank Duveneck. Here was a large, fair fellow with long and drooping moustache, who liked good talk and lolled about giving an impression of indifference and indolence but who lifted the creative spirits of all who came to learn from him.

After returning from hard labor in the Munich school of hard knocks, Duveneck took on all at once with a most successful show of his red-blooded colors in Boston in 1875 when he was twenty-seven. Hunt had barely preceded him, captivated the town by gentle storm and gave the younger artist a huge boost with his enthusiasm for the show. Duveneck's talent for teaching may or may not have been larger than his genius for creating, but it slowly got the better of his nature anyway. He returned to Europe for more study, and then teaching there, mostly American students — his "boys," the "Duveneck boys" — including that most unpaternal "father" of American Impressionism, John Henry Twachtman. Back from Italy, Duveneck became engaged in 1879 to a pupil, formerly Hunt's, Elizabeth Boott of Boston. They did not wed until 1886; a son, Frank, was born in December, and she died two years later.

Although Duveneck's biographers don't place him in Gloucester until 1899, his son, who was raised by his mother's family in Boston, remembers staying with him in a rented house on Eastern Point as early as the summer of 1893. And Lester Stevens wrote that the artist hit upon Cape Ann as a sketching ground in the mid-1870s with Hunt and rented the Niles farmhouse on Eastern Point for the season before 1880; his local obituary in 1919 had him summering in Gloucester for more than forty years. William Niles, an elder son of curmudgeon Thomas, ran the farm after his father's death in 1872 but was more avidly an amateur painter and may have been the agent of Duveneck's tenancy.

Several artists besides Duveneck are recorded as renting the picturesque old homestead on the harbor, beginning with Reginald Cleveland Coxe, the etcher and illustrator, in 1890 and including one "Eisham" in 1895, no doubt the critic and historian who knew them all, Samuel Isham. Duveneck was definitely there for the summer of 1898 with an unidentified fellow artist from Cincinnati, possibly his close friend Twachtman, who died suddenly, estranged from his large family, in 1902 while staying at the Harbor View Hotel on Wonson's Cove. And so Frank Duveneck may have fallen for Cape Ann almost as early as William Morris Hunt did and more than twenty years before his biographers have dared locate him there.

This amiable artist for many years kept studios at both Bass Rocks and Rocky Neck to take advantage of the morning and evening light across sea or harbor. His canvases are evocative, warm, comfortable, and full of color and light. He painted Brace Rock, off the back shore of Eastern Point, ten or twelve times at different hours, as Lane did, for the effects of the light. He could always find an excuse not to paint. One day he was set up on a wharf when someone offered him $1,500 on the spot before the oil was dry, and was turned down with, "I've got to take it back with me to show my boys that I've been working." In fact, home in Cincinnati, he placed the finished canvas in the Art Club exhibition for $800 so the club would get the commission.

As an aesthetic chauvinist at a time when collectors in this country were still buying third-rate European over first-rate American, this co-rediscoverer of Lane's Cape Ann with Hunt and Homer introduced a number of painters who would be widely influential in their own right to its always shifting theatricality as an arena of nature, one of the world's great basins of the plein air, a nursery of American art on no less a scale than the Hudson River valley and the Southwest.

Among these disciples who saw something new through the eyes of Duveneck were Joseph R. De Camp, Theodore Wendell, Edward H. Potthast and Lewis H. Meakin. All studied in Cincinnati, all but Meakin with Duveneck in Munich. All followed him to Cape Ann. De Camp and Wendell settled in Boston as landscapists (the former a portraitist as well), Potthast in New York specializing in bright beach scenes, Meakin remaining in the Midwest as a locally well known producer of landscapes and still lifes. So too, Ross E. Turner, who trailed De Camp to Boston from Munich in 1882, taught thousands of students watercolor over a long career, settled in Salem and came early to Cape Ann to sketch, as did the flamboyant, innovative, emancipative William Merritt Chase, who studied with Duveneck and Twachtman in Venice.

Like Duveneck of German parentage (the families were friendly in Cincinnati), Twachtman was twenty-two when the two traveled to Munich to study in 1875. He didn't return to America to settle until 1889, when he joined the coterie of painters infected with the work of Monet and the new European Impressionism, and affected by the snide expatriate Whistler, and that summer was drawn to Gloucester, probably by Duveneck. Twachtman in turn is the likely culprit in Gloucester's seduction of his close friend, the even-tempered, beloved and not terribly exciting J. Alden Weir.

Frederick Childe Hassam and Twachtman developed an undoubtedly productive and in some respects supportive friendship. One, Maine-born, athletic, a devotee of the outdoors, was as physically dynamic as the other was ostensibly enervated, temperamental and unstable in all but what his inner eye conveyed to him. The two palled around together, drank too much together and painted the New England shore together, with a common partiality for the Connecticut coast around Greenwich, and for Gloucester. Twachtman was much the painter's painter, and was joined in the plein air and in attendance in 1895 at the classes of Charles A. Winter for the first of many summers by another rising luminist, Willard L. Metcalf out of Lowell.

"Muley" Hassam (so nicknamed by Frederick Remington) often claimed the credit, though Twachtman with his scraggly beard is just as likely the moving spirit — but in 1898 Twachtman, Hassam, De Camp, Weir, Metcalf and Edmund C. Tarbell, Boston portraitist and pillar of the Museum School then painting in Annisquam on occasion, broke away from the Society of American Artists, itself a splinter from the National Academy, and with four friends — Frank W. Benson, Salem portraitist and etcher of waterfowl, Thomas W. Dewing of Boston, limner of dreamy damsels, and the muralists Robert Reid of Stockbridge and Edward Simmons of Concord — organized as the "Ten American Painters," commonly "The Ten," showing more or less together for another twenty years, William Merritt Chase replacing Twachtman on the latter's death in 1902.

Childe Hassam had a studio in East Gloucester up the dusty road from the old Fairview Inn, where in the 1880s the Philadelphia etcher Stephen Parrish boarded with his teenage son, Maxfield, more famed illustrator-to-be, and chum, Charles Adams Platt, artist and architect-to-be. They sketched and etched and painted the bustling harbor that so inspired Rudyard Kipling, Fairview boarder of ten years thence, to write *Captains Courageous,* though one short and queasy sail on a lurching fishing schooner down from Boston was enough for him. And that greatest of Gloucester yarns was the talk of the waterfront when the future "female Sargent," Cecilia Beaux, took a room at the Fairview to paint in 1897, nine years before she built her "Green Alley" farther out on Eastern Point; Bo had a studio next to Parrish's in Philly but was too awed to introduce herself.

After the turn of the century the influx seemed to gather impetus almost exponentially until the independent folk of East Gloucester and its pendant Rocky Neck looked around one fine luminescent morning to find themselves, to their surprise and sometimes dismay (pocketbooks excepted), harboring *the* art colony north of Boston, perhaps *the* summer art colony of America.

Here was the heart of it all, the wharves stalling the patient schooners in still waters, the helter-skelter sprawl of fishing establishments and shoreside emporia and acres of flake yards of pungent salt codfish spread to dry, the cozy inner harbor contrasts of bustle and serenity, the comings and goings of gray canvas in the breeze, the snug clapboard houses, Five and Ten Pound islands, lighthouses, salt ships from Sicily airing out patched squaresails in the sun, steam-puffing tugboats, lobstermen, dorymen, beachcombers and bathers, sailing yachts and naphtha launches, tall rows of trees, upland meadows, Dogtown scrub and boulder, the Back Shore in an easterly, wild as the coast of Maine.

Above all, literally, the light over and around, enveloping, permeating, insinuating, suffusing the Olympian amphitheatre of Gloucester Harbor and the very water itself, as if *under* . . . that evanescent presence of airy, heaven-sent light almost as palpable, it strikes one who has dwelled within its embrace for twenty years, as the hard rock shore. As well as any, John Wilmerding tried to put his finger on this famous glow "which seems always to clarify, even press against the configurations of land and sea. The contours of a landscape, however memorable, do not alone insure their appeal to an artist; but in combination with a seemingly present quality of atmosphere they can inspire the artist to consider aesthetic problems he may never discover elsewhere."

Not infrequently this landlocked, almost, bowl of the damnedest light you ever experienced, in its thousand shifting nuances from day to night and night to day, scowl to smile, season to season, has been compared with the Bay of Naples alone. And many the traveler has rounded the world, only to return, gaze about him, breathe a deep sigh, and announce as if he had the tablets in hand at last that there was nowhere, anywhere, for that interplay of land and sea and sky and inhabitants to surpass the old, old fishing port of Gloucester, on the North Shore of Massachusetts Bay.

Here Prendergast was drawn back summer after summer to dip and dab on paper the dreamy colors of an open-air tea party above the harbor (a *dauber,* scoffed the traditionalists of the colony). To honest Gloucester came honest yeomen of the brush, solid marinists the likes of Walter Dean, who would as happily sail as paint, Frederick Mulhaupt from far-away Missouri, Swedish-born Theodore Victor Carl Valenkamph and A. W. Bühler, well-trained painter and etcher, who shifted his ground from Annisquam in 1898 because there was more to paint over at East Gloucester and the Neck, more of the fishermen

Frank Duveneck galvanizes an audience, 1909. Duveneck House, Covington, Kentucky

The Ten American Painters. Front, Edward Simmons, Willard L. Metcalf, Frederick Childe Hassam, J. Alden Weir, Robert Reid; rear, William Merritt Chase (who replaced John H. Twachtman after the latter's death in 1902), Frank W. Benson, Edmund C. Tarbell, Thomas W. Dewing and Joseph R. DeCamp. Benson collection, Essex Institute

John Sloan and friends at the cottage on East Main Street, Gloucester, probably 1915. Seated, painter Paul Cornoyer of St. Louis and composer Paul Tietjens in straw hats, and Sloan; standing, clockwise from left, painters Stuart Davis of New York, F. Carl Smith of Washington, Agnes F. Richmond of New York and Alice Beach Winter, pianist Katherine Groschke of New York, and Dolly Sloan. Charles Allen Winter photo, Cape Ann Historical Association

Gallery-on-the-Moors, East Gloucester, photographed from the stage. Cape Ann Historical Association

and the way of life he so singularly preserved on canvas. And Leonard Craske, creator of that noble bronze colossus, *The Man at the Wheel,* watchman over the harbor.

Bühler found Annisquam as a young man in 1885, as the Parrishes and Beaux would, briefly, after their Fairview days, and as Homer did in 1886 when he and Tarbell, Bolton and Frank Jones, Henry Gallison and a few others called themselves "The Regulators." To Squam was magnetized the Vermonter William L. Picknell, fresh, strong, uncomplicated landscapist who dealt with canvases so broad and with such zest he had a boy trundle his outfit behind him in a wheelbarrow and squeeze his paint for him like a one-boy tube brigade. And Maurice Prendergast, writing his hostess, Mrs. Oliver Williams, of his 1905 visit — "the country and the seashore, the fine location of the house, the flowers, and the neighbors and the solitary tent on the dunes across the bay . . ." More than a Regulator, less than a native, was Anna Vaughan Hyatt, the sculptress of Gloucester's anomalously heroic Joan of Arc, rear to the traffic, mounted on a local firehorse; Anna was the daughter of the famous summering oceanographer Alpheus Hyatt.

Every summer a trolley guidebook directed riders to Annisquam, where "may be seen a score of artists at work on the beach, sketching some of the gray-bearded old followers of the sea who work away on their nets apparently unconscious that they are attracting attention." Not so unconscious, some of them. Lester Stevens wrote of one graybeard who learned that his portrait had fetched a good price during the winter and declined to pose for the artist the next time around " 'cause prices has ris'."

East of Annisquam and the granite quarries of Lanesville, near Folly Cove on broad, blue Ipswich Bay, settled Charles Grafly in 1904, from Philadelphia winters. Grafly was Cape Ann's first summer sculptor, foremost in his day, considered the leading American portraitist of men (among them Duveneck, De Camp and Hassam), mentor of George Demetrios, Paul Manship, Walker Hancock, who all stayed and worked their roots into the Lanesville ledge. Farther east yet, to Pigeon Cove in the north of Rockport in the 1880s, came John Joseph Enneking, Cincinnati-educated Impressionist, early influence on the young Hassam, getting the hang of the New England landscape that would bring him fame; and there, too, strolled Duveneck in desultory search of subjects. But Cape Ann's far shore was rough and lee and sparked inspiration in only the sturdiest though not necessarily flintiest of souls.

For the more easily inspired in these frontier days of the colony, the quaint fishing and lobstering and quarrying village of Rockport lay complacently ahead. Down on the shore in 1873 a self-taught young fellow of twenty-one, Gilbert Tucker Margeson, set up his easel in a shack, sharing with Homer the rediscovery of Cape Ann if not the honors, and he was still at it seventy-two years later, bringing up the rear of the parade he had led.

The day came when the fishermen could not afford not to sell their shanties on Bearskin Neck to that parade, the originality of whose marching song was emblazoned on the marching mile of canvas as the too-familiar red wharf shed derided by one bored art teacher as "Motif Number One." And the day came, too, in 1978, when the Rockport colonists and their symbiotic swarm of crafts- and tradespersons could not afford not — so they swore — to replace this too-common trademark of the lowest denominator with an exact copy (the measurements had already been taken against such a catastrophe) when the "Motif" disintegrated at the height of a storm. But of course alluring Rockport, like picturesque Provincetown and charming Rocky Neck, has attracted many the fine artist impassive or private enough to shrug off such stigmata of the market.

For all its visual attractions, its intimacy, its undoubted paintability, Rockport has so far not been gifted with the chemistry for greatness. Gloucester was, and is. She was and is dirty, dazzling and dynamic. Had Winslow Homer and Gilbert Margeson traded easels that summer of 1873, the course of marine painting . . . that summer . . . would have been different.

Their own veils lifted in Europe, the Impressionists had opened America's eyes inward, to dreams of life as God had wrought it to be, to Gardens of Eden populated by exquisitely kissable young women floating across mauve meadows in the early morning haze of the American happy land. Odd bedfellows, some of them, but The Ten — so happily Gloucesterized, most of them — had struck a blow for the tariff: Buy American, they declaimed, and were heeded.

Along came "The Eight" in 1908 in a single show (thereafter they hung separately) assembled by the progressive New York art teacher Robert Henri. What a contrast to The Ten! "What shocked the world of art was a preoccupation with types, localities, and incidents to which Americans were conveniently deaf and blind," art historian Oliver W. Larkin has written with a nice irony. "A degree of strenuousness could be forgiven in the days of Teddy Roosevelt; but to paint drunks and slatterns, pushcart peddlers and coal mines, bedrooms and barrooms was somehow to be classed among the socialists, anarchists, and other disturbers of the prosperous equilibrium." But the *Ashcan School!* Ridiculous!

And again, there was the common thread of Cape Ann. Of The Eight, mild Maurice Prendergast, with a foot in both camps, had to be the sentimental favorite. Three of the others as well, John Sloan and his pal William Glackens, and Ernest Lawson (who absorbed his technical nuances from Twachtman and Weir) were influenced to varying degrees of profundity by their exposure to the land of light, whose effects, if any, on George Luks, Arthur Davies, Everett Shinn and Henri are moot.

And then, along came Europe again — always Europe — crudely nude, disarticulating down an abstract tumble of stairs at the Armory Show. That bombshell of modernism exploded in mid-Manhattan in 1913, and in the back alleys of John Sloan's head, clearing his visual landscape in one clean sweep that propelled him to Gloucester, which must already have been beckoning through his friends and those he wanted to know there.

Square-jawed John and Dolly Sloan, and Charles Winter (old teacher of Twachtman, bridge to The Eight) and his artist wife Alice, took for the 1914 season a cottage that is still standing on East Main Street in East Gloucester above the causeway to Rocky Neck. Next summer they were joined by the much younger Stuart Davis, even more mind-blown by the Armory Show, for the first of his many years in Gloucester with his wild brush and poster colors.

Sloan spent but five summers in Gloucester, spanning the war in which he was too old to serve, but they were the most productive of his life, the fork in a career that led him from the monotones of the big city to the full spectrum of land and sea at Cape Ann, and finally of desert and mountain in the Southwest — five summers that "immeasurably enriched his own production," in the estimate of James O'Gorman, who has shed new light on the development of the Cape Ann art colony as no other has, "and significantly brightened America's artistic heritage."

But how truly was the Great War a Great Divide in time and place, separating the rightness in some things and the wrongness in others!

There is noble irony in the appearance, in the middle of it, on the East Gloucester scene of a pair of patrons dedicated to forward movement in the arts whose very intentions bore the seeds of their disappointment. These were William Atwood, a civilized Connecticut textile manufacturer and amateur artist, and his gracious wife, Emmeline.

Finding the artists all roundabout trying to seduce the muse (and the custom) in waterfront warrens of "dark little lofts, old outhouses, chicken coops, stables, tiny rooms, poorly lighted and unattractive," the Atwoods took the extraordinary step of buying upland above the Sloan-Davis-Winter cottage and engaging the Boston architect Ralph Adams Cram to design and build the medieval-revival "Gallery-on-the-Moors," and nearby, their own summer home, "House-on-the-Moors." In the midwar year of 1916 the Gloucester colony's first genuine gallery opened, with high promise. A Duveneck was the centerpiece. The Atwoods would accept no commissions. All was for the artists' sake.

As so frequently is the reward for the Samaritan who pokes his nose into the business of those beside the wayside, the benefactors within a couple of seasons were being roundly if sotte voce muttered at by many and possibly most of the nose-bent colonists who found their work excluded from the new gallery by the well-intended efforts of the owners to decorate their walls according to certain standards.

It is said that Sloan had sold one painting before he came to Gloucester, and that at the Atwoods' gallery he sold none. The market was seeking its own level. East Gloucester was alive with artists . . . or dying from them, as one writer lamented, the new bungalows "elbowing out" the old fisherman who "clings to the olden days. These radical changes almost make him weep. He is oftentimes seen lost in contemplation of the 'curse' that has overtaken Rocky Neck." For the solitary painter there was hardly anywhere left to be alone. Gone were the days when my Great-Granduncle Will Niles would disagreeably turn his easel around at the approach of an innocent kibitzer, and William Morris Hunt draped himself with sandwich boards advising I CAN'T TALK and I CAN'T HEAR. Even gregarious Lester Stevens was wont to pine for his boyhood when he and his art teacher "would wander all day through the fields, or along the shore, and never meet another painter."

Sloan gave up painting in the streets of Gloucester after a disagreeable encounter with a drunken fisherman (no more ashcans for him!) and fared no better with his peers, complaining to his friend Van Wyck Brooks that he had no use for art colonies (though he could not stay long away from them), that "there was an artist's shadow beside every cow in Gloucester, and the cows themselves were dying from eating paint-rags," and that he could see why the natives called the summer people "summer vermin."

By the summer of 1919 the war was over. John and Dolly Sloan abandoned Gloucester forever for Sante Fe. Stuart Davis took off for Cuba. Frank Duveneck died, and so did Alden Weir, the third of The Ten to pass away, The Ten who were by now almost passé.

And the Atwoods surrendered. The show that season was hung by a jury selected by the colony and dominated by landscapes executed, according to one caustic critic, "to catch the eye of the wealthy tourist." For three more seasons the Atwoods compromised their tastes.

There would be lonely exceptions wandering across the landscape — Edward Hopper, Marsden Hartley and a few others. But Gloucester was overrun, now that the war was over, with the Pharisees of the familiar, of the endless surf upon an endless shore, of the seagull and the saccharin, of blue canvas and green paper.

In 1922 the artists organized the North Shore Arts Association, bought a hulking old warehouse on Reed's Wharf with acres of walls. The Gallery-on-the-Moors tiptoed out with a last small show. Deftly, the victors installed the Samaritan as their first president.

But of course painters paint to be hung, as writers who are not critics write about painters to be drawn and quartered!

18

All the Shore's a Stage

AS FOR THE ATWOODS, DEFEATED IN THEIR QUIXOTIC TILT WITH THE WIND-milling jury system of the Gloucester art establishment, they carried, as luck would have it, a spare lance. By 1918, when already they could see how the breeze was blowing, they were planning a community theatre, these two, in their Gallery-on-the-Moors — rather in the forefront, too, of the summer theatre movement, close behind Ogunquit and Detroit.

Happily for Cape Ann and the theatre at large, Florence Cunningham, a Gloucester-born graduate of Vassar College then teaching spoken English at Smith to the barbarian girls of Northampton, heard of the couple's plan, offered promptly to take charge, and was gratefully taken up. With the catching enthusiasm that carried her through a long and distinguished career, she recruited a local cast behind the almost too professional and unforgivably handsome Leslie Buswell, that young English actor returned from ambulance-driving in France and residing, for the nonce, with his friend John Hays Hammond, Jr., on the other shore of Gloucester Harbor in Jack's "Bungalow," a precipitous drop below the family's "Lookout Hill."

After getting off to a patriotic start that final summer of the war with an outdoor pageant for the benefit of "Bundles for Britain," the gallery in its evening dress as the "Playhouse-on-the-Moors" presented three one-act plays, beginning with *Land of Heart's Desire* by Yeats. Success overnight. The director lady had a knack for matching types with roles, such as the Gloucester policeman she followed on his beat one day until she screwed up the courage to recruit him for the cop in *Two*

Crooks and a Lady. The artist John Sloan, on the other hand, was too shy to tread the Playhouse boards, though he convulsed his intimates with his pantomimes and his impersonations of Woodrow Wilson.

Eastern Point's Dabsville and friends, naturally, patronized this so interesting experiment occurring just on the edge of their pale. Buswell had been one of Mrs. Jack Gardner's favored young men ever since she saw him in a juvenile lead. She got Leslie to read aloud to her to improve her diction, not that it needed it. He, in turn, got the players to put on a pair of one-acters as a delayed birthday present in the Gothic Room at Fenway Court on the eleventh of June, 1922; Isabella had been eighty-two for two months.

"Mrs. Atwood and I went to make the arrangements with Mrs. Gardner," Florence Cunningham recalled to the journalist Paul Kenyon years afterwards. " 'We shall need a small table and a few chairs,' I said, 'but we can easily find those in this room.'

" 'Oh no,' said Mrs. Gardner. 'You may not use anything in this room.' It was the large room of the Rembrandts, now protected in white cloths, the room used for concerts by well known musicians.

" 'No difficulty,' I said. 'We can get the little umbrella stand from Mrs. Evans's school; we can get everything we need there.' [Florence Evans ran a speech and diction school in Boston.]

" 'The performance must begin at exactly 25 minutes after two on Sunday afternoon,' said Mrs. Gardner as she took her seat in the elevator going to her rooms on the third floor.

"And so it was that we gathered about lunchtime in a kind of laundry room on the first floor to go over lines of an act from Maeterlinck's *Monna Vanna* and Lord Dunsany's *A Night at an Inn,* in which Leslie Buswell played the lead. I cannot remember the other actors except one portly Irish woman who was most indignant because we had to bring our own lunches and enter by the kitchen door. No one was paid, of course.

"On the dot at 2:25 we began our show before an elite audience. Harvard's President Lowell, also Henry Cabot Lodge, I believe, and a few others of their stature. Mrs. Gardner wore a lovely white gown and the Catherine of Russia pearls. Everyone had a front seat as there were only about a dozen guests. . . . The actors left as quietly as they had come and they delivered the umbrella stand and the chairs to Mrs.

Evans's school on Beacon Street on their way back to Gloucester." A thunderstorm had obligingly swept across the Fenway during the storm scene in *Monna Vanna*. Mrs. Jack always traveled, or stayed at home, first class.

Magnet as it was for a mixture of amateur and professional talent, the Playhouse-on-the-Moors was strong up front but weak backstage. Always resourceful, Cunningham rang in Evans, the quite-as-resourceful diction teacher and drama coach. The two Florences rented the huge paint shop of the Rocky Neck Marine Railways and opened the Gloucester School of the Theatre in this old place of interesting odors in the summer of 1919.

Like its companion playhouse, which the indefatigable Cunningham continued to direct by day, the "Little Theatre" — as everyone was soon calling it — was by night one of the first of its kind in the country. One-act plays on the ground floor at first to a small audience, then on to full productions when the upper stories were removed for a regular stage and a whitewashed auditorium seating two hundred always-enthralled goers.

The incredible firetrap of a paint shop projected partly on piles — "spiles" they call them in Gloucester — over the reeking inner harbor. From a deck, the enchanted patrons had cool summer-evening-wafted smells and views and sounds of the water, the lit city across the channel, the riding lights of the fishing vessels and the twinkling stars above. Usherettes wore sailor suits, and the curtain was raised like a sail to the nautical clang of a ship's bell. One night, as if responding in some ghostly fashion to O'Neill's stage directions for *Anna Christie,* the fog rolled in and a passing schooner's blast sent spine-tingling thrills through the theatre. 'Twas magic, pure magic.

Nearby guesthouses were commandeered as men's and women's dormitories, and a dining room and entr'actes snack bar. "Early in the game," Miss Cunningham wrote the author several years before her death in 1980 at the age of ninety-two, "Delacroix Eurythmics was in our curriculum, and the girls wore Annette Kellerman bathing suits. This shocked — and interested — the fishermen around the wharves."

Although nationally known and respected in the more than three decades of its existence before Florence Cunningham's reputation brought her a summons to Hollywood as a dramatic and linguistic coach for the stars in 1950, Gloucester's Little Theatre catapulted no great names onto the marquees. But Russel Crouse, summer resident of Annisquam, hung around productions of his plays, and so did Thornton Wilder. The poet May Sarton braved the footlights. So did Ruth Hanna, daughter of the Ohio Republican boss Mark Hanna; she arrived in Gloucester with her maid and had Cunningham at her wits' end trying to keep her practical joke of a fake elopement out of the papers. And Mary Steichen Calderone, future leader in the sex-education field, whose famous photographer father, Edward, froze one of the early plays with his camera.

Child of the Playhouse-on-the-Moors, the Gloucester School of the Theatre — the Little Theatre — was a force on the American summer drama workshop circuit for thirty-two years. The playhouse, having been given up as an art gallery by the Atwoods, gave way as a theatre of equal originality to its robust offspring after eight seasons and closed its doors to an unpredictable world in 1925.

Again the scenario changes, and the scene shifts.

Florence Cunningham's male reliance, the Englishman Leslie Buswell, had been playing in East Gloucester and, in a way, West Gloucester too, where he was still abiding with Jack Hammond in Jack's "Bungalow" above the harbor.

In October of 1922 the brash and in some ways really quite brilliant, young, very evidently tough Benito Mussolini and his tough friends who called themselves *Fascisti* seized power from the faltering monarchy in Italy. The next year Hammond sold patent rights worth half a million to the Radio Corporation of America and put architects to work on a sort of castle, a donjon at any rate, adjacent to the "Bungalow" to house the gigantic organ that was taking shape, pipe by pipe, in his fugal imagination.

While all this was going on, Leslie Buswell acquired thirty-three acres of the wooded height directly above the Hammond estate. He dammed the brook to make a pond, on which he conferred the name of Buswell, and was soon overseeing the construction of a rambling reproduction of a seventeenth-century English country home on the crest of the hill with a manorial command of Gloucester Harbor, on over Eastern Point and out to sea beyond.

Early in 1924 Mussolini, now Il Duce and the dictator of Italy, summoned America's electronic genius to create for him a secret radio communications system for no less a stated purpose than the consolidation of his authority.

In April Hammond and his Buswell sailed for Rome. In three months the job was done with such dispatch, the deviser admitted to a magazine writer thirty-six years later, that "I was really sold on dictatorship as a way of running a government efficiently." Of course he was not alone, but almost immediately Jack was disillusioned, according to this article in *True* of November 1960: the network's first major mission, in reality, was to entrap important anti-Fascists, "and among those who were snared by the system were a good many of Hammond's friends."

Back in Gloucester that fall, Buswell's Jacobean estate, practically completed in his absence, was opened for inspection by the press while Hammond's donjon rose stone by stone above the high-tide mark. Meanwhile, Jack "wooed and won" Irene Fenton, an artist; after her divorce they were married in the summer of 1925, incurring such disapproval from the inventor's parents, as historian James O'Gorman reconstructs the scene (and it must have been some scene), that he had to abandon altogether any thoughts of bringing a divorced woman to live on Hammond family turf. Work on the donjon organ house ceased abruptly, and a mile and a half toward Magnolia, above Norman's Woe Rock, he purchased on the very brink of a Wagnerian cliff a rocky tract to which he transferred his castellar ambitions.

Was Freudian rivalry rearing its unsavory head? Old Man Hammond was dismayed: "I dropped in to see the site of your new house and I fear you do not realize the *staggering* sum you will have to provide. [By 1928, with twenty years of work still ahead, young Jack had spent more than $350,000.] This is a very costly site to develop — You should go slowly! A small, inexpensive house with money in the bank is better than a costly house mortgaged to death!!! I am very much worried about you and your affairs." It may be noted that Hammond, Sr., had built his own costly battlemented stone tower to Arthur Shurtleff's design three years earlier at "Lookout Hill" and was not a man to be upstaged lightly, least of all by a precocious offspring.

The summer of 1925 dropped the final curtain on the Playhouse-on-

Director Florence Cunningham on the grounds of the Little Theatre, Rocky Neck, Gloucester. Ruth Cunningham Bolger

The Flail Dance—a feature of the Greek Festival staged outdoors at the Playhouse-on-the-Moors in East Gloucester for French war relief, August 9, 1918. Cape Ann Historical Association

The Playhouse-on-the-Moors moves across Gloucester Harbor to play G. K. Chesterton's Magic, *starring Leslie Buswell as the hooded Conjurer, in the Gothic Room of Jack Hammond, Jr.'s, "Bungalow" on what he playfully called "Point Radio" below his father's "Lookout Hill," August 1922. Cape Ann Historical Association*

Trying out Jack Hammond's invention for extracting new tonal effects from the piano at the "Bungalow" in 1925: Leslie Buswell, now manager of the Hammond Laboratories, Hammond, conductor Leopold Stokowski and pianist Lester Donahue. Hammond Castle Museum

"This is a very costly site to develop—you should go slowly!" So Jack Hammond, Sr., warned his son and namesake. Building a castle on and from the rock, February 13, 1927. Hammond Castle Museum

the-Moors. The next April Leslie Buswell's mother died in England. She was the daughter of Admiral Henry Croft of Stillington, Yorkshire, and a cousin of Lord Plummer, the King's Master of the Rolls. Her son called his new turf "Stillington." In July 1926 Buswell completed an addition, Stillington Hall, a vaulted manor hall with a stage at one end, professionally equipped in every respect, seating a hundred and seventy. While doing so, he organized his own amateur troupe, the Stillington Players.

Summer theatre on Cape Ann in the dramatis personae of the Stillington Players, without the lapse of even a season, reopened in the hills of West Gloucester in the most Gothic setting imaginable the third week in August, 1926, with the French comedy, *She Had to Know*. The heavy cream of North Shore society June-to-September was packed in behind Governor and Mrs. Alvan T. Fuller, who had been entertained at dinner across the harbor on Eastern Point in his slightly spooky "Red Roof" by Congressman Piatt Andrew and doubtless the doyens of Dabsville.

Leslie Buswell, torchbearer, trouper, creator, producer, director, host and star, was never more magnetic. A week later the musical side of Stillington burst harmoniously upon the dream world of the North Shore with a recital by the virtuoso violinist Ephraim Zimbalist.

For his second season as impresario Buswell presented the American Opera Company in *Faust, The Barber of Seville* and *I Pagliacci*, among others, while the Players introduced *The Intimate Stranger* with the Manchester socialite actress Mrs. Fitzwilliam Sargent, who would play again and again opposite Leslie, in the female lead. A stuffed house every night. The *in* thing on the Shore.

Buswell's coup of the decade, and the night of nights for the Stillington Players, came in 1929 with their world premiere of *Christopher Rand* by Mrs. August Belmont and her collaborator on an earlier success, Harriet Ford. Leslie undoubtedly knew where the choirs of angels sang. An actress once herself, this grandest of the New York and Newport *dames,* wife of the ridiculously rich financier, was already long a legend in society, charity, music and the arts, and she had a long way to go, for she died in 1979 at 100.

Mrs. Belmont stayed at the Oceanside in Magnolia for rehearsals and the opening. The critic for the *North Shore Breeze* ventured, concerning *Christopher Rand,* that "certainly, with the exception of the rather infelicitous curtain of Act II, it is difficult to see how any company could have done more for this drama of the mines, and this is the more noteworthy, when one realizes that practically all of Mr. Buswell's previous productions might roughly have been classed as 'society plays.'"

One can almost imagine the indestructible lady descending into one of her husband's coal mines researching her play. She had ascended some distance since that turn-of-the-century day when the beautiful young actress Eleanor Robson, hardly more than an ingenue, was beckoned by the maid from the window of a Beacon Street town house as she passed. She paused. And Mrs. Jack Gardner appeared at the door, declared, "Walk erect, young woman!" and disappeared back inside. Mrs. Jack had been dead five years when her young man Leslie premiered Eleanor's latest.

Collapsed the stock market upon the land, and in 1930 (until 1938, anyway, when Buswell and Mrs. Sargent reopened briefly) so did the curtain upon the cameo stage of Stillington Hall. Always, though, there was someone to pick up the torch — this time a carpenter at the Oceanside who with a few other Buswell veterans started up the Oceanside Theatre with a series of one-acters that were still wowing 'em in 1935.

The castle that issued stone by stone from Jack Hammond's solid-state imagination above Longfellow's sacred Norman's Woe — "Abbadia Mare," Abbey-by-the-Sea — one of the truly unauthentic architectural anachronisms of the North Shore, was built around a Great Hall right out of Camelot, the sort and size his friend Mussolini would have set himself at one end of on an elevated dais if he had only thought of it first. A hundred feet long and sixty high, the Great Hall was Arthurian in conception, Twainian in the realization, and designed acoustically to amplify to the limit of aural tolerance the product of every one of the ten thousand pipes of his magnificent organ that would be twenty years in the completion.

But this organ (no relation to the electric make), one of the universe's more pretentious musical instruments, was not the only bizarre feature of Hammond's moated, drawbridged, portcullised, battlemented, parapeted and towered castle, home and — after 1930 — museum as well. He had great fun working into it all sorts of secret passages and bedrooms, peepholes, peekaboos and such naughty niceties and narcissistic knickknacks first favored by his friends Doc Andrew and Harry Sleeper. What acronymic antics they engaged in, those four — Buswell, Andrew, Sleeper, Hammond — what BASHes!

Further, among the furnishings and even into the walls the inventor incorporated "art treasures and architectural specimens that today are almost priceless museum pieces." So instructs *The Hammond Museum Guide Book* of 1966, which goes on to explain as ingenuously as it can that "he brought these treasures from Europe as he collected them in his travels."

The matter of the provenance of the treasures of Italian origin, at least, is raised by the "immediacy" of Jack Hammond's recollected disillusionment with Il Duce after the entrapment of his anti-Fascist friends.

Three years after installing Mussi's radio network, in 1927, Hammond was praising the dictator to the heavens in an interview in the *Breeze*. Nine years after, in 1933, a *Breeze* article revealed all — or almost all — stating that if Benito Mussolini ever visits America, Jack Hammond's "will be one of the first roofs to shelter him. An electrical engineer in connection with Italy's complicated system of secret defense, Hammond was thrown in close contact with the powerful Premier. They shared a common enthusiasm for Italian antiquities. Masonry, furniture and bibelots of medieval birth have been brought to Gloucester to give the stamp of authenticity to Hammond's portcullised home."

Twelve years after the rendition of the son's considerable favor to the Fascisti, in 1935, John Hays Hammond, Sr., wrote in his *Autobiography* of his own interview with the "beneficent" dictator in 1926. He described the Duce and his movement and methods with enthusiasm as heroic bulwarks against Communism in Europe, observing proudly that Mussolini had made Jack, Jr., a Grand Officer of the Crown, and concluded: "I have not seen him since but have kept directly in touch with him through my son, Jack, who installed for him a selective system of radio which he uses in communicating with his representatives in Italy and Africa."

Thus is history made, and written, and rewritten. Visitors to the

Hammond Castle Museum in search of the treasures of Italy, *nota benito*.

On a terrace overlooking the entire North Atlantic Ocean Jack Hammond erected a much-larger-than-life statue of himself, heroically posed, gazing in bronze condescension over the sea, naked as the day he was born. He died in 1965 at the age of seventy-six, lord of quite a lot he had surveyed, at that, and had himself buried a few feet away. Though not a Catholic, he left his castle to the Archdiocese of Boston, which in a while found it too much of a secular care and sold it. Most of Jack's books went to the Sawyer Free Library in Gloucester. En route, they were stored in the basement of the First Baptist Church in the next block until shelf space could be found. None of the pornography made it to the library, which would have given him a chuckle, for like his father, he was a bit of a rascal at heart.

19

ontinuity

THE WILLIAM H. COOLIDGES, JR., SHARED THE ROLLING ACRES OF "BLYNMAN Farm," back of Coolidge Point in Manchester-by-the-Sea, with the William H. Coolidges, Sr., who wintered at the Hotel Somerset in Boston.

In the spring of 1927 (castles, as we have seen, being rather in the vogue thereabouts around then) the younger Coolidges built one on top of the hill for their three children, all under nine. It was a single stone tower three stories high. An inside staircase spiraled up to the timber and stucco aerie at the top, which was furnished with a view fit for a king and for a Coolidge. Here there was a stone fireplace, and there were electric lights, and a kitchen with an electric stove and running water.

The Coolidges had a very definite sense of the continuity of things.

A century is longest in the life of a family, not long in the history of a nation, and but a moment in the course of a civilization. Yet the tenacity of a social phenomenon as inherently ephemeral, not to say frivolous, as a summer resort to hang on and around for a hundred years amounts to hoariness unto senility.

By the 1920s the North Shore had survived ten decades since Colonel Perkins opened Boston's summery window on the sea with the Nahant Hotel, a century of much change (the "American Century") and some progress (a lot of it either deplorably or excitingly revolutionizing in nature and direction). Three generations and the beginning of a fourth

had witnessed the opening up of the West and the attendant (and caus-
ative) shift of culture and control from the increasingly effete (so
Westerners thought) East, the disruption (and rejuvenation) of two
major wars, the desolation of income taxes, waves of ethnic adulteration
from across the sea, and inundations of motor cars whose presence on
Route 1A was a curse or a blessing depending on who was behind the
wheel.

Cold Roast warmed over? A hundred years later a summer census of
leading families surprised no one who already knew: Nahant contained 106 from Boston, five from Washington, one each from New
York and Chicago, one from Philadelphia, and one each from inde-
terminate locations in Connecticut, Illinois, Ohio and Florida. Greater
Boston continued to dominate every colony on the Shore while tolerating, if not exactly welcoming, hinterlanders from the vast unknown
beyond nearby Dedham, and the postwar trend toward year-round
suburban living of a sort was gaining favor.

There was a characteristically cautious feeling by 1928 that the depression (we would call it a "recession" today) following the Armistice
was finally being overcome and that business conditions were improving. To all this the *North Shore Breeze* was tempted to "almost yell
hurrah!" It voiced careful optimism, however, that house sales were
picking up but thanked God the Shore had been "spared from the aggressive ruinous propaganda of real estate exploiters and boomers."

Caution, Boston caution, resisted the temptation (not always, but
often enough) to sell off the family acres acquired by Great-Grand-
father from families who couldn't resist the temptation to make, they
had thought, a killing. Caution built the dynasties that built Boston's
North Shore — and cautious trust funds of bonds and playhouses of
stone — and maintained its grip on the coast for a hundred years —
and would for another fifty after all came Crashing down around it,
and perhaps another fifty after that . . . well, Cold Roast Caution
transfused regularly, lest we forget, with the hot blood of the patriarchal gamblers from Perkins to Prince.

Caution built continuity — that and a proper marriage, to be sure.
Caution, and Concern for the Customer.

The firm of S. S. Pierce, which provided every proper pantry in

Boston By Appointment, inaugurated "City Service at the Seashore" in the early Twenties. Salesmen would call for orders regularly, in person, or they could be phoned or mailed in. The company's own motor trucks, with facilities for icing perishables, would deliver anywhere between Boston and Cape Ann and even beyond. H. A. Hovey, "The Oldest Butterhouse in Boston," with headquarters at the Faneuil Hall market, was a little more chary and promised delivery of the choicest butter and eggs on standing order, from Nahant to Bass Rocks. Langley-Wharton guaranteed fresh Russian Beluga caviar via your North Shore service entrance, packed in ice at twenty-eight degrees Fahrenheit.

And after all was cleared away ("So many covers were laid at Mrs. So-and-So's 'Atavistic Acres' in Beverly Farms on Tuesday," the *Breeze* never tired of regaling its readers), the man from the Pilgrim Laundry would pick up and deliver without fail, while Lewandos — with its feline laundress and her children painted so amusingly on the panel of every truck — packed milady's "good" linens separately in blue tissue.

For a coming-out party, Jefferson-Johnson Orchestras on Tremont Street in Boston advertised in *The North Shore Blue Book and Social Register:* "Superior Colored Players — Jazz Bands and Entertainers." While for cautious continuity of a less bouncy cadence, summer as well as winter, the *Boston Evening Transcript* with uncharacteristic belligerence (perhaps feeling so comfortably buffered within the cold, fraternal pages of the *Blue Book*) termed itself "as nearly perfect a daily newspaper as it is possible to print."

Caution, Continuity — and Bunny Woods.

Bernard J. Woods — "Bunny" to thousands of North Shore, Boston-based, Best-of-Brood "Chicks," as he called the children lovingly placed under his wing — was to their instruction in the manly and womanly ways of the outdoors what Marguerite Souther, the dreadnaught proprietress of the Eliot Hall dancing school in suburban Jamaica Plain, was to their indoctrination in the arts of the anteroom. Both were pillars in the institutional structure of Boston Society, Miss Souther for fifty-five years, Bunny Woods from 1899 until well into the 1930s.

The Cement of Continuity. There *are* rules governing social intercourse. The formidable spinster, a perfect flagship on the dance floor, once commanded a fearfully shy young fellow, with a twinkle in her eye: "LEAD me! As if I were FLESH and BLOOD, not a cigar store INDIAN!" And an ex-chick of the male sex wrote Bunny late in his career "first of all to tell you how wonderful I think you are, and second, to say that I would give a good deal to be back at that age myself, for nothing ever comes up to the fun I had with you in those days, and I don't believe you ever realize how much you did for me. You may not remember how I suffered from shyness at first, but I'll never forget how kind you were to me, nor will I forget a party at George Lyman's when I won my first cup. I have always felt that was a turning point in my life, and nothing has ever been so hard again, and I attribute that all to your help and tact. One of the regrets of my life is that you haven't had a hand in bringing up my boys, for I consider it a rare and lasting privilege."

This benign Pied Piper started instructing children in sports and gymnastics at a New York State resort and was inveigled to Boston during the winter, inevitably following his chicks summers to their North Shore habitat, where the contagion for him was such that before long estate owners were vying for the privilege of hosting his "outing classes," and mothers from far-off New Jersey were pressuring their spouses to summer on the North Shore of Boston and pulling strings to get their babes enrolled with him.

Early patrons were the C. G. Rices in Ipswich. Pupils from as far as Nahant would be conveyed to the Beverly depot, nearly filling the coach that tumbled them out at Ipswich, where all piled into carriages and wagons for the bumpy ride to "Turner Hill Farm." The Rices turned a floor into a gym. Sixty or seventy happy chicks splashed in the pool and gobbled their lunches at a long outdoor table presided over by the gentle Bunny.

Games, folk dances and "stunts" designed to teach chicks to be "real true sports" were the fare for the under-six classes on the lawn of the Beverly Cove estate of Dr. and Mrs. Henry F. Sears, their own children included. Opening day, each initiate was brought up to Mr. Woods and shook hands or curtsied. "Some told their names, but usually the nurses helped out in answer to Bunny's question, 'What little chick is this?'" Hard to believe, but in 1919, after only twenty years of it, Bunny thought he might have taught over 100,000 children.

The Great Depression was settling in when on that same greensward, in 1931, Sears grandson George Cabot Lodge was the nominal host. Fluttered the *Breeze:* "Little tots from three to six or seven come to George's class. Bunny welcomes them with a handshake; then the sports starts — baseball, tennis, games and gymnastic work, with everyone having the best time ever. Too soon the closing hour arrives, when nurses or mothers come for their charges. Then it's 'Goodbye, Bunny! Come again, Bunny!' And away they go in their cars."

An unchallengeable rationale for such early discipline, if one were needed, had long since been provided by Mrs. S. Burt Wolbach of Pride's Crossing, wife of the eminent Harvard pathologist, who revealed that she had made a special study of youngsters under five and found that "the children of wealthy parents are often undernourished and improperly fed, and underweight, as well as the children from homes of limited means."

Kindergartenmeister, all-around athlete, coach and trainer, innovator in physical education and therapy, builder of character, but above all a kindly referee between the generations, Bunny Woods coaxed his little ones, as he had their fathers and mothers, from the Rice barn and the Sears lawn and the Higginson hayfield and the icy waters of West Beach to Harvard Stadium, the battlefields of France and the United States Senate. And the movie moguls, finally, tried to coax *him* onto the screen. But his old chicks would have none of it. "He is ours," fumed one, "and we do not want to lose him. Going to Hollywood is the beginning of the end, but we want the end here."

For every wholesome intergenerational influence of a Bunny Woods on the more thoughtful, and stable, of the privileged families of the North Shore there were dozens of yacht club stewards and sailing instructors instilling respect for the sea, joy in the mastery of the wind, and the fervor of the race into these same chicks, noses peeling, sunbleached hair stiff with salt.

There was something about the Twenties, the confused, crazy — not so often roaring — *childish* Twenties that was especially of and for and perhaps by the children — children of the Great War, children like fresh poppies forever springing from a thousand Flanders Fields — innocents in the linen, lace and ribbons of the summer — the great-grandchildren of Victoria — the children Prendergast and Beaux and

Time and anniversaries roll on at Nahant . . . the fiftieth in 1903 and the seventy-fifth in 1928. Nahant Public Library

Continuity. Frederick Ayer at the Myopia Hunt around 1909 . . . and twenty years later, his son-in-law, Major George S. Patton, Jr., and his grandson, George S. Patton IV, four-star and two-star generals-to-be. Patton album

Sargent could not resist putting on canvas, wide-eyed and cherry-lipped.

. . . The Twenties, in the middle of which Mary Northend passed on to her sweet garden in the sea-blue sky, Mary whose horticultural questionings were of no more and of no less import than all the others in the *Breeze:* "What Shall We Do with Our Shady Corners?" — "Where Shall We Plant Our Vines?"

How many of the children of the Twenties would be children always — puzzled by the shady corners of their elders, heads aswim with bathtub gin, crowded by the gathering social, political and philosophical catastrophe toward the only conceptual precipice left, economic calamity?

The North Shore of Boston was after all a mere verandah above an enchanting sea, a verandah to a verandah to a certain hotel, long gone, built by a cynical old man who loved his little grandson.

There is a continuity to verandahs, and a caution.

Early in 1927 Beatrice Ayer Patton bought "Green Meadows," the lovely, rolling George Burroughs estate in Hamilton picked up the previous fall by a group of Myopians for the protection of the chase in the heart of the Essex County hunting country. Her husband was in charge of operations planning in Hawaii. It would be their permanent home. For all her remarkable devotion, support, assistance and sacrifice, as Martin Blumenson sized up their relationship, Beatrice, "without meaning to do so, robbed him of an essential facet of his masculinity. They lived on her income. He needed neither his Patton inheritance [his father died that spring] nor his Army pay. That too spurred him to achieve greatness, something that no amount of money could purchase. And that too is probably why he needed to project an image so strong and aggressive and masculine."

Major Patton was definitely suffering from interbellum boredom.

In April of 1929 Bill Swan, the dean of New England yachting writers, checked forty-three boatyards along the North Shore and reported that they were building 325 yachts of respectable dimensions at a total cost of more than eight million dollars. The Shore was moving into the biggest yachting season in history. Swan had to admit, however, that ninety percent of the activity in the yards was in pleasure craft and "very little construction for commercial purposes can be found."

Who now can say how many of that great armada of dreams were launched on a sea of watered stock?

It was midsummer of the last year of the Lost. Absolutely everybody and everything were on the rise, without a shadow of a doubt. Spirits, prices, real estate, elevators, stocks, heels, murders, indices, savings and the bubbles in the bootleg champagne.

For weeks the great secret had been the fantastic bash in the making at "Rocklea," the summer mansion of the Lyon Weyburns (he was a Boston lawyer) at Pride's Crossing. In dubious honor of the dubious hotel that glowered sootily over the B & M yards from on top of North Station, the Weyburns cast the party to end all parties as "Opening-Closing Night of the Manger Night Club" and turned over the vast carriage room of their barn for it.

The preparations were letter-perfect. Not a word leaked out. But you could tell from the hour on the invitation that it was one of those late starters that portend a red, white and blue wing-ding.

The cabaret got under way at eleven-thirty with a "screamingly funny skit that completely brought the house down." (The *Breeze* was there — who else?) Then everyone out on the floor for a tango and a waltz, with the help of Ruby Newman's orchestra, after which "a most amusing playlet in which Mrs. Daniel Comstock from her chaise longue carried on a typical society matron telephone conversation with Mrs. Lloyd Nichols seated at her desk. It brought gale after gale of laughter, as the indiscretions and idiosyncrasies of one person after another on the Shore were blandly discussed over the wire."

Two society dames in little girl outfits belted out four numbers, followed by Mr. Edward A. Weeks of Montserrat leading his partner "through the intricate steps of a maxixe, and several interpretive dances — in fact he danced all around her with great agility, accompanied by the roars of laughter from the onlookers. His partner was a coquettishly painted broomstick."

More dancing, more acts, more of the joys of the Twenties, an' aroun' happast three in th' mornin' ole Ruby Newman himself, in person, arrived to take over th' bat'n 'f his orch'stra. Th' Mang'r Nite Club shrut s'doors som'er 'roun fur-thutty 's the first wide-awake milkman came clip-clopping briskly down Hale Street.

The same summer of '29 a gaily anonymous contributor to the *Breeze,* which has insinuated so much of the vitality of the times into this chronicle, penned so unintentionally, so innocently, so eloquently, their obituary:

"Seven-thirty! Cocktail hour! The 'clear call that may not be denied' is sounded, and from all up and down the shore, from Marblehead to Rockport, the nightly hegira of the Faithful has begun.

"Turning out from spacious driveways, from tiny side-streets, from country estates, cars of every description join the ever-growing procession on the highway.

"At Del Monte's, the first cars draw up to the door — the thin wail of a violin being tuned floats out through the night. From across the quiet water, lights on the Burrage yacht *Aztec* flare up — launches, hurrying back and forth from shore to ship, like water bugs, carrying dinner guests — gay voices, laughter, music!

"In front of a beautiful Tudor home two policemen have taken their stand. A car stops — saxophones, a violin, drums, are lifted out. The orchestra. The Jack Clunies are giving a dance! Some jovial members of a patriotic war organization, climbing the stairs to the second floor of a barn — later the strains of 'Sweet Adeline' will make the night hideous in Beverly Farms.

"Down in a little cove, past Pride's, a loving father and his four-year-old son have anchored a speed-boat, and hand in hand, the tall man and the little boy climb the hill, through the fast gathering dusk, to a long, low, white house.

"The group of languid gentlemen who hold up the front of some of the shops in Manchester are slowly assembling. Never do to miss any of the passing show! Legend has it that they sleep like the bears all winter, and it must be true, for they never put in an appearance until the first daffodil and the first Rolls-Royce come out in the spring!

"At Calderwood's boat yard, the Lloyd Nichols, with a gay party, are starting for their boat, *Stornaway,* out in the harbor — a moonlight sail is on!

"A huge lavender machine with 'New York City' written in large and impressive letters across the front, purrs by — exactly the shade of the Sen-Sen tablets we used to chew in order to disguise the odor of nicotine from watchful parents, in the far-off days, before the Emancipation of Youth.

"Betty Barrell, Connie Percival and two young men turning in at Essex — the most utterly dilapidated Ford touring car, churning along with a young couple, apparently oblivious to the incongruity of evening dress, in such a contraption!

"And so they go. The whole world is on the move, for it's cocktail hour along the North Shore."

After three and a half more months of such engaging giddiness, on October 29, 1929, the stock market collapsed.

Boston's North Shore survived rather well, all things considered. Not too surprisingly, either. And it survives to this day, not surprisingly, even charmingly in many places.

But since Black Friday it has been, somehow, déjà vu, don't you agree?

Bibliography

GENERAL

Abbott, Katharine M. *Trolley Trips on a Bay State Triangle.* Lowell, Mass., 1897.
Abbott, Marshall K. *Myopia Songs and Waltzes.* Cambridge, Mass., 1897.
—— *Along the North Shore.* Boston and Northern Street Railway Company. Boston, 1905.
Amory, Cleveland. *The Last Resorts.* New York, 1952.
—— *The Proper Bostonians.* New York, 1947.
—— *Who Killed Society?* New York, 1960.
Appleton Farms Tercentenary, 1638–1938. N.p., 1938.
Aub, Joseph C., and Ruth K. Hapgood. *Pioneer in Modern Medicine: David Linn Edsall of Harvard.* Boston, 1970.

Babson, Thomas E. "Evolution of Cape Ann Roads and Transportation." *Essex Institute Historical Collections,* October 1955.
Bacon, Edwin M. *Walks and Rides in the Country Round About Boston.* Boston, 1898.
Baedeker, Karl. *The United States. New York,* 1893.
Beaux, Cecilia. *Background with Figures.* Boston, 1930.
Beebe, Lucius. *The Lucius Beebe Reader.* New York, 1967.
—— *Mansions on Rails.* Berkeley, Calif., 1959.
Benson, Henry Perkins. "Half Century of Motoring in Essex County." *Essex Institute Historical Collections,* July 1949.
Bergan, William M. *Old Nantasket.* Quincy, Mass., 1969.
Beverly Farms Island Inn (flyer). N.p., 1905.
Blumenson, Martin. *The Patton Papers 1885–1940.* Boston, 1972.
Bollman, Henry. "The Little Theatre." Gloucester, Mass., *Daily Times,* Sept. 27, 1956.
Boston Looks Seaward: The Story of a Port, 1630–1940. WPA Writers Program. Boston, 1941.
Boyd, Ellen B. R. *Adventures in Sharing.* Newburyport, Mass., 1964.
Boyle, Richard J. *American Impressionism.* Boston, 1974.
Brann, E. H. *Sketches of Nahant.* Nahant, Mass., 1911.
Brooks, Van Wyck. *John Sloan, A Painter's Life.* New York, 1935.
Buswell, Leslie. *Ambulance No. 10.* Boston, 1916.

Carroll, Lewis. *Alice's Adventures in Wonderland*. London, 1865.

Choate, Craig Cogswell. "New Life on Old Cape Ann." *Boston Herald*, July 16, 1895.

Clarke, George C. "The Story of Revere Beach." Part I of *Kiwanis History of Revere*. Mimeographed, 1966. At Revere, Mass., Public Library.

Collins, Lou, and George Hardy. "Salem Willows for Mine Waltz." Salem, Mass., 1919.

Curtis, George William. *Lotus-Eating: A Summer Book*. New York, 1852.

Deveney, James J. History of Bass Point, Nahant. Series in Lynn, Mass., *Item*, June 1953.

Dictionary of American Biography. New York, 1964.

Donaldson, Frances. *Edward VIII*. Philadelphia, 1974.

Duveneck, Josephine W. *Frank Duveneck — Painter-Teacher*. San Francisco, 1970.

Eliot, T. S. *Four Quartets*. New York, 1943.

Estaver, Paul E. "Castle on the Coast." *The Shoreliner*, July 1952.

Falt, Mary Taylor. 'Rocky Neck's Development as a Summer Resort." *North Shore Breeze*, Sept. 29, 1911.

Fein, Albert. *Frederick Law Olmsted and the American Environmental Tradition*. New York, 1972.

Ferguson, David L. *Cleopatra's Barge: The Crowninshield Story*. Boston, 1976.

Floyd, Frank L. *Manchester-by-the-Sea*. Manchester, Mass., 1945.

Forbes, Allan. "Early Myopia at Winchester." *Essex Institute Historical Collections*, January 1942.

—— "Early Myopia at Brookline, Dedham, Framingham, Southboro and Milton." *Ibid.*, April 1942.

—— "Early Myopia at Hamilton." *Ibid.*, July 1942.

—— "Early Myopia Festivities." *Ibid.*, October 1942.

Foster, Mrs. E. G., and Alice W. Foster. *The Story of Kettle Cove*. Magnolia, Mass., 1899.

Frank Duveneck. Chapellier Gallery. New York, n.d.

Fraser, Mrs. William S. "Manchester Becomes a Resort." Manchester, Mass., *Cricket*, serialized 1961.

Frothingham, Eugenia B. *Youth and I*. Boston, 1938.

Fuess, Claude M. *Calvin Coolidge: The Man from Vermont*. Boston, 1940.

Gallup, Donald. "The 'Lost' Manuscript of T. S. Eliot." *The Times Literary Supplement*, Nov. 7, 1968.

Garland, Joseph E. "Dry Run at Manchester by the Sea." Gloucester, Mass., *Daily Times*, March 8, 1968.

—— *Boston's North Shore: Being an Account of Life among the Noteworthy, Fashionable, Wealthy, Eccentric and Ordinary, 1823–1890*. Boston, 1978.

—— *Eastern Point: A Nautical, Rustical and Social Chronicle of Gloucester's Outer Shield and Inner Sanctum, 1606–1950*. Dublin, N.H., 1971.

—— *The Gloucester Guide: A Retrospective Ramble*. Gloucester, Mass., 1973.

Gibson, Sally. "How Presidents Enjoyed the North Shore." *North Shore '74*, Nov. 2, 1974.

Gould, Bartlett. "Burgess of Marblehead." *Essex Institute Historical Collections*, January 1970.

Grant, Robert. *The North Shore of Massachusetts*. New York, 1896.

Green, Eleanor. *Maurice Prendergast*. College Park, Md., 1976.

Hammond, John Hays. *The Autobiography of John Hays Hammond.* 2 vols. New York, 1935.

Harbor View Hotel (brochure). Gloucester, Mass., n.d.

Hartt, Hildegarde T. *Magnolia Once Kettle Cove.* Magnolia, Mass., 1962.

Harvey, George. *Henry Clay Frick: The Man.* New York, 1928.

Harwood, Reed. "The History of Misery Island." *Essex Institute Historical Collections,* July 1967.

——— "The Ill-fated Misery Islands." *Yankee,* August 1966.

Heermann, Norbert. *Frank Duveneck.* Boston, 1918.

Here and There by Trolley from Salem. Boston and Northern Street Railway Company. N.p., n.d.

Hill, Benjamin D., and Winfield S. Nevins. *The North Shore of Massachusetts Bay* (guidebooks). Salem, Mass., 1879–1894.

History of the American Field Service in France. "Friends of France" 1914–1917. Told by its members. 3 vols. Boston, 1920.

House, Edward M. *The Intimate Papers of Colonel House.* Ed. Charles Seymour. 4 vols. Boston, 1926.

Jewett, Amos Everett. "The Tidal Marshes of Rowley and Vicinity with an Account of the Old-Time Methods of 'Marshing.' " *Essex Institute Historical Collections,* July 1949.

Kenny, Herbert A. *Cape Ann: Cape America.* Philadelphia, 1971.

Kenyon, Paul B. "The Playhouse and the School of the Little Theatre." Gloucester, Mass., *Daily Times,* March 20, 1976.

Kipling, Rudyard. *Captains Courageous.* New York, 1896.

Kline, Naomi Reed. *The Hammond Museum — A Guidebook.* Gloucester, Mass., 1977.

Lamson, D. F. *History of the Town of Manchester, Essex County, Massachusetts, 1645–1895.* Boston, 1895.

Larkin, Oliver W. *Art and Life in America.* New York, 1966.

Lawrence, William. *Memories of a Happy Life.* Boston, 1926.

Lord, Priscilla Sawyer, and Virginia Clegg Gamage. *Marblehead: The Spirit of '76 Lives Here.* Philadelphia, 1972.

Lowell, James Russell. *Letters of James Russell Lowell.* Ed. Charles Eliot Norton. New York, 1894.

Lyons, Louis M. *Newspaper Story: One Hundred Years of The Boston Globe.* Cambridge, Mass., 1971.

McCauley, Peter. *Revere Beach Chips.* Revere, Mass., 1979.

Mansur, Frank L. "Swampscott, Massachusetts: The Beginnings of a Town." *Essex Institute Historical Collections,* January 1972.

Masconomo House (brochures). Manchester, Mass., 1899 and 1906.

Mason, Edward S. *The Street Railway in Massachusetts: The Rise and Decline of an Industry.* Cambridge, Mass., 1932.

Mason, Herbert N., Jr. *The Lafayette Escadrille.* New York, 1964.

Miller, Richard H. "John Hays Hammond: Electronic Sorcerer." *True,* November 1960.

The Misery Island Club. *Announcement of the Second Annual Regatta.* N.p., Aug. 7, 1901.

The Misery Island Club (flyer). N.p., 1900.

Montserrat (brochure). N.p., 1897.

Montserrat Highlands (brochure of Montserrat Syndicate). N.p., 1910.

Morison, Samuel Eliot. *The Maritime History of Massachusetts, 1783–1860.* Boston, 1921.

Nahant, or "The Floure of Souvenance." Philadelphia, 1827.

New England Aviators 1914–1918: Their Portraits and Their Records. Intro. A. Lawrence Lowell. 2 vols. Boston, 1919.

The North Shore Blue Book and Social Register. Boston, 1893 on.

Northend, Mary H. "The Summer Home of Mr. Eben D. Jordan." *Town and Country,* June 10, 1905.

Ocean House (brochure). Swampscott, Mass., 1896.

O'Gorman, James F. "Architectural Action Was His Disease." Gloucester, Mass., *Daily Times,* Feb. 17, 1979.

————— *This Other Gloucester.* Boston, 1976.

————— "Twentieth-Century Gothick: The Hammond Castle Museum in Gloucester and Its Antecedents." *Essex Institute Historical Collections,* April 1981.

Parks, Groves, Seashore Resorts. Boston and Northern and Old Colony Street Railway companies. Boston, 1903.

Phillips, James Duncan. "Commuting to Salem and Its Summer Resorts Fifty Years Ago." *Essex Institute Historical Collections,* April 1944.

Picturesque Cape Ann (booklet). Gloucester, Mass., 1909.

Pierce, Patricia Jobe. *Edmund C. Tarbell and the Boston School of Painting, 1889–1980.* Hingham, Mass., 1980.

————— *The Ten.* Hingham, Mass., 1976.

Pleasant Rides and Pleasure Spots on the Lynn and Boston Railroad. Lynn, Mass., 1897.

Prendergast, Maurice. *Watercolor Sketchbook, 1899* (facsimile). Notes by Peter A. Wick. Cambridge, Mass., 1960.

Preston Hotel (brochure). Swampscott, Mass., 1907.

The Priceless Gift (Wilson letters). Ed. Eleanor Wilson McAdoo. New York, 1962.

Pringle, Henry F. *The Life and Times of William Howard Taft.* 2 vols. New York, 1939.

Rantoul, Robert S. "The Misery Islands and What Has Happened There." *Essex Institute Historical Collections,* July 1902.

Rhys, Hedley H. *Maurice Prendergast, 1859–1924.* Cambridge, Mass., 1960.

Robinson, Morris B. "Some Artists Who Called Squam, Lanesville and the Folly 'Home.'" Gloucester, Mass., 1973. Typescript at Sawyer Free Library, Gloucester.

Rowsome, Frank, Jr. *Trolley Car Treasury.* New York, 1956.

Shepley, Hayden. *Automobiles Built in Essex County.* Toughkenamon, Pa., 1976.

Shurcliff, Margaret H. M. *Lively Days.* Taipei, 1965.

Shurcliff, Sidney N. *Upon the Road Argilla.* Boston, 1958.

Solley, George W. *Alluring Rockport.* Manchester, Mass., 1924.

Souvenir of Salem Willows. Salem Willows Merchants Association. Salem, Mass., 1929.

Stevens, W. Lester. "Cape Ann — An Artists' Paradise." *North Shore Breeze,* April 29, 1921.

The Story of Essex County. Ed. Claude M. Fuess. 4 vols. New York, 1935.

Taft, Mrs. William Howard. *Recollections of Full Years*. New York, 1914.

Tharp, Louise Hall. *Mrs. Jack*. Boston, 1965.

Townsend, Charles W. *Beach Grass*. Boston, 1923.

——— *The Birds of Essex County, Massachusetts*. Cambridge, Mass., 1905.

——— *Sand Dunes and Salt Marshes*. Boston, 1913.

Trolley Trips. Bay State Street Railway Company. Boston, 1912.

Trolley Trips. Boston and Northern and Old Colony Street Railway companies. N.p., May 1910.

Van de Water, Frederic F. *The Real McCoy*. New York, 1931.

Waters, Harold. "King of Rum Row." *The Compass*, Fall 1974.

Waters, T. Frank. "Candlewood." *Ipswich Historical Society Publications*, 1909.

——— "A History of the Old Argilla Road." *Ibid.*, 1900.

——— "Ipswich in the Massachusetts Bay Colony." *Ibid.*, 1917.

——— "Jeffrey's Neck and the Way Leading Thereto." *Ibid.*, 1912.

——— "The Old Bay Road from Saltonstall's Brook and Samuel Appleton's Farm." *Ibid.*, 1907.

Weeks, Edward. *Myopia, 1875–1975*. Hamilton, Mass., 1975.

Whitehill, Walter Muir. *Boston: A Topographical History*. Cambridge, Mass., 1968.

——— *Museum of Fine Arts Boston: A Centennial History*. Cambridge, Mass., 1970.

Whitehouse, Arch. *Legion of the Lafayette*. New York, 1962.

Who's Who Along the North Shore. Manchester, Mass., ca. 1907ff.

Williams, John. *The Other Battleground: The Home Fronts — Britain, France and Germany, 1914–18*. Chicago, 1972.

Willoughby, Malcolm F. *Rum War at Sea*. Washington, 1964.

The Willows (brochure). Salem, Mass., 1900.

Wilmerding, John. "Interpretations of Place: Views of Gloucester, Mass." *Essex Institute Historical Collections*, January 1967.

Wilson, Fred A. *Some Annals of Nahant*. Boston, 1928. Reprinted by the Nahant, Mass., Historical Society, 1977.

Wise, DeWitt D. *Baker's Island Now and Then*. Salem, Mass., 1940.

——— *Now, Then Baker's Island*. Salem, Mass., 1964.

Witham, Corinne B. *The Hammond Museum Guide Book*. Gloucester, Mass., 1966.

NEWSPAPERS AND PERIODICALS

Boston Transcript; Boston Globe; Boston Herald; Boston Post; Cape Ann Weekly Advertiser; Gloucester Daily Times; Ipswich Chronicle; Lynn Item; New Ocean House (later *North Shore*) *Reminder; North Shore Breeze; New York Times; Revere Journal; Salem News; Salem Gazette; Salem Willows Budget; Town and Country; Town Topics; True*

Index